*By Barbara Gibbons and the
Editors of Consumer Guide®*

Delicious Recipes for the
Healthy Stay-Slender Life

HARPER & ROW, PUBLISHERS

NEW YORK

Cambridge
Hagerstown
Philadelphia
San Francisco

London
Mexico City
São Paulo
Sydney

1817

Contents

It's true! You can eat delicious meals and stay slim, too. And, it's easy. All you have to do is cook the *Lean Cuisine* way. *Lean Cuisine* shows you how to strip excess calories from what you eat while retaining all the taste-tempting goodness. How do you do that? You just avoid eating fat, which is much higher in calories than either protein or carbohydrate.

If you don't buy those excess calories, they won't end up on your dinner table—or on you! *Lean Cuisine* shows you how to become a fat-fighting food shopper.

Start the day with protein-powered waker-uppers like Blender Cheese Pancakes, French Sausage Patties, High-Protein French Toast, Cottage-Cheese Scramble, Fried Sausage and Apples, or any of the other *Lean Cuisine* breakfast dishes. Then move on to a satisfying low-calorie lunch such as Main Course Spanish Omelette, Corned Beef Reubenesque, Frittata Foo Yung, High-Fibre Bread Quiche; just a partial list of *Lean Cuisine* midday meal treats.

Think that appetizers and party foods are off-limits to dieters? Think again. You can enjoy Aspargus Tips In Blankets, Ambrosia Fruit Cocktail, Tuna Stuffing For Mushrooms Or Celery, Sunshine Cheese Ball, French Deviled Eggs, and many more tempting treats.

Ladle up everything from hearty main-dish soups to light and elegant soups—all prepared the *Lean Cuisine* low-calorie way. You'll find recipes for Minestrone With Meatballs, Asparagus Vichyssoise, Lamb-Barley Soup, Chinese Egg Drop Soup, Tuna Chowder, Jellied Gazpacho, Curried Chicken Gumbo Soup, and many more.

Get your vitamins and other important nutrients (including fiber!) in such unusual and zesty salads as Mushroom Vinaigrette Salad, Chicken Salad Hawaiian-Style, Deli-Marinated Salad, Polynesian Shrimp-Stuffed Papaya, Beef Stroganoff Salad, and others. Then top off your salad creation with Chianti Dressing, Creamy Caesar Salad Dressing, Lemon Sweet-And-Sour Dressing, or any of the other delicious dressings in the *Lean Cuisine* repertoire.

Copyright © 1979 by Publications International, Ltd.
All rights reserved
Printed in the United States of America

Published by
Harper & Row, Publishers
10 East 53rd Street
New York, New York   10022

Published simultaneously in Canada
by Fitzhenry & Whiteside Limited, Toronto,
Ontario, Canada.

Library of Congress Catalog Card Number: 79-1663
ISBN: 0-06-090737-1 (paper)
       0-06-011498-3 (cloth)

This book may not be reproduced or quoted in whole or in part by mimeograph or any other printed means or for presentation on radio or television without written permission from:

Louis Weber, President
Publications International, Ltd.
3841 West Oakton Street
Skokie, Illinois   60076

Permission is never granted for commercial purposes

About the Author:
Barbara Gibbons, United Features' popular, nationally syndicated columnist, is the author of several cookbooks, including *The Slim Gourmet, The International Slim Gourmet* and *Diet Watchers Cookbook*. Ms. Gibbons put her slenderizing guidelines into practice some years ago when she lost 80 pounds by fighting fat in her own kitchen.

If You Love To Eat And Hate To Diet, Discover Lean Cuisine

To Avoid Fat, *Avoid Fat!*

That's the safe, simple secret of slim cookery. No hocus pocus, no mumbo jumbo, just simple math: fat is the most fattening food element there is, containing more than twice the number of calories in either protein or carbohydrate. So "getting the fat out" is the most efficient approach to eliminating those unwanted *excess* calories in the foods you eat. Much of the fat we eat unknowingly is just tasteless grease or oil that adds nothing but calories to food.

How Fattening Is Fat?

Pure fat contains nine calories per gram while so-called pure carbohydrate and protein contain only four calories. Or, to translate these statistics into pounds, a pound of oil or shortening contains about 4,000 calories, while a pound of pure carbohydrate or protein contains only 1,800. (Actually no food is pure, unadulterated carbohydrate or protein. Sugar comes closest, being 96 percent pure carbohydrate. Most meat protein foods contain more fat calories than protein calories. The purest familiar protein food ingredients are plain, unflavored gelatin, 86 percent protein, and egg whites, 80 percent protein.)

To put it in another perspective, a pound of fat — eaten over and above your calorie needs — can produce *more than its own weight in body fat*. It takes about 3600 extra calories to add (or lose) a pound of weight. So, every time you trim the fat off a steak or skim the grease from gravy, it's comparable to trimming the fat right off your own hips or waistline. That's where those excess calories would go eventually!

The Healthy Bonus of *Lean Cuisine*

Even though slipping into a smaller size is your prime motivation, becoming a *Lean Cuisine* cook offers more important long-range health benefits. In the past century, the average American's fat intake has grown to nearly 45 to 50 percent of total calories consumed. Yet fat accounts for only 10 to 15 percent of caloric intake in those primitive societies where people eat little meat, lots of vegetables and live long lives. In its *Dietary Goals for the U.S.,* the Senate Select Committee on Nutrition urged a cutback in fat intake to a maximum of 30 percent *from all sources.*

Fight Fat Three Ways: When You Shop, Cook and Dine

By shopping wisely, you can leave thousands of excess calories behind in the store. The calories that don't go into your grocery bag won't end up on the table.

By preparing foods with *Lean Cuisine* techniques, you eliminate fat rather than add it. The fat that doesn't reach your plate will never reach your lips or hips!

By dining wisely and well, on filling, appetite-satisfying foods, rather than those that are concentrated and calorie-rich, you won't be as likely to overeat.

Fat Facts: Some Straight Talk about Overweight

Overweight is caused by taking in more food energy (calories) than your body can use. Nobody knows with absolute certainty why some people consume more than they need while others eat only enough and remain slim or maintain normal weight with no problem. There are scores of theories from different experts. Possible explanations include heredity, overfeeding in infancy and early childhood, overprotective parenting, too little exercise, mother's rich cooking, junk foods — even sexual fears. You'll get a medical answer from a doctor, a psychological explanation from a psychiatrist, a genetic theory from a biologist and an exercise program from a gym teacher. (If you ask a lawyer or an architect, you may very well get a legal opinion or an indictment of too many elevators and too few stairs.)

There's probably a little bit of truth in all of these opinions. The basic answer, however, is still this: people become overweight because they consume more calories than they can use. Exactly why they consume too many remains open to debate, but the only cure for overweight is to eat fewer calories or use more. A combination of both is preferable: fewer calories and more activity.

You Can Eat Fewer Calories without Eating Less Food

You need not go hungry to lose weight. There are bulky foods that take longer to eat and fill your stomach quickly, providing a sensation of fullness without excess calories. On the other hand, there are the concentrated, high-calorie, high-fat foods that are easily and quickly consumed. They provide a lot of calories yet take up very little space in the stomach, leaving a void that demands to be filled. For example, a 50-calorie portion of lettuce represents a whole head, and a 50-calorie serving of mayonnaise represents a half-tablespoonful. One would be hard pressed to make room for anything else after eating a whole head of lettuce; however, a half-tablespoonful of mayonnaise goes unnoticed on a sandwich!

High-Protein (Alias High-Fat) Diets Don't Work

Protein usually coexists with fat. For that reason, the so-called high-protein diets of the past decade were high-fat diets as well. The person who fills up on high-protein foods, such as steaks, chops, hamburgers, cheese and the like, is actually filling up on fat because the fat calories in those foods exceed the protein calories. A 400-calorie quarter-pound hamburger can contain as few as 100 calories in protein and as many as 300 calories in fat.

Those diets appeared to work on a short-term basis because of the temporary dehydration caused by the absence of sufficient carbohydrate foods. A person needs at least 100 grams of carbohydrate a day, and these diets often cut the intake to 30 grams or less, causing the body to flush water from the system. The water loss registers as a weight loss on the scale, an unhealthy self-deception. Once the diet is abandoned and normal carbohydrate intake resumed, body tissue refills itself with needed moisture and the pre-diet weight returns. Sometimes additional weight is gained due to the excessive calorie intake in the form of high-fat (high-calorie) foods.

Fasting Can Be Dangerous, and It Doesn't Work Anyway

Most diet-conscious readers are familiar with the newspaper reports of sudden deaths associated with certain extreme fasts. Fewer are aware of some follow-up studies conducted on patients who had lost considerable weight under well-supervised, medically directed fasts. One follow-up study revealed that 50 percent of the patients gained back every pound they had lost. After seven years only 5 percent remained at their reduced weight.

The problem with fasting — or even extreme dieting — is that it fails to teach the person how to deal with food on a lifelong basis. You can't learn how to eat properly by not eating. *Lean Cuisine*, on the other hand, is a permanent, lifelong commitment to less fatty, less fattening ways of shopping, cooking and eating.

Some Commonly Asked Questions about Fat

Q. *Isn't a no-fat diet dangerous? Don't I need to add some fat or oil to my menu?*

A. Yes and no. A *no*-fat diet is dangerous, but a *low*-fat diet needn't be. And, no, you don't need to add extra fat to your foods or menus, because all the fat you really need is already present, in abundance, in many foods. Some fat *is* essential for the body to utilize fat-soluble vitamins, but that amount is small — about two tablespoons. Unless you are on an extreme vegetarian diet restricted to just a few foods — or if you limit your food intake to near-starvation level — it would be hard not to get enough fat in what you eat, even with the *Lean Cuisine* approach. Remember, in many societies people eat only 10 percent fat. And some therapeutic post-cardiac diets today limit fat to just 10 percent.

Q. *Don't I need a lot of fat in my diet to prevent wrinkles and dry skin?*

A. No. Dryness of the skin has less to do with fat than moisture. The object of applying creams to the skin is to prevent the loss of moisture (water, not oils) from the skin. Dry skin is caused by many factors — heredity, environment (steam heat, sunshine, pollution), age, hormone level and general nutrition. It's usually the lack of vitamins and minerals on a strict fad diet that can affect skin texture, not the lack of sufficient fat.

Q. *Aren't vegetable fats less fattening than animal fats? Isn't margarine less fattening than butter?*

A. No. Fat is fat. Margarine (vegetable fat) and butter (animal fat) both contain 100 calories per tablespoon. The emphasis on vegetable fat for diet purposes has nothing to do with cutting calories or losing weight but rather with what seems to be the cholesterol-lowering ability of polyunsaturated vegetable fats *when used in place of* animal fats. Studies have shown that it's possible to lower a person's cholesterol level by substituting polyunsaturated fats for animal fats.

The cholesterol-lowering advantages of products high in polyunsaturates have been heavily advertised and promoted and the message is often misunderstood. The casual reader or television-viewer sometimes gets the mistaken idea that a health advantage can be gained simply by *increasing* the amount of soft margarine or corn oil, without simultaneously cutting down on other fats. Simply eating more margarine or using more oil will only *add* calories to your diet and cause weight gain.

Vegetable fats are no less fattening than animal fats, and simply substituting margarine for butter will not result in calorie savings. If your cholesterol level is low or normal, and you want to use ployunsaturated fats simply as a precaution, be sure that you use them *as a replacement for* — not an addition to — animal fats.

Q. *What are the differences between animal and vegetable fats?*

A. While the calories are the same, there are basic differences in the chemical structure of different types of fats. Fats are divided into three types: saturated, monounsaturated and polyunsaturated. Saturated fats are generally believed to be the villains that help raise cholesterol levels. Saturated fats are usually solid at room temperature; they include all forms of animal fat, including butter, the fat in milk, cream and cheese, and the fat encasing and marbled through meats. Poultry fats and fish oils are softer than meat fat and less saturated, but just as fattening. Some vegetable fats are also highly saturated: for example, coconut oil, cocoa butter and hydrogenated vegetable fats (solid shortenings).

Olive oil and peanut oil are high in monounsaturated fats. They are neutral in effect, neither raising nor lowering your cholesterol level. Polyunsaturated fats, on the other hand, have been demonstrated to help lower cholesterol levels. These are usually liquid oils of vegetable origin and include safflower, corn, cottonseed, sesame and sunflower seed oils. Safflower oil is the highest in polyunsaturates.

Q. *Is a low-fat, low-calorie diet the same as a low-cholesterol diet?*

A. They are not exactly identical. As we have said, the number of calories does not vary with the type of fat. A low-fat diet seeks to eliminate exccess calories by reducing the amount of fat consumed. However, as indicated above, it appears that different types of fat do have varying effects on cholesterol level.

Cholesterol itself is a normal constituent of the cells of animals and fish. Therefore, foods of animal and fish origin contain cholesterol in varying degrees. However, foods of plant origin — such as fruits, vegetables, grains, legumes, nuts and even highly saturated coconut oil — do *not* contain cholesterol. The amounts of cholesterol and saturated fat in a particular food need not be directly related to each other. For example, one large egg contains approximately 2 grams of saturated fat and 250 milligrams of cholesterol, while one cup of whole milk contains approximately 5 grams of saturated fat and only 34 milligrams of cholesterol.

Thus, a cholesterol-lowering diet is one in which the total amount of fats consumed is generally decreased, and of this total, the proportion of saturated fats is reduced, while the proportion of polyunsaturated fat intake is increased. At the same time, foods containing substantial amounts of cholesterol are used in moderation. Although the role of cholesterol-lowering diets in preventing heart disease remains controversial, as a prudent measure, the small amounts of fats or oils called for in the recipes in this book are primarily polyunsaturated safflower or corn oils or margarines made from them.

At this point, it would be advantageous to clear up what seems to be a rather widespread misconception concerning the amount of cholesterol found in shellfish. Except for shrimp, other commonly eaten shellfish — oysters, clams, scallops, lobster and crab — are not off-limits to those on cholesterol-restricted diets. These shellfish can be used interchangably with allowable types of meat. Shrimp is moderately high in cholesterol — unlike organ meats, such as liver, kidney, heart and brains, which are very high in cholesterol content — and, therefore, its consumption should be limited.

Special Help for "Special" Dieters

This is *not* intended as a medically therapeutic cookbook and in no way takes the place of your doctor's recommendations for special diet problems. The primary purpose of this book is to help healthy people get or stay slim the low-fat way, thereby increasing their chances of avoiding obesity and the degenerative diseases associated with overweight (and with America's overindulgence in fatty, fattening foods).

If you are on a doctor-prescribed cholesterol-lowering,

sodium-restricted or diabetic diet, note the special "alerts" to recipes and ingredients that are likely to be off-limits on your special diet. In these instances, we may suggest an alternative ingredient which would be allowable on that particular diet. Where no appropriate substitution could be made, it is usually suggested to omit the ingredient. In those cases where a substitution or deletion of a particular ingredient is not possible—perhaps because it is the main ingredient or because the recipe would not turn out satisfactorily—the entire recipe itself is "alerted" as not recommended for one of these special diets.

Substitutions recommended for one type of special diet may not be appropriate for another type of diet. For example, it is usually indicated to use liquid egg substitute in place of eggs for a low-cholesterol diet. However, 1/4 cup of liquid egg substitute (the normal quantity used to replace one large egg), contains approximately 130 milligrams of sodium, while the actual fresh egg contains only about 60 milligrams of sodium.

Certain ingredients may contain a much larger amount of an offending constituent than do other ingredients. When the quantity called for in a recipe is quite small and the ingredient contains a moderate amount of the constituent, it may not be alerted. For example, soy sauce contains approximately 1100 milligrams of sodium per tablespoon, while hot red pepper sauce contains approximately 104 milligrams of sodium per tablespoon. Any quantity of soy sauce is noted with a "High Sodium Alert," while a dash of hot red pepper sauce is not alerted, even though both foods are usually restricted on a low-sodium diet. However, when a low-sodium or unsalted product is available for a particular ingredient, we do alert that item and recommend the substitution even if the quantity called for in the recipe is small.

In the final analysis, we must stress the importance for individuals on highly restrictive or selective diets to verify recipes with their physician's recommendations.

Nutrition Figures for Each Recipe

Every recipe in this book is accompanied by a chart that lists the nutrition content of the total recipe and of each serving. Included are figures for grams of protein, carbohydrate and fat (the three basic food elements), along with figures for grams of saturated fat and milligrams of cholesterol and sodium. And, of course, the number of calories is also given.

All of these figures should be considered approximate, although we have attempted to be as exact as possible. The figures are based on findings of the U.S. Department of Agriculture, except for a few products for which information was obtained from manufacturers.

The figures for a recipe include all the ingredients listed in the main body of the recipe, *except* for those indicated as "optional." If an ingredient is listed with one or more alternatives, such as "1 red or green bell pepper" or "1 cup fresh, frozen or canned crab meat," the first item is used to calculate the nutrition figures for the recipe. Thus, in the two examples just cited, the recipe totals include figures for 1 red bell pepper and 1 cup fresh crab meat. Also, if a recipe calls for previously cooked vegetables, pasta or rice, for example, the total sodium figures are based on these foods having been cooked in water to which a moderate amount of salt has been added in accordance with normal cooking practices or common directions given on a manufacturer's package.

*A final reminder on the nutrition charts is that the figures include only ingredients listed in the main body of the recipe (except optional items). They do **not** reflect any substitutions or deletions that are recommended in the "alerts."*

Shoppers Guide To Lean Cuisine

FIGHTING FAT IN THE MARKETPLACE

The fight against excess fat in the kitchen really begins at the store. If you lose the first skirmish in the grocery aisle or at the meat counter, it could very well mean losing the whole war. To illustrate how smart shopping can cut calories, consider two bags of similar groceries each of which costs approximately $40. The first bag contains an assortment of foods that might be on any shopper's typical weekly marketing list: meat, canned goods, bread, ice cream, frozen vegetables, snacks, sandwich fillings, condiments and other standard items. The second bag contains the less fattening alternatives: leaner steak and hamburger, low-fat ice milk, low-fat high fiber bread, low-fat mayonnaise and salad dressings, plain frozen vegetables instead of those packed in calorie-laden cream sauces, turkey bologna instead of regular high-fat cold cuts, part-skim-milk cheeses, and so on. The calorie savings are startling. The first bag contains close to 50,000 calories while the second bag totals closer to 28,000. Since you need to save only 3,600 calories to lose a pound, this sample shopping trip represents a theoretical loss of six pounds for the people who might consume the second bag of groceries.

Look for the Fat and Calorie Price Tags: the Nutrition Label

Price tags? That's our term for the nutritional and ingredient information on package labels, the fine print that can tell us what we want to know. If you're a bargain hunter by instinct, you're used to reading labels, comparing packages and prices, weights and measures, to figure out which item is the best buy for the money. It's easy to transfer those same skills to become a calorie-comparison shopper. Only now, instead of looking for the most for your money, you're looking for the most nutrition for your calories. That approach can save you literally hundreds of thousands of calories a year.

About Nutrition Labels. Now that many foods are labeled with nutritional data, it's easier than ever to make calorie and fat comparisons among competing grocery items. By law, any product that makes a nutrition claim ("lower in fat," "higher in protein," "high in vitamin C," for example) must also include complete nutritional information in accordance with a legally defined format.

When There Is No Nutrition Label

If the manufacturer makes no nutritional claims for its product, then nutritional labeling is voluntary. Many food-makers include nutritional data, even though not required. Obviously, a food company willing to disclose complete information about its product inspires more confidence than one that doesn't. A shopper is inclined to believe that the nutritionally labeled food offers more vitamins and minerals, more protein and less fat and probably fewer calories than the product of the competitor who isn't willing to disclose the information.

Look for the ingredient list. Even in the absence of nutrition labels, the calorie-cautious consumer can still get a clue from the ingredient list. By law, the manufacturer must list ingredients in order of quantity. So, if the first word on the list is sugar, as it is on packages of many breakfast cereals, you know that the product contains more sugar than anything else.

If a product contains more fat than anything else, you know it has to be fattening. Remember, too, that fat can be listed in a number of ways—as shortening, butter, margarine or any form of vegetable oil. You can probably assume that a product that lists either sugar or fat (in any of their various forms) at or near the top of its ingredient list has a substantial number of calories.

In comparison shopping, consider two ingredient lists for plain tomato sauce and for spaghetti sauce. If the tomato sauce contains no fat in any form, while the spaghetti sauce contains oil, you know that the tomato sauce is likely to be lower in calories than the spaghetti sauce. It's the seasonings that give spaghetti sauce its special flavor, not the fat. You can always add your own oregano, basil, garlic and onion. Hot pepper can turn tomato sauce into a spaghetti sauce with substantial savings.

Canned tuna is an example of food that can be purchased either packed in oil or packed in water or brine (salted water). A seven-ounce can of oil-packed tuna contains 570 calories; the same brand, packed in water, contains only 250. The difference doubles the calorie count.

The bread counter is another place where label reading can lead you to the less fattening choices. Most breads contain fat or

shortening in some form. But true French and Italian breads do not; nor do they contain any sugar. French or Italian bread traditionally is made simply with flour, salt, leavening and water. Sometimes French- and Italian-style breads, labeled to imply authenticity, will contain added fat or sugar. By reading the fine print you can save fat and sugar calories and locate the real thing.

Don't Be Misled by Labels That Imply a Low-Fat or Low-Calorie Content

Look beyond the words "dietetic," "lower in fat," "lower in saturated fat," "no butterfat," "non-dairy," "part skim" and "sugar-free." While such products may indeed be lower in fat or calories, check the nutrition label and be sure. Dietetic foods may simply be salt-free, or sweetened with Sorbitol sweetener which is useful for diabetics but no lower in calories than sugar. Some dietetic foods are just as fattening, or *more* fattening, than nondietetic foods. A product may be lower in fat, but not much. The product itself could still be relatively high in fat and calories. Some products that are non-dairy, lower in saturated fat or labeled "no butterfat" may contain vegetable oil instead and be just as fattening as others. Even products that are truly low-fat may be high in calories because of added sugar. And sugar-free products can be high in calories because of added fat. The real bottom line to look for is the calorie count and how it compares with a competing product. Since such claims do trigger the requirement for complete nutritional data, it should be available on the label.

Beware of Verbal or Other Unsubstantiated Claims

If the person behind the cheese counter tells you a certain variety is low in fat, if the proprietor of a health food or diet food shop claims that his or her sausage or cold cuts are nonfattening, ask to see supporting information on the product's box or package. Beware also of verbal claims and hand-lettered signs. Ask that informal claims be substantiated.

IN THE GROCERY AISLES

General Rules for Smart Shopping

1. Look for the nutrition label. Check competing products and select the item with the least calories and lowest fat content per serving.

2. If not nutritionally labeled, look for the "list of ingredients." Ingredients are listed in order of quantity. Avoid products which show forms of fat or sugar among the first few ingredients.

3. Purchase plain foods rather than those packaged in or with sauces, which usually contain added fat and calories. Avoid convenience foods; it's more economical in cost and calories to purchase the ingredients and make your own.

4. To save calories, look for alternative items that are lower in fat or sugar such as low-sugar jams and jellies, juice-packed fruits, seafood packed in water instead of oil.

5. Make a shopping list and stick to it.

6. Don't go shopping on an empty stomach.

7. Buy large economy sizes only if you're certain that you can use the contents within a reasonable time. Big packages are no bargain if you throw half away. Worse yet is overeating to avoid waste. Be sure that the larger package really costs less per ounce than a smaller one (check the unit pricing code).

8. Don't buy sale or coupon items unless you really need them and then only if they're nutritious, low in fat and calories.

LEAN CUISINE GUIDE TO CREAM AND CREAM SUBSTITUTES*

Cream or Substitute	Calories	Carbohydrate (g)	Protein (g)	Total Fat (g)	Saturated Fat (g)	Cholesterol (mg)	Sodium (mg)
Cream, half & half	20	0.6	0.4	1.7	1.1	6.0	6.0
Cream, light (coffee or table cream)	29	0.6	0.4	2.9	1.8	10.0	6.0
Cream, medium	37	0.5	0.4	3.8	2.3	13.0	6.0
Frozen non-dairy coffee whitener, containing hydrogenated vegetable oil and soy protein	20	1.7	0.2	1.5	0.3	0.0	12.0
Frozen non-dairy coffee whitener, containing lauric acid oil and sodium caseinate	20	1.7	0.2	1.5	1.4	0.0	12.0
Powdered non-dairy coffee whitener	32	3.2	0.3	2.1	1.9	0.0	10.6
Cream, heavy whipping cream	52	0.4	0.3	5.6	3.5	21.0	6.0
Cream, heavy whipping cream whipped	26	0.2	0.2	2.8	1.7	10.0	2.8
Pressurized whipped cream	8	0.4	0.1	0.7	0.4	2.0	4.0
Pressurized non-dairy whipped topping	11	0.6	trace	0.9	0.8	0.0	2.0
Frozen non-dairy whipped topping	13	0.9	0.5	1.0	0.9	0.0	1.0
Non-dairy powdered whipped topping mix, prepared with whole milk	8	0.7	0.1	0.5	0.4	trace	3.0
Sour cream, half & half	20	0.6	0.4	1.8	1.1	6.0	6.0
Sour cream	26	0.5	0.4	2.5	1.6	5.0	6.0
Non-dairy imitation sour cream	30	1.0	0.3	2.8	2.6	0.0	14.7

Source: U.S. Department of Agriculture; Agricultural Research Service, *Composition of Foods: Dairy and Egg Products — Raw, Processed, Prepared* (Agriculture Handbook No. 8-1), 1976.

All figures are based on a volume of one tablespoon. Figures will vary according to specific brands.

9. If possible, shop alone. Don't allow yourself to be influenced to deviate from your shopping list by a relative or neighbor, your spouse or children.

10. Avoid temptation. Stay away from the store areas where snacks, sweets and junk foods are displayed.

AT THE DAIRY COUNTER

Once upon a time there were only three kinds of milk, and they all came in the same bottle: the kind at the top, the kind at the bottom, and the kind you got when you shook up the bottle.

Today the milk section has expanded into an enchanted dairyland of real and fake eggs, creams, coffee lighteners, non-dairy substitutes, whipped toppings, yogurts, ice milks and dietetic frozen desserts. There are cheeses from all corners of the world, plus imitation cheeses, processed cheeses and so-called cheese foods. There are at least a dozen ways to buy milk: skimmed, non-fat, low-fat, dried, canned, evaporated, condensed, sweetened, cultured, malted, flavored, with 2 percent butterfat, with 1 percent butterfat, with added Vitamins A and D and nonfat dry milk solids.

This bewildering assortment of dairy and non-dairy alternatives is in response to the consumer's wish to cut down on fat, saturated fat, cholesterol and/or calories. The confusion arises be-cause not all consumers are out to exorcise the same villains. So a variety of products has emerged, often at cross purposes. Unless you have a clear idea of what you need to avoid it's easy to pay a premium price for an alternative you thought was low in calories, only to discover after months of usage that it's even more fattening than the real thing. You may select a cholesterol-free non-dairy imitation product, not knowing that it's full of cholesterol-raising saturated oil.

Luckily, most of the information you really need to know is on the label—in small print.

How to Buy Milk

We are often told that we never outgrow our need for milk. Since most of the important nutrients in milk are available elsewhere, or in other dairy products, that statement is open to debate. Nevertheless, milk is a significant source of low-cost protein and calcium, which can also be low-fat and low-calorie if you choose a defatted or low-fat version. Skim milk has about half the calories of whole milk, yet it contains just as much protein and calcium. Only the fat (and fat calories) have been removed.

Because dairy products are available in different regions under a variety of brand names, our *Lean Cuisine* Milk Guide is based on the types of products generally available. Read the labels of the products available in your area to determine which is which.

LEAN CUISINE MILK GUIDE*

Milk Product	Calories	Carbohydrate (g)	Protein (g)	Total Fat (g)	Saturated Fat (g)	Cholesterol (mg)	Sodium (mg)
Whole milk	157	11.4	8.0	8.9	5.6	35.0	119.0
Low-fat (2%) milk	121	11.7	8.1	4.7	2.9	18.0	122.0
Low-fat (2%) milk, with nonfat milk solids added	125	12.2	8.5	4.7	2.9	18.0	128.0
Low-fat (1%) milk	102	11.7	8.0	2.6	1.6	10.0	123.0
Low-fat (1%) milk, with nonfat milk solids added	104	12.2	8.5	2.4	1.5	10.0	128.0
Skim milk	86	11.9	8.4	0.4	0.3	4.0	126.0
Skim milk, with nonfat milk solids added	90	12.3	8.8	0.6	0.4	5.0	130.0
Buttermilk	99	11.7	8.1	2.2	1.3	9.0	257.0
Chocolate whole milk	208	25.9	7.9	8.5	5.3	30.0	149.0
Chocolate low-fat (2%) milk	179	26.0	8.0	5.0	3.1	17.0	150.0
Chocolate low-fat (1%) milk	158	26.1	8.1	2.5	1.5	7.0	152.0
Eggnog	342	34.4	9.7	19.0	11.3	149.0	138.0
Goat's milk	168	10.9	8.7	10.1	6.5	28.0	122.0
Canned Milk							
Condensed milk, sweetened	982	166.5	24.2	26.6	16.8	104.0	389.0
Evaporated whole milk	338	25.3	17.2	19.1	11.6	74.0	266.0
Evaporated skim milk	198	28.9	19.3	0.5	0.3	10.0	294.0
Milk Substitutes							
Imitation milk containing blend of hydrogenated vegetable oils	150	15.0	4.3	8.3	1.9	trace	191.0
Imitation milk containing lauric acid oil	150	15.0	4.3	8.3	7.4	trace	191.0

Source: U.S. Department of Agriculture, Agricultural Research Service, *Composition of Foods: Dairy and Egg Products—Raw, Processed, Prepared* (Agriculture Handbook No. 8-1), 1976.

*All figures are based on a volume of one cup of fluid milk. Figures will vary according to specific brands.

About Powdered Milk. The calorie, fat and cholesterol data for reconstituted (water added in accordance with package directions) nonfat dry milks are approximately the same as that for fresh skim milk.

There are two types of nonfat dry milk available. Instant nonfat dry milk, sold in supermarkets, is heat-treated so that it dissolves easily in cold water. Non-instant is harder to find, but its flavor is superior, much closer to that of fresh milk. (Non-instant, non-heat-treated nonfat dry milk is usually sold in health food stores.) It takes less of the non-instant powder to make one cup of milk—only ¼ cup compared with ⅓ cup of the dry instant milk.

When reconstituted according to package directions, both milks have approximately the same nutritional and caloric content as fresh skim milk. All three kinds can be used interchangeably in any recipe that calls for fluid milk.

How to Lighten Your Coffee. To our way of thinking, the most nutritious, least fattening way to lighten coffee (or tea) is with low-fat fresh milk. A tablespoon contains only about 6 calories and ½ gram of cholesterol.

Questions and Answers about Yogurt

Yogurt, plain and simple, is fermented milk that has no more nutritional value than the milk it was made from. Since yogurt is usually (but not always) made from low-fat milk, it would be a good snack to eat if people really did eat it plain and simple. Actually most of the yogurt sold in this country has been calorie-inflated with sugary fruit preserves. The flavorings and sweeteners can double the calorie count.

Q. *My friends like to diet by eating a container of fruit yogurt for lunch. They say it's high in protein. Is yogurt a high-protein lunch?*

A. No. Fruit-sweetened yogurt has nutritional value roughly comparable to a glass of chocolate milk. An eight-ounce container usually offers only nine grams of protein. Because yogurt is milk, predigested by bacteria, it takes only an hour to assimilate. Fresh milk takes three or four hours. And the added sugar in fruit-sweetened yogurt is a waste of calories. For a more satisfying and nutritious dairy lunch, you should consider a small container of low-fat cottage cheese topped with fresh, unsweetened fruit.

Q. *What is yogurt?*

A. Yogurt is milk that has been commercially fermented by the addition of "friendly" bacteria. These bacteria predigest the milk, thickening it somewhat and changing its taste from fresh to slightly tart or sour. This makes the milk easier to digest, helpful for people who can't digest fresh milk. The friendly yogurt bacteria also help to fight off harmful bacteria in the digestive tract, thereby providing added health benefits. Because of its tart, sour-cream-like taste, yogurt is a handy ingredient in cooking; but high

LEAN CUISINE CHEESE GUIDE*

Cheese	Calories	Carbohydrate (g)	Protein (g)	Total Fat (g)	Saturated Fat (g)	Cholesterol (mg)	Sodium (mg)
Natural Cheeses							
Blue	100	0.7	6.1	8.2	5.3	21.0	396.0
Brick	105	0.8	6.6	8.4	5.3	27.0	159.0
Brie	95	0.1	5.9	7.9	N.A.	28.0	178.0
Camembert	85	0.1	5.6	6.9	4.3	20.0	239.0
Cheddar	114	0.4	7.1	9.4	6.0	30.0	176.0
Cheshire	110	1.4	6.6	8.7	N.A.	29.0	198.0
Colby	112	0.7	6.7	9.1	5.7	27.0	171.0
Cottage, creamed	29	0.8	3.5	1.3	0.8	4.3	115.0
Cottage, low-fat (2%)	25	1.0	3.9	0.5	0.3	2.4	115.0
Cottage, low-fat (1%)	21	0.8	3.5	0.3	0.2	1.3	115.0
Cottage, dry curd	24	0.5	4.9	0.1	0.1	1.9	82.0
Cream	99	0.8	2.1	9.9	6.2	31.0	84.0
Edam	101	0.4	7.1	7.9	5.0	25.0	274.0
Feta	75	1.2	4.0	6.0	4.2	25.0	316.0
Fontina	110	0.4	7.3	8.8	5.4	33.0	N.A.
Gjetost	132	12.1	2.7	8.4	5.4	N.A.	170.0
Gouda	101	0.6	7.1	7.8	5.0	32.0	232.0
Gruyere	117	0.1	8.4	9.2	5.4	31.0	95.0
Limburger	93	0.1	5.7	7.7	4.8	26.0	227.0
Monterey	106	0.2	6.9	8.6	N.A.	N.A.	152.0
Mozzarella	80	0.6	5.5	6.1	3.7	22.0	106.0
Mozzarella, low-moisture	90	0.7	6.1	7.0	4.4	25.0	118.0
Mozzarella, part skim	72	0.8	6.9	4.5	2.9	16.0	132.0
Mozzarella, low-moisture, part skim	79	0.9	7.8	4.9	3.1	15.0	150.0
Muenster	104	0.3	6.6	8.5	5.4	27.0	178.0
Neufchatel	74	0.8	2.8	6.6	4.2	22.0	113.0
Parmesan, hard	111	0.9	10.1	7.3	4.7	19.0	454.0
Parmesan, grated	130	1.0	13.0	8.3	5.2	25.0	410.0
Port du Salut	100	0.2	6.7	8.0	4.7	35.0	151.0
Provolone	100	0.6	7.3	7.6	4.8	20.0	248.0
Ricotta	49	0.9	3.2	3.7	2.4	14.4	24.0
Ricotta, part skim	39	1.5	3.2	2.2	1.4	8.8	36.0
Romano, hard	110	1.0	9.0	7.6	5.9	29.0	340.0
Romano, grated	130	1.0	11.0	9.0	7.0	35.0	405.0
Roquefort	105	0.6	6.1	8.7	5.5	26.0	513.0
Tilsit	96	0.5	6.9	7.4	4.8	29.0	213.0
Pasteurized Process Cheeses							
American	106	0.4	6.3	8.9	5.6	27.0	406.0
Pimiento	106	0.5	6.3	8.9	5.6	27.0	405.0
Swiss	95	0.6	7.0	7.1	4.6	24.0	388.0
Pasteurized Process Cheese Foods							
American	93	2.1	5.6	7.0	4.4	18.0	337.0
Swiss	92	1.3	6.2	6.8	N.A.	23.0	440.0
Pasteurized Process Cheese Spread,							
American	82	2.5	4.7	6.0	3.8	16.0	381.0

Source: U.S. Department of Agriculture, Agricultural Research Service, *Composition of Foods: Dairy and Egg Products — Raw, Processed, Prepared* (Agriculture Handbook No. 8-1), 1976.

*All figures are based on one ounce of cheese. Figures will vary according to specific brands.

N.A.: Information is not available, but constituent is believed to be present in measurable amount.

heat kills the bacteria present, as does deep freezing for long periods of time.

Q. *Is all yogurt low-fat and low-calorie?*

A. No. The average 8-ounce container of low-fat plain yogurt has about 125 calories. Normally, some nonfat milk solids have been added, which provides extra protein but adds no extra fat. But there are also brands of yogurt made with whole milk or extra-rich milk, and these may have double the amount of fat and an increased calorie count. Most yogurts on the market are sweetened with fruit preserves and sugar, which can double the calorie count.

Shopping for Cheeses

For the serious fat-fighter, most cheeses are a caloric extravagance to be used sparingly, more as a seasoning than a food. The one big exception is, of course, cottage cheese, which well deserves its reputation as the fat-fighter's friend. You'll find low-fat cottage cheese used as a stand-in for more fattening ingredients throughout the recipes of this book. When low-fat cottage cheese is indicated, use 99 percent fat-free cheese.

Hard cheeses are often sold unlabeled, or labeled with store-made signs that describe certain imports as low-calorie, made from skim milk, or in similar phrases that suggest reduced fat content. The cheese itself may even be labeled "made from partially skimmed milk," but with no further information about fat or calorie content. We have investigated a number of these so-called low-calorie cheeses and found, in most cases, that there is no significant reduction in fat and calories. Many hard cheeses made from partially skimmed milk have additional butterfat added. So the supposed fat and calorie savings are only an illusion.

Soft part-skim-milk cheeses—mozzarella and ricotta—*are* lower in fat and calories, which is good news for fans of Italian cuisine! Feta cheese and Neufchatel cheese are also somewhat lower in fat and calorie content.

Don't Be Turned Away by the Word "Imitation." There is a real need for cheeses with a reduced fat and calorie content, and a number of brands are available in different sections of the country. They must be labeled "imitation cheese" only because they contain less butterfat than required by the official stan-dards for cheeses. In other words, if you make a Cheddar that's identical to other Cheddars in every way except that it contains less fat, your cheese must be labeled "imitation,"—even though your cheese is nutritionally superior, and has more protein than the so-called real Cheddar.

Q. *Are all imitation cheeses low in fat and calories?*

A. No. Some reduced-butterfat cheeses have polyunsaturated fats added. Although these might be useful to a cholesterol-watcher without a weight problem, a person who is trying to reduce overall fat intake and calories will not save anything by buying them. These cheeses are usually well labeled. Look for fat and calorie data if losing or maintaining weight is your primary concern.

Q. *Are low-fat, low-calorie cheeses also low in sodium?*

A. No. Because salt (sodium chloride) is used in manufacturing cheese, it tends to have a higher sodium content than many foods. Fat and calorie contents are not an accurate guide to sodium content in cheese. There are low-sodium cheeses (so labeled) on the market. In these cheeses, a salt substitute (usually potassium chloride) is used in the manufacturing process as partial replacement for the sodium chloride. Persons on sodium-restricted diets should note the sodium alerts in the recipes in this book and omit cheese when necessary or substitute a low-sodium cheese.

IN THE DIETETIC DEPARTMENT

You might expect to find a safe oasis among the diet foods—away from the potato chips, cheese dips and frozen chocolate pies. Don't count on it. Label reading is even more important here, because not every so-called dietetic product will spare you from excess fat and calories but will probably cost you more money than a nondietetic product.

The word dietetic doesn't necessarily mean low-calorie. Any product suitable for any one of a number of special diets might be labeled as diet or dietetic. That could simply mean it is salt-free or specially formulated for diabetics.

All the information you need to know is on the label, but unless you take the time to read it, you might mistakenly assume that a sugar-free candy is low-calorie, or that dietetic peanut butter or mayonnaise is low-fat. The sugarless candy might be sweetened with Sorbitol sweetener, a slow-metabolizing sweetener for diabetics that has just as many calories as sugar. Saccharin-sweetened products, on the other hand, generally are lower in calories, but not always. The dietetic peanut butter may simply be salt-free but no lower in fat or calories. The specially formulated mayonnaise substitute might be made without eggs, or with polyunsaturated oil, but still be no less fattening than ordinary mayonnaise.

To compound the confusion, many dietetic products use fanciful names that imply slimness, and some decorate their labels with shapely silhouettes or other illustrations that convey the idea of weight loss. The casual shopper can easily be misled, but thanks to federal regulations, the pertinent information is usually available on the label for those willing to read the fine print.

Beware of Unlabeled Products

Unlabeled products in diet shops and health food stores represent a potential trap. Don't trust the verbal claims of clerks or hand-lettered signs claiming that the veal sausage, beef bologna or artichoke spaghetti are low-calorie. Perhaps the particular product being sold *is* substantially lower in calories. If so, the store manager should be able to support the claim with a packing crate label or other information from the manufacturer—in print. The deception is often unintentional; the clerk or counterperson may honestly believe that the product is low in calories.

Low-Calorie Diet Foods

Look for calorie-saving products on the diet shelf in categories such as those listed below. A variety of brands is available, but do be sure to read the label for calorie content.

Canned Fruits Packed in Juice Instead of Syrup. These can contain less than half the calories of syrup-packed fruits.

Low-Calorie, Low-Fat Diet Salad Dressings. Choose those formulated with less oil.

Diet Sodas and Soft Drinks. Choose those that are made without sugar.

Sugar-Free Iced Tea Mix.

Sugar-Free, Low-Fat Hot Cocoa and Milkshake Mixes. Choose brands made with nonfat milk powder.

Sugar-Free Gelatin and Pudding Mixes.

Calorie-Reduced Cake Mixes. It is especially important to read the label and choose a calorie-reduced brand that's low in fat and sweetened with fructose (fruit sugar), rather than a sugar-free brand for diabetics, sweetened with Sorbitol sweetener.

Low-Calorie Pancake Mixes and Sugar-Free Pancake Syrup.

Diet Cheeses. Purchase only the cheeses specially formulated to be low-fat and clearly labeled with pertinent information.

Low-Sugar and Sugar-Free Jams, Jellies and Preserves.

Diet Margarine. It contains half the calories of regular margarine or butter, but that's still 50 calories per tablespoon.

Low-Calorie Frozen Desserts. These include ice milks and frozen yogurt. Look for a brand with less than 2 percent fat and a labeled calorie count under 100 per half-cut serving.

Diet Frozen Dinners. Purchase those that have complete nutritional information on the label. Be sure that the dinner offers more grams of protein than grams of fat.

AT THE BREAD COUNTER

Generations of dieters have shunned bread needlessly, when the real calorie culprit was what they put on it! With bread goes butter or margarine—at 100 calories per level tablespoon—or

LEAN CUISINE GUIDE TO BREAD PRODUCTS *

Bread Product	Calories	Carbohydrate (g)	Protein (g)	Total Fat (g)	Saturated Fat (g)	Cholesterol (mg)	Sodium (mg)
White bread	1247	227.7	40.8	17.2	3.9	18.0	2245.0
Whole-wheat bread	1102	216.4	47.6	13.6	2.7	18.0	2390.0
Cracked-wheat bread	1193	236.3	39.5	10.0	2.1	9.0	2400.0
Vienna bread	1315	251.3	41.3	13.6	3.0	14.0	2631.0
French or Italian bread	1252	255.8	41.3	3.6	N.A.	5.0	2654.0
Raisin bread, plain	1188	243.1	29.9	12.7	2.9	14.0	1656.0
Rye bread	1102	236.3	41.3	5.0	N.A.	5.0	2527.0
Pumpernickel bread	1116	240.9	41.3	5.4	N.A.	5.0	2581.0
High-fiber bread	795	154.4	40.1	9.1	N.A.	0.0	2543.0
High-protein bread	1200	224.0	56.0	16.0	N.A.	0.0	2480.0
Hard rolls, white	1415	269.9	44.5	14.5	3.2	18.2	2835.0
Soft hamburger and hotdog buns	1352	240.4	37.2	25.4	6.0	22.7	2295.0
Brown-and-serve rolls	1356	229.5	35.8	30.8	7.4	25.9	2200.0
Bagels, egg	1362	231.0	49.5	16.5	4.1	N.A.	N.A.

Sources: U.S. Department of Agriculture (Agricultural Research Service) and information supplied by manufacturers.

All figures are based on one pound of commercially made enriched products. Figures will vary according to specific brands.

N.A.: Information is not available, but constituent is believed to be present in measurable amount.

peanut butter at 95 calories and jelly at 50 calories.

Avoid unnecessary calories by eating bread without a spread. Use bread and bread products as a sandwich-wrapping filled with high-protein lean meat, poultry or seafood. Bread is also a good meat stretcher: top it with slices of lean roast and low-fat gravy for a hot sandwich main course to be served with side dishes of vegetables and salad.

There are differences in breads, and the would-be waistline-watcher should choose the types made with a nutritious flour and a minimum of added fat and sugar or none at all. Be sure to read the label for nutrition information.

Calorie and fat contents vary according to the size of the loaf or the thickness of the slice. The best way to compare bread products is by the pound.

AT THE HEALTH FOOD STORE

Remember, the word natural is no guarantee that a product is good for you. If you wish to avoid excess calories—fat and sugar—keep in mind that even natural foods can be fattening. Some health foods contain more fat and sweetening ingredients than their supermarket counterparts. Granola-type cereals, for example, are sprinkled with oil before toasting and contain nearly 500 calories a cupful compared with 110 calories in corn flakes or 90 in Kellogg's Special K breakfast cereal. While granola is a nutritious treat, its high fat and calorie contents would make it more suitable for youngsters, athletes or other highly active slim people not engaged in fighting excess weight.

At health food stores, as everywhere, informed buying—through label reading—is important. Despite their higher price, some health food products are real calorie bargains. Look for the following:

Dried Fruits. Those prepared without sugar are great for making *Lean Cuisine* sweets and treats. Health food stores generally offer a wider variety of dried fruits.

Natural Fruit Juices and Concentrates. Health food stores generally offer varieties made without sugar, honey or other sweeteners not otherwise available at retail stores.

Soy Flour and Soy-Flour Pancake Mixes. These products are higher in protein than wheat flour. Adding low-fat protein to your menus in this form allows you to eat less high-fat meat protein.

Soy Meat-Extenders. Called TVP, textured vegetable protein made from high-protein soy can be mixed with ground beef in making hamburgers, meatballs, meatloaf and other ground-meat dishes. With soy extender added, you get more servings with less fat and calories but the same amount of protein.

Non-Instant Nonfat Dry Milk. When reconstituted, this is better-tasting and more like fresh skim milk than the heat-treated instant-mixing products sold in supermarkets.

Whole-Grain Flours and Cereals. Whole-wheat flour, stone-ground cornmeal, brown rice, natural oatmeal, grits and other minimally processed grain products are higher in fiber and nutrition than the refined supermarket products. Be wary, however, of mixes. The mixes generally contain added oils and sweeteners, more than you would use preparing the item from basic ingredients the *Lean Cuisine* way.

Fruit Sugar (Fructose). For the same calories, fruit sugar is 1 1/2 times sweeter than table sugar when used to sweeten fruits and other acid foods. This makes it a better choice than ordinary table sugar, because you can use less. Like sucrose, fructose is pure calories and should be used sparingly. Avoid raw sugar and turbinado sugar; they are no sweeter than table sugar and the miniscule amounts of nutritional substances they may contain do not make up for their high calories.

THE LEAN COOK'S KITCHEN

Is your kitchen equipped to fight fat? Without the proper weapons, the campaign is tougher than it has to be. But with the proper tools, cooking the *Lean Cuisine* way can be a joy. Expensive, elaborate kitchenware really isn't necessary. Luckily, many of the handiest gadgets are relatively inexpensive. Following is a list of some necessities and niceties for the Lean Cook:

Adequate Refrigerator and Freezer Space. Even if your family size is very small, a roomy refrigerator-freezer is a real work-saver for the cook with little time for frequent shopping trips. *Lean Cuisine* focuses on low-fat meat, poultry and seafood, abundant fruits and vegetables, creative use of leftovers, home-made frozen dinners and other do-it-yourself convenience foods—and you'll need a place to keep them all.

Nonstick Cookware. This is an absolute must. You needn't buy the most expensive brand. The nonstick finish is the important factor. Your cookware should be of sufficient quality to stand up to scouring, yet cheap enough that you feel free to toss it out when the finish loses its smoothness and requires added fat for cooking.

Good, Sharp Knives. These are essential for trimming the fat from meat, slim-slicing roasts and making short work of preparing salad greens, fruits and vegetables. (Unless you're willing to hand-wash and dry the carbon-steel variety, look for stainless-steel knives with dishwasher-safe handles.)

Measuring Cups and Spoons. There is no substitute for accuracy in measuring.

Kitchen Scale. This is handy not only for weighing por-

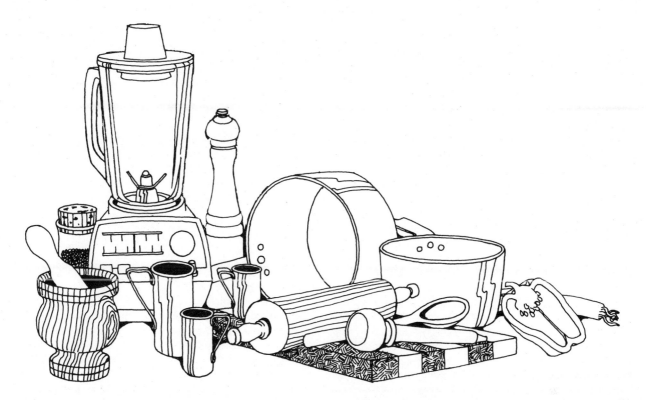

tions, but it takes all the guesswork out of measuring most basic ingredients as well. For instance, a cup of flour can vary if it's sifted or unsifted, level or rounded, but 8 ounces of flour by weight is a uniform measurement, exactly the same every time. (A small postal scale can serve just as well.)

Blender. This appliance is handier than an electric mixer for most *Lean Cuisine* recipes. If you have to choose between the two, opt for the blender. Look for a big-enough container and a powerful motor; these features are more important than a multitude of buttons.

Bulb-Type Baster, with Needle. The baster looks like an oversize eye dropper with a rubber bulb at one end; it is useful not only for basting but also for skimming the fat off the top of broth. Some basters come equipped with a screw-on hollow needle that makes it possible to inoculate lean roasts with tenderizer solution (a meat tenderizer dissolved in water).

Fat Mop. This handy gadget has an absorbent mop head of plastic fibers. If you've noticed how grease adheres to plastic, then you know how this mop works. You simply swish it through a stock or stew and the plastic collects the fat. The mop is washable and reusable.

Pressure Cooker. This cooks food in one-third the time it takes by conventional methods—one of the most convenient gadgets ever invented for busy cooks. And now that the cook is busier than ever, the pressure cooker is enjoying a great revival. Today's pressure cookers have built-in safety features that make them virtually foolproof. Look for a model with a nonstick finish.

Egg Separator. An egg separator makes short work of separating whites from yolks, with little chance of mishap.

Shredder. You can shred vegetables with an inexpensive grater from the housewares department, with an attachment to a standing mixer, with an electric shredder designed for that purpose, or with the shredding disc on a food processor. Whichever kind you choose, a shredder is a necessity in *Lean Cuisine*.

Thermometers. A meat thermometer is the one sure way to know when a roast is done to perfection. Without one, you're simply guessing. And an oven thermometer is the only definite way to determine that food is baking or roasting at the right temperature.

Barbecue Grill. Since grilled foods are so calorie-wise, the lean cook can really make happy use of barbecue equipment, whether it's simply an inexpensive charcoal grill from the hardware store or a fancy gas or electric rotisserie with permanent briquettes that can be used indoors or out.

Nice but Not Necessary. Any gadgetry that makes cooking simpler or more enjoyable is worth having, if you can afford it. On that basis you might like to treat yourself to a microwave oven, an ice cream machine (it makes low-fat frozen yogurt and low-calorie ice milk as well), a food processor, a set of decorative copper molds for all those gelatin desserts (and for enhancing the kitchen walls), an electric slicing machine (for wafer-thin slicing of roasts), a yogurt maker (which pays for itself if you use a lot of yogurt).

EATING OUT

Americans seem to be eating out more. The ever-increasing share of America's food dollars being spent in restaurants (especially fast-food chains, luncheonettes and diners) rather than in supermarkets and food stores is related to the increase in working wives, singles, childless couples, fragmented families and business travel. Many of the meals eaten out are due to necessity not choice.

So there are two types of eating out to consider: the routine refueling stops—lunch at the office or breakfast on the road—and the kind you do for the fun of it—dinner with friends, trying a new restaurant, sampling the local specialties on vacation, celebrating a special occasion.

Of the two, the routine refueling stops represent the greater threat of excess fat and calories. By their very nature, fast-food places specialize in the quick-cooking, deep-fried, starchy fare with the most fat and calories and the least substance.

New York has regulations covering the type of foods that can go on a "diet plate," but few restaurant operators are even aware these regulations exist. California has a truth-in-menu law. Theoretically, the law would make it illegal to put a high-calorie food on the "low-calorie plate."

But as a practical reality, the restaurant patron has little assurance that the dieter's menu will save any calories over wisely selected choices from the regular menu. Quite often the opposite is true. The familiar cottage cheese-hamburger combination is a case in point: an ad agency handling food accounts once did a survey for a client and found that the cottage cheese-hamburger plate in its study averaged close to 600 calories. The hamburger is often the same ground meat served other patrons, not extra lean. And it may be grilled the same way. The cottage cheese is usually the regular creamed type, not low-fat. We have seen so-called diet plates piled with syrup-packed canned fruit, fruit-flavored gelatin cubes, even sugary sherbets, salads drowned in oily dressings, tuna or salmon well laced with mayonnaise.

There's really very little to prevent restaurant operators from putting together any combination of food they think is low-calorie (or that they think that *you* will think is low-calorie). With the increasing interest in leaner cuisine, some restaurants are doing a better job, offering more imaginative menus with creative combinations that truly *are* low-calorie. If in doubt, talk with the manager and ask for an explanation. What foods are used and how are they prepared? What makes a particular entrée low-calorie?

No-Frills Fare in the Air

For no extra charge, travelers on U.S. airlines can opt for special meals at the time they make their airline reservations. Choices include meals that are low-calorie, low-cholesterol, diabetic and salt-free. Many knowledgeable travelers order the low-calorie meal even if they aren't dieting. Although it costs you nothing ex-

tra, the low-calorie meals are better quality—made with more expensive protein foods, less starchy fillers and junk food than the regular airline meals. Typical low-calorie choices might include broiled tenderloin steak, chicken or fish for the main course, two vegetables, a salad and piece of fresh fruit for dessert.

Lean Cuisine Menu Guide for Routine Meals Away from Home

Breakfast. GOOD CHOICES: fresh fruit, cereal with milk (especially a high-protein cereal), poached or soft-boiled egg (unless you're cholesterol-watching). The least fattening breakfast meats available in commercial eating places are Canadian bacon and ham. Order unbuttered toast or English muffins; or better yet, bagels—they're higher in protein. AVOID: fried eggs (they're almost always fried in too much fat), pancakes or French toast with syrup, bacon, sausage, Danish pastries, prebuttered toast, bread or rolls, and jams or jellies.

Quick Lunches. GOOD CHOICES: chef's salad with dressing on the side (only add a tablespoon), cottage cheese with fresh fruit (avoid canned or sweetened fruit), sandwiches made with sliced turkey, roast beef, chicken roll or boiled ham—ask for a pickle on the side, or lettuce and tomato. AVOID: hot dogs, hamburgers, French fries and anything else deep-fat fried. Avoid all lunchmeats because anything available at the average lunch counter is likely to be high in fat and calories. Avoid salad fillings made with mayonnaise.

Dinner. GOOD CHOICES: broiled seafood or chicken, roast turkey, veal steak or chops, lean roast beef, liver (if you are not on a cholesterol-restricted diet), small tenderloin steak, flank steak, London broil. Try to find a place with a good salad bar, and supplement your entrée with salad greens, raw tomatoes, carrots, celery and other *crudités*—and only one tablespoon of salad dressing. AVOID: anything breaded and deep-fat fried, most casserole-style combination dishes made with sauces or cheeses, steak and prime ribs, most chops, meatloaf, creamed soups and sauces, salads already coated with dressings, fried potatoes and onion rings—or any other fried side dish.

How to Eat Out for the Fun of It, without Adding Pounds

You needn't pass up the pleasure of a special-occasion dinner in a good restaurant just because you're waistline-watching. Sampling new foods or ethnic specialties needn't be off-limits. The key words here are sample and special occasion. Remember, you can indulge in anything—if both the quantity and frequency are kept in control.

Opt for a seafood place, if possible. If you can't afford calories, then indulge yourself with something expensive, for instance, lobster, shrimp, crab or scallops. Or order an expensive fish such as Dover sole. Ask for several lemon or lime wedges instead of melted butter or tartar sauce. Clams, oysters and mussels are low-calorie, too, especially steamed.

Head for a Chinese or Japanese restaurant. Most Oriental dishes are made with a high percentage of vegetables in proportion to meat and fat. Ask for a translation before you order so you will know to avoid the deep-fried fare and sweet sauces.

Dine out less, but better. Make dining out a first-class experience. Don't settle for second-rate places and routine fare. It's better to eat out less often, but really enjoy it. Boring food, indifferently prepared, will cost you just as much in calories, possibly more, than fine food, well prepared and nicely served.

Lean Cuisine At Breakfast And Lunch

ALL ABOUT EGGS AND EGG SUBSTITUTES

At only 80 calories apiece and less than 12 percent fat, eggs are certainly one of the leanest, least fattening main courses a calorie-counter could choose—and one of the most controversial! The problem, of course, is the cholesterol. The fact that the yolk of an egg contains about 250 milligrams of cholesterol has prompted the American Heart Association to suggest limiting egg-yolk consumption to no more than three a week. (The white of the egg does not contain cholesterol.) The egg industry has countered with promotion campaigns assuring shoppers that eggs are a valuable, nutritious food, and that there's no proof that curtailing egg consumption will save you from developing heart disease. There are eminent scientists on either side of the fence.

What should *you* do about eggs? If you have a cholesterol problem, you should follow your doctor's recommendations. Most of the recipes in this book can be made without eggs or with egg substitutes. If you are young, female, blessed with a low cholesterol count or feel you have no need to limit eggs, this chapter will show you how to prepare them with a minimum of fat and calories.

Questions and Answers about Eggs

Q. *Why do some eggs have cloudy whites?*

A. Cloudy or milky whites are a feature of freshly laid eggs. They indicate that the carbon dioxide naturally present in fresh eggs has not yet escaped through the shell. As this gas escapes, the white becomes clearer. Fresh eggs are often treated with mineral oil to help maintain freshness. This process seals many of the shell pores and slows down the loss of carbon dioxide. Cloudiness is a normal characteristic indicating that the egg is fresh.

Q. *Why do some hard-cooked eggs have discolored yolks?*

A. You may get a greenish coating around the yolks of hard-cooked eggs if you have cooked the eggs at too high a temperature, or for too long a time or if you do not cool them rapidly following cooking. The greenish color comes from sulphur and iron compounds in the egg. These compounds from at the surface of the yolk when eggs are overcooked. Even though the greenish color appears, the eggs may be eaten. They are wholesome and nutritious, and the flavor is unaffected.

Q. *What are the stringy white pieces in egg white?*

A. These are perfectly normal components of eggs—the chalazae. The chalaza is the thick, white, ropelike material that appears on opposite sides of the yolk during formation of the egg. They anchor the yolk in the white. Presence of chalazae indicates high quality eggs. As eggs become poorer in quality (older), the chalazae tend to disappear.

Q. *Why are some hard-cooked eggs difficult to peel?*

A. Frequently shells do not peel easily from very fresh hard-cooked eggs. As eggs are stored, they lose carbon dioxide and become easier to peel when hard-cooked. Buy eggs for hard-cooking several days in advance.

Q. *What are blood spots?*

A. Blood spots are caused by the rupture of a blood vessel on the yolk surface during formation of the egg. About one percent of all eggs have blood spots. Most of these eggs are removed during the grading, but occasionally one is overlooked. These spots are more difficult to detect in freshly laid eggs. The spot is harmless and can be removed with the tip of a knife.

Q. *Why are some yolks lighter in color than others?*

A. The color of the yolk depends on the feed the hen eats. Birds that have access to grass, pasture or have yellow corn or alfalfa in their diet, tend to produce darker-colored yolks. Since commercial laying hens are confined, lighter and more uniformly colored yolks are being produced. Yolk color does not affect nutritive value or cooking characteristics.

Q. *What about shell color?*

A. Some cooks prefer brown eggs to white—or vice versa. Actually, the only difference is in the shell itself. The shell color is determined by the breed of hen. If hens have been fed the same rations, the eggs will be nutritionally equivalent, regardless of shell color. They will also have the same flavor, the same keeping quality and the same whipping and cooking characteristics.

Q. *Are eggs always wholesome?*

A. Fresh eggs are wholesome, but if they are stored in a soiled condition, become cracked or are otherwise mishandled, they may become contaminated with bacteria. Even then, unless they are actually spoiled, adequate cooking makes them safe to eat. Since eggs are nutritious for bacteria as well as for man, foods containing eggs will support bacterial growth if they are not handled properly or are not refrigerated—and may cause food poisoning. Cracks in eggs permit entry of bacteria that are ordinarily stopped by the shell membrane. Once inside the shell, bacteria can thrive. If eaten raw or undercooked, such eggs may cause illness. Cracked or chipped eggs should be used at once and only in foods that are to be thoroughly cooked.

To Hard-Cook Eggs

Put the eggs in a single layer in a saucepan, and cover with cold water. Bring the water to a boil, then turn off the heat and cover the pan. Leave eggs in the water for 15 minutes, then cool under cold running water. Chill in the refrigerator.

To Soft-Cook Eggs

Put the eggs in a single layer in a saucepan, and cover with cold water. Bring the water to a boil, then turn off the heat and cover the pan. Leave eggs in the water for 2 to 4 minutes, depending on doneness desired.

To Poach Eggs

Pour 2 inches of water into a shallow saucepan. Heat to boiling, then lower to a steady simmer. Break each egg into a shallow saucer (without breaking the yolk), then tilt the saucer so the egg slips into the simmering water. Simmer 3 to 5 minutes, depending on firmness desired. Remove with a slotted spoon or pancake turner.

To Fry Eggs without Fat

Choose a nonstick skillet with a smooth, unmarred surface—you might like to reserve one just for egg cookery. Spray it with cooking spray until slick and wet.

For scrambled eggs: fork-blend with 1 tablespoon water or skim milk per egg. Heat a sprayed nonstick skillet over medium heat. Add eggs all at once. Use a wooden spoon, coated spatula or rubber scraper to lift and move eggs gently while they cook. Cook

4 to 5 minutes for moist eggs, 6 to 8 minutes for drier eggs. Season to taste.

For eggs sunny-side up: break the eggs (without breaking yolk) into a cold, sprayed, nonstick skillet. Cover pan with a lid or plate. Cook for 2 to 3 minutes. Lift eggs gently with a spatula onto a prewarmed plate.

For eggs once over lightly: follow directions for eggs sunny-side up. Once tops of eggs are firm or set, gently lift the eggs with spatula and turn them over. Cook, uncovered, over low heat 1 more minute. Carefully remove with spatula to a prewarmed plate.

For easy omelet: fork-blend 2 or 3 eggs with 4 to 6 teaspoons water (and salt and pepper to taste if desired). Use a small, nonstick omelet or crepe pan with sloping sides. Spray with cooking spray, and heat over moderate heat. Add egg mixture all at once. Cook undisturbed for 30 seconds, then shake pan gently. Use a coated spatula or rubber scraper to lift egg mixture gently, allowing uncooked egg to run underneath. After eggs are set, tilt the pan and lift one edge of the cooked egg mixture with the spatula or scraper. Carefully roll the omelet over and out of the pan onto a prewarmed plate.

You can also make omelets in a hinged, 2-part omelet pan. Spray both sections with cooking spray. Heat pan over medium heat. For a 2-egg omelet, pour all the egg mixture in one side. Cook and lift with scraper or spatula until nearly set, then close the pan and turn it over to cook the other side until set. Turn onto a prewarmed plate. For a larger omelet, divide the mixture between both sides of the hinged pan. Center the pan over the heat so both sides cook equally. When eggs are nearly set, close the pan and turn off the heat. Wait 1 minute before opening. Turn onto a prewarmed plate.

About Egg Substitutes

For the cholesterol-conscious or egg yolk-allergic, egg substitutes are a boon that allows the enjoyment of scrambled "eggs" for breakfast or an omelet for lunch or supper. These products are formulated to look, taste and cook like eggs, so they can be used in place of eggs in many recipes where whole eggs are used as a binder.

Check the Calorie Counts. Convenient as they are for cholesterol-watchers, some brands of egg substitute are no bargain for calorie-counters. Some egg substitutes contain more fat and calories than an equivalent amount of eggs. However, egg substitutes with less fat and fewer calories than contained in fresh eggs are available under a variety of brand names in different areas of the country. All egg substitutes are nutritionally labeled, so check the calorie and fat information and pick the brand with the least calories. (Keep in mind that one large fresh egg has about 80 calories, 6 grams of protein and 6 grams of fat.)

Adapting Recipes. Substitute ¼ cup liquid egg substitute for each beaten egg in any recipe listing whole eggs. If a recipe calls for separated eggs, you may use 3 tablespoons egg substitute for each egg yolk, plus the fresh egg whites called for in the recipe. (The cholesterol is in the yolk, not the whites, so egg whites need not be eliminated.)

TRIM TOPPINGS FOR PANCAKES AND FRENCH TOAST

Using the *Lean Cuisine* recipes in this chapter, there is no reason why you cannot enjoy the irresistible flavors of pancakes or French toast. Toppings for these traditional favorites, however, can add many unwanted calories. Remember, butter and margarine have 100 calories per *level* tablespoon. You don't really need them. Diet margarine, at 50 calories per tablespoon, is not really necessary either. Maple syrup and most syrup blends range between 50 and 60 calories per tablespoon; honey is 60 calories per tablespoon. Most of the common toppings are pure calories: fat and sugar. Some slenderizing, more sensible alternatives follow.

Crushed Fresh Fruit, such as sweet, ripe peaches, strawberries or other berries, gently warmed in their own juices, make an unbeatable topping. Off season, use defrosted unsweetened berries or other fruit from the freezer.

Homemade Chunky Applesauce (unsweetened, of course), warmed, spiced with cinnamon or apple-pie spice or sprinkled with golden raisins, makes a nice change of pace.

Juicy Crushed Pineapple straight from the can or warmed is refreshing. To avoid sugar and calories, choose juice-packed rather than syrup-packed pineapple.

Fruit-Juice Syrups, made with unsweetened fruit juice, are colorful and low in calories. Combine 1 cup juice with a scant teaspoon cornstarch or arrowroot; cook and stir over low heat until the consistency of syrup. To make with fruit-juice concentrates, simply defrost juice and thin with a little boiling water. (Try pineapple or orange juice spiked with pumpkin-pie spice or try apple juice with cinnamon). Or simmer low-sugar jams with equal parts water. These, of course, contain sugar. Diabetics and others on sugar-free diets can use the same trick with dietetic jams and jellies.

Dietetic Pancake Syrups are available on the diet shelf for sugar-free dieters. To make your own *low-sugar* Calorie-Reduced Syrup, mix 1 tablespoon cornstarch with 1 cup cold water, 1/3 cup honey and 2 teaspoons maple flavoring. Cook and stir over low heat until thickened to syrup consistency. Store in refrigerator; reheat before serving.

Adding fruit to the pancakes themselves can also be a welcome treat. You can add any of the following to the pancake recipes in this chapter: 1/2 cup rinsed and drained fresh blueberries; 1 apple, pared, cored and chopped (sprinkled with cinnamon, if desired); or 1/2 cup juice-packed crushed pineapple, well-drained (press out as much moisture as possible).

Blender Cheese Pancakes•

Makes 8 servings

2 eggs ■
1 cup low-fat cottage cheese
2/3 cup skim milk
1/2 tsp. vanilla extract
1 cup sifted all-purpose flour
1/2 tsp. baking soda
1/2 tsp. salt

● *HIGH SODIUM ALERT — Not recommended for low-sodium diets.*

■ *HIGH CHOLESTEROL ALERT — Use 1/2 cup liquid egg substitute.*

Combine eggs, cottage cheese, milk and vanilla in blender container. Cover; blend until smooth. Add flour, baking soda and salt. Blend on low speed just until mixed. Spray nonstick skillet with cooking spray. Heat over moderate heat. Spoon the batter into hot skillet to make 4-inch pancakes. Cook over low heat until bubbles form on surface. Turn; cook other side until bottom is golden brown.

Total		Per Serving
857.5	Calories	107.2
109.5	Carbohydrate (g)	13.7
61.0	Protein (g)	7.6
15.0	Total Fat (g)	1.9
5.2	Saturated Fat (g)	0.6
526.7	Cholesterol (mg)	65.8
2581.7	Sodium (mg)	322.7

German Puff Pancake■

Makes 6 servings

1 cup all-purpose flour
1/2 tsp. baking powder ●
1/2 tsp. salt ●
1 cup skim milk
5 eggs
2 tsp. safflower or corn oil
3 cups fresh fruit (sliced peaches, nectarines, strawberries or blueberries)

● *HIGH SODIUM ALERT — Use low-sodium baking powder. Omit added salt.*

■ *HIGH CHOLESTEROL ALERT — Not recommended for low cholesterol diets.*

Sift flour, baking powder and salt into mixing bowl. Stir in milk; beat in eggs 1 at a time. Spray large skillet or metal-handled omelet pan with cooking spray. Wipe with safflower oil. Heat over moderate heat. Pour in batter all at once. Cook 1 minute. Transfer skillet to a preheated 425° oven. Bake uncovered 20 minutes, or until pancake is golden and puffy. Top with fruit and slice into 6 wedges to serve.

Total		Per Serving
1225.3	Calories	204.2
156.9	Carbohydrate (g)	26.1
55.0	Protein (g)	9.2
40.9	Total Fat (g)	6.8
10.7	Saturated Fat (g)	1.8
1265.0	Cholesterol (mg)	210.8
1671.5	Sodium (mg)	278.6

Low-Fat Whole-Wheat Cakes

Makes 8 servings

1 1/4 cups whole-wheat flour
2 1/2 tsp. baking powder ●
1/2 tsp. salt ●
1 egg, slightly beaten ■
1 1/4 cups skim milk

● *HIGH SODIUM ALERT — Use low-sodium baking powder. Omit added salt.*

■ *HIGH CHOLESTEROL ALERT — Use 1/4 cup liquid egg substitute.*

Combine flour, baking powder and salt in mixing bowl. Mix together egg and milk; stir into flour mixture until just moistened. (Batter will be lumpy.) Spray nonstick skillet with cooking spray. Heat over moderate heat. Spoon the batter into hot skillet to make 4-inch pancakes. Cook over low heat until bubbles form on surface. Turn; cook other side until bottom is golden brown.

Total		Per Serving
696.5	Calories	87.1
123.4	Carbohydrate (g)	15.4
37.2	Protein (g)	4.6
8.5	Total Fat (g)	1.1
2.0	Saturated Fat (g)	0.2
258.2	Cholesterol (mg)	32.3
2113.2	Sodium (mg)	264.1

Alert Symbols: ● Sodium   ■ Cholesterol   ▲ Sugar

Soy Pancakes

Makes 8 servings

3/4 cup all-purpose flour
1/3 cup low-fat soy flour
2 1/2 tsp. baking powder ●
1/2 tsp. salt ●
1 egg ■
1 1/3 cups skim milk

● *HIGH SODIUM ALERT — Use low-sodium baking powder. Omit added salt.*

■ *HIGH CHOLESTEROL ALERT — Use 2 egg whites or 1/4 cup liquid egg substitute.*

Sift flour, soy flour, baking powder and salt into mixing bowl. Stir egg and milk together; stir into flour mixture until moistened. (Batter will be lumpy.) Spray nonstick skillet with cooking spray. Heat over moderate heat. Spoon the batter into hot skillet to make 4-inch pancakes. Cook over low heat until bubbles form on surface. Turn; cook other side until bottom is golden brown.

Total		Per Serving
649.5	Calories	81.2
100.1	Carbohydrate (g)	12.5
40.4	Protein (g)	5.0
8.7	Total Fat (g)	1.1
2.3	Saturated Fat (g)	0.3
258.7	Cholesterol (mg)	32.3
2121.3	Sodium (mg)	265.2

High-Protein French Toast

Makes 4 slices

2 eggs ■
2 tbsp. water
4 slices high-protein bread ●
Cinnamon (optional)

● *HIGH SODIUM ALERT — Use low-sodium bread.*

■ *HIGH CHOLESTEROL ALERT — Use 1/2 cup liquid egg substitute.*

Beat eggs and water together and pour into a shallow dish. Soak each bread slice in egg mixture until completely saturated, turning bread frequently with a spatula. Spray nonstick skillet or electric frypan with cooking spray. Heat over moderate heat. Use spatula to transfer the soaked bread to the skillet. Brown bread slices on both sides over low heat. Sprinkle with cinnamon, if desired.

Total		Per Slice
440.0	Calories	110.0
48.0	Carbohydrate (g)	12.0
28.0	Protein (g)	7.0
14.0	Total Fat (g)	3.5
4.0	Saturated Fat (g)	1.0
504.0	Cholesterol (mg)	126.0
742.0	Sodium (mg)	185.5

Low-Fat Mock Croque-Monsieur

Makes 1 serving

1 slice high-fiber bread, toasted ●
2 oz. (2 slices) lean baked or boiled ham ● or white-meat roast chicken or turkey
2 tsp. low-calorie, low-fat mayonnaise ●
1/2 oz. (1 thin slice) Swiss cheese ● ■

● *HIGH SODIUM ALERT — Use unsalted mayonnaise and low-sodium bread and cheese. Use chicken or turkey, not ham.*

■ *HIGH CHOLESTEROL ALERT — Use low-fat cheese.*

Spray a flat broiler tray or nonstick pie pan with cooking spray. Place toast on tray; top with ham. Spread with mayonnaise and top with cheese. Broil just until cheese is melted. Slice diagonally and serve immediately.

Total		Per Serving
245.8	Calories	245.8
9.0	Carbohydrate (g)	9.0
16.9	Protein (g)	16.9
15.8	Total Fat (g)	15.8
6.2	Saturated Fat (g)	6.2
70.3	Cholesterol (mg)	70.3
973.7	Sodium (mg)	973.7

French Breakfast Sausage Patties

Makes 12 patties

1 1/2 lb. lean boneless pork, trimmed of fat, ground
1/4 cup shaved ice
1 tsp. salt ● (optional)
1/4 tsp. pepper
1/4 tsp. ground allspice
1/4 tsp. paprika
1/8 tsp. thyme

● *HIGH SODIUM ALERT — Omit added salt.*

Combine all ingredients and mix lightly. Shape into 12 patties. If not to be used immediately, wrap, label and store in freezer. This sausage is

1 tsp. = 5 mL   1 tbsp. = 15 mL   1 cup = 250 mL   1 oz. = 30 g

uncured. Frozen patties may be broiled or grilled without defrosting (be sure to cook until well done). Thawed or unfrozen patties can be fried in a nonstick skillet sprayed with cooking spray. Cook on both sides until cooked through, with no trace of pinkness remaining.

WARNING: Do not taste raw or uncooked pork sausage for seasoning. If you would like to taste-test before completing the seasoning, fry a small sample.

Total		Per Patty
1320.0	Calories	110.0
0.0	Carbohydrate (g)	0.0
141.9	Protein (g)	11.8
68.1	Total Fat (g)	5.7
24.4	Saturated Fat (g)	2.0
420.0	Cholesterol (mg)	35.0
376.5	Sodium (mg)	31.4

Main-Course Spanish Omelet for Four

Makes 4 servings

8 eggs ■
1/4 cup water
1/4 cup minced onion or 4 tsp. instant minced onion
8-oz. can plain tomato sauce (check label for no added oil) ●
1 red or green bell pepper, minced, or 1/2 cup defrosted frozen chopped pepper, or 3 tbsp. dried pepper flakes
Salt or garlic salt ● and coarsely ground pepper to taste (optional)
Dash red pepper sauce or pinch cayenne pepper

● *HIGH SODIUM ALERT — Use unsalted tomato sauce. Omit added salt or garlic salt; use garlic powder if desired.*

■ *HIGH CHOLESTEROL ALERT — Use 2 cups liquid egg substitute.*

Spray a 10- or 12-inch nonstick skillet (for 1 large omelet) or a smaller skillet (to make 2 omelets one at a time) with cooking spray. Heat over moderate heat. Beat eggs and water together. Add all at once to large skillet, or pour half the mixture into smaller skillet. When set at edges, gently lift eggs with spatula to allow uncooked portion to run underneath. When eggs are set,

fold over and remove to plate. Cover with a pie pan to keep warm. (Repeat procedure if using small skillet.) Combine remaining ingredients in the skillet. Increase heat to high. Cook and stir 2 minutes. Divide eggs into 4 servings; pour sauce over eggs.

Total		Per Serving
756.2	Calories	189.0
26.6	Carbohydrate (g)	6.6
53.2	Protein (g)	13.3
48.5	Total Fat (g)	12.1
16.0	Saturated Fat (g)	4.0
2016.0	Cholesterol (mg)	504.0
2035.0	Sodium (mg)	508.7

Manicotti-Style Omelet with Tomato Sauce

Makes 3 servings

4 eggs, lightly beaten ■
1 cup low-fat cottage cheese ●
1 tbsp. grated extra-sharp Romano cheese ● ■
1/2 tsp. pizza seasoning or oregano
Salt or onion salt ● and pepper to taste (optional)
8-oz. can plain tomato sauce (check label for no added oil) ●
Chopped fresh parsley

● *HIGH SODIUM ALERT — Use low-sodium cheeses and unsalted tomato sauce. Omit added salt or onion salt.*

■ *HIGH CHOLESTEROL ALERT — Use 1 cup liquid egg substitute. Substitute low-fat cheese for Romano, or omit.*

Spray nonstick skillet with cooking spray. Heat over moderate heat. Add eggs. Spread cottage cheese over surface of eggs and sprinkle with Romano, pizza seasoning, salt and pepper. When egg mixture is set, fold omelet in half and turn. Cook over low heat until cheese is just heated through. Remove to platter; cover and keep warm. Heat tomato sauce in the skillet over high heat; pour over omelet. Cut into thirds to serve. Garnish with parsley.

Total		Per Serving
601.6	Calories	200.5
24.1	Carbohydrate (g)	8.0
59.4	Protein (g)	19.8
28.0	Total Fat (g)	9.3
10.5	Saturated Fat (g)	3.5
1033.8	Cholesterol (mg)	344.6
2678.6	Sodium (mg)	892.9

Frittata Foo Yung

Makes 4 servings

6 eggs, lightly beaten ■
16-oz. can mixed Chinese vegetables, drained ●
1 cup cooked cubed roast turkey, pork or drained cooked or canned small shrimp ● ■
Foo Yung Sauce (optional) (recipe in this chapter)

● *HIGH SODIUM ALERT — Use unsalted vegetables. Do not use shrimp.*

■ *HIGH CHOLESTEROL ALERT — Use 1 1/2 cups liquid egg substitute. Do not use shrimp.*

Spray large nonstick skillet with cooking spray. Heat over moderate heat. Add eggs. Cook without stirring 2 minutes. Spread vegetables and meat over surface of egg. Reduce heat; cook covered 2 minutes. Cut the frittata into 4 wedges. With a pancake turner, gently turn each wedge over. Cook uncovered over low heat 2 minutes. Serve with Foo Yung Sauce, if desired.

Total		Per Serving
833.6	Calories	208.4
14.6	Carbohydrate (g)	3.7
86.5	Protein (g)	21.6
44.5	Total Fat (g)	11.1
14.5	Saturated Fat (g)	3.6
1636.6	Cholesterol (mg)	409.2
3002.0	Sodium (mg)	750.5

Foo Yung Sauce

Makes 1 cup

1 cup fat-skimmed beef broth, canned or, preferably, homemade ●
2 tbsp. soy sauce ●
2 tsp. cornstarch or arrowroot

● *HIGH SODIUM ALERT — Use unsalted broth. Omit soy sauce.*

Heat broth to simmering. Mix together soy sauce and cornstarch; stir into broth. Cook, stirring constantly, until sauce thickens and clears.

Total		Per 1/4 Cup
69.3	Calories	17.3
9.7	Carbohydrate (g)	2.4
7.0	Protein (g)	1.8
0.0	Total Fat (g)	0.0
0.0	Saturated Fat (g)	0.0
24.0	Cholesterol (mg)	6.0
2980.0	Sodium (mg)	745.0

Alert Symbols: ● Sodium ■ Cholesterol ▲ Sugar

Cheese Omelet Florentine

Makes 1 serving

2 eggs, lightly beaten ■
1/2 oz. shredded Swiss cheese ● ■
1/2 cup cooked chopped spinach, well drained ●
1/8 tsp. ground nutmeg or mace
  Salt ● and pepper to taste (optional)

● *HIGH SODIUM ALERT — Use low-sodium cheese. Cook spinach in unsalted water. Omit added salt.*

■ *HIGH CHOLESTEROL ALERT — Use low-fat cheese. Use 1/2 cup liquid egg substitute.*

Spray small skillet or omelet pan with cooking spray. Heat over medium-high heat. Add eggs. When set at edges, gently lift eggs with a spatula to allow uncooked portion to run underneath. When eggs are almost set, sprinkle with cheese, spinach, nutmeg, salt and pepper. Fold over onto plate; serve immediately.

Total		Per Serving
233.0	Calories	233.0
3.5	Carbohydrate (g)	3.5
18.6	Protein (g)	18.6
16.2	Total Fat (g)	16.2
6.2	Saturated Fat (g)	6.2
518.0	Cholesterol (mg)	518.0
498.0	Sodium (mg)	498.0

Protein Lasagna without Pasta

Makes 4 servings

5 eggs, lightly beaten ■
2 cups low-fat cottage cheese ●
1/4 cup grated Romano cheese ● ■
1 tsp. parsley flakes
1 tsp. dried oregano
1/4 cup water
16-oz. can plain tomato sauce (check label for no added oil) ●
1/2 tbsp. bread crumbs

● *HIGH SODIUM ALERT — Use low-sodium cheeses and unsalted tomato sauce.*

■ *HIGH CHOLESTEROL ALERT — Use 1 1/4 cups liquid egg substitute. Substitute low-fat cheese for Romano or omit.*

Combine 1 egg, or 1/4 cup substitute, with the cottage cheese, Romano, parsley, and oregano. Mix well; reserve. Beat the remaining eggs with water until light and fluffy. Spray large nonstick skillet with cooking spray and heat over low heat. Add eggs. Cook covered over very low heat until eggs are set. Remove from heat; cool. Cut into 1-inch strips. Layer the egg strips with reserved cheese mixture and the tomato sauce. Top with tomato sauce and sprinkle with bread crumbs. Bake in a preheated 325° oven 45 to 50 minutes.

Total		Per Serving
1024.7	Calories	256.2
51.2	Carbohydrate (g)	12.8
105.3	Protein (g)	26.3
41.5	Total Fat (g)	10.4
17.5	Saturated Fat (g)	4.4
1324.4	Cholesterol (mg)	331.1
5347.4	Sodium (mg)	1336.9

Unfattening Fondue

Makes about 2 cups

16 slices low-fat American cheese ●
1 cup skim milk
1 tsp. prepared mustard ●
1/2 tsp. Worcestershire sauce
  Salt ● and pepper to taste (optional)
2 or 3 tbsp. low-calorie low-carbohydrate beer
  Melba toast (optional)

● *HIGH SODIUM ALERT — Use low-sodium cheese. Substitute dry mustard to taste for prepared mustard. Omit added salt.*

Combine cheese, milk, mustard and Worcestershire in medium saucepan. Cook and stir over low heat until cheese melts. Sprinkle with salt and pepper. Transfer to fondue pot and keep warm. Thin with beer 1 tablespoon at a time until of desired consistency. (You may use Melba toast for dipping.)

Total		Per Tablespoon
502.6	Calories	15.7
21.1	Carbohydrate (g)	0.7
65.4	Protein (g)	2.1
16.3	Total Fat (g)	0.5
16.0	Saturated Fat (g)	0.5
85.0	Cholesterol (mg)	2.7
3657.9	Sodium (mg)	114.3

High-Fiber Bread Quiche

Makes 8 servings

4 slices high-fiber bread, preferably stale ●
1 cup low-fat cottage cheese ●
2 onions, minced
13 1/2-oz. can evaporated skim milk
3 eggs ■
1 tbsp. minced parsley
  Salt ● and pepper to taste (optional)
2 tbsp. bacon bits ● ■ (optional)

● *HIGH SODIUM ALERT — Use low-sodium bread and cheese. Omit added salt and bacon bits.*

■ *HIGH CHOLESTEROL ALERT — Use 3/4 cup liquid egg substitute. Substitute bacon-flavored bits for the bacon.*

1 tsp. = 5 mL   1 tbsp. = 15 mL   1 cup = 250 mL   1 oz. = 30 g

Line 10-inch pie pan with bread. Spread with cottage cheese and onions. Combine remaining ingredients, except bacon bits, in blender. Cover; blend until smooth. Pour over onion layer. Sprinkle with bacon bits. Bake in a preheated 425° oven 35 to 40 minutes. Cut into squares to serve.

Total		Per Serving
1039.5	Calories	129.9
111.6	Carbohydrate (g)	14.0
92.7	Protein (g)	11.6
22.0	Total Fat (g)	2.7
7.2	Saturated Fat (g)	0.9
896.9	Cholesterol (mg)	112.1
2139.5	Sodium (mg)	267.4

French Toasted Turkey and Cheese Sandwiches

Makes 1 serving

1 oz. (2 thin slices) Swiss cheese ● ■
2 slices high-fiber bread ●
2 oz. sliced roast turkey breast
  Salt or celery salt ● and pepper to taste (optional)
1 egg, lightly beaten ■

● *HIGH SODIUM ALERT — Use low-sodium cheese and bread. Omit added salt or celery salt.*

■ *HIGH CHOLESTEROL ALERT — Use low-fat cheese. Use 1/4 cup liquid egg substitute.*

Place 1 slice of cheese on 1 slice of bread. Top with turkey, seasonings, second slice of cheese and bread. Place the sandwich in a shallow dish with the egg. Turn frequently until all the egg is absorbed and both sides are well coated. Spray nonstick skillet with cooking spray. Heat over moderate heat. Place sandwich in skillet; cook, turning once, until bread is browned and cheese is melted.

Total		Per Serving
385.3	Calories	385.3
19.5	Carbohydrate (g)	19.5
37.6	Protein (g)	37.6
17.2	Total Fat (g)	17.2
7.0	Saturated Fat (g)	7.0
323.9	Cholesterol (mg)	323.9
623.7	Sodium (mg)	623.7

Corned Beef Reubenesque ●

Makes 1 serving

1 oz. (2 thin slices) Swiss cheese ■
2 slices high-fiber bread
2 oz. thinly sliced lean corned beef round (not brisket)
2 tsp. brown mustard
1 tsp. horseradish or to taste (optional)

● *HIGH SODIUM ALERT — Not recommended for low-sodium diets.*

■ *HIGH CHOLESTEROL ALERT — Use low-fat cheese.*

Place 1 slice of cheese on 1 slice of bread. Spread with mustard and horseradish. Top with the meat, second slice of cheese and bread. Spray small nonstick skillet with cooking spray. Grill sandwich, turning once, until bread is golden and cheese is melted.

Total		Per Serving
423.2	Calories	423.2
20.2	Carbohydrate (g)	20.2
26.5	Protein (g)	26.5
26.8	Total Fat (g)	26.8
12.7	Saturated Fat (g)	12.7
64.9	Cholesterol (mg)	64.9
1175.9	Sodium (mg)	1175.9

Eggless Salad

Makes 4 servings

1 cup liquid egg substitute
5 tbsp. low-calorie low-fat mayonnaise ●
2 tbsp. minced celery
2 tbsp. minced green pepper (optional)
1 tbsp. minced onion
1/2 tsp. prepared mustard ● (optional)
  Salt ● and pepper to taste (optional)
  Dash red pepper sauce, or pinch red pepper (optional)

● *HIGH SODIUM ALERT — Use unsalted mayonnaise. Substitute dry mustard to taste for prepared mustard. Omit added salt.*

Cook egg substitute covered in nonstick skillet over very low heat about 10 to 15 minutes, or until the egg substitute thickens and is set. Remove from heat and cool slightly. Dice or shred the cooked egg substitute; combine with remaining ingredients. Chill.

Total		Per Serving
266.5	Calories	66.6
18.5	Carbohydrate (g)	4.6
28.3	Protein (g)	7.1
10.0	Total Fat (g)	2.5
0.0	Saturated Fat (g)	0.0
40.0	Cholesterol (mg)	10.0
634.9	Sodium (mg)	158.7

Alert Symbols: ● Sodium   ■ Cholesterol   ▲ Sugar

Cottage Cheese Scramble

Makes 2 servings

- 3 eggs ■
- 2 tbsp. water
  Salt ● and pepper to taste (optional)
- 1/2 cup low-fat cottage cheese ●
  Dash red pepper sauce (optional)

● *HIGH SODIUM ALERT — Omit added salt. Use low-sodium cottage cheese.*

■ *HIGH CHOLESTEROL ALERT — Use 3/4 cup liquid egg substitute.*

Beat eggs and water together. Sprinkle with salt and pepper. Spray nonstick skillet with cooking spray. Heat over moderate heat; add eggs. Cook over low heat, stirring occasionally, until thick. Stir in cottage cheese and pepper sauce. Cook until eggs are set.

Total		Per Serving
330.0	Calories	165.0
3.0	Carbohydrate (g)	1.5
33.0	Protein (g)	16.5
19.0	Total Fat (g)	9.5
6.6	Saturated Fat (g)	3.3
765.7	Cholesterol (mg)	382.8
598.0	Sodium (mg)	299.0

High-Fiber French Toast

Makes 8 slices

- 2 eggs ■
- 3/4 cup skim milk
- 1 tsp. vanilla
- 1/2 tsp. salt ● (optional)
- 8 slices high-fiber bread ●

● *HIGH SODIUM ALERT — Omit added salt. Use low-sodium bread.*

■ *HIGH CHOLESTEROL ALERT — Use 1/2 cup liquid egg substitute.*

Beat eggs, milk, vanilla and salt together. Pour into a shallow rectangular pan. Arrange bread in pan in a single layer. Turn bread frequently with a spatula until all slices are completely saturated. Spray a large nonstick skillet or electric frypan with cooking spray. Heat over moderate heat. Transfer bread to skillet. Brown bread slices on both sides over low heat.

Total		Per Slice
628.0	Calories	78.5
85.0	Carbohydrate (g)	10.6
38.7	Protein (g)	4.8
16.0	Total Fat (g)	2.0
4.0	Saturated Fat (g)	0.5
507.7	Cholesterol (mg)	63.5
1477.2	Sodium (mg)	184.7

Cottage Cheese Sandwich Spread

Makes enough for 4 sandwiches

- 1 cup low-fat cottage cheese ●
- 1/2 cup chopped green pepper
- 1/2 cup shredded carrot
- 2 tbsp. chopped dill pickle ●
- 2 tbsp. chopped onion
  Salt ● and pepper to taste (optional)
  Dash red pepper sauce

● *HIGH SODIUM ALERT — Use low-sodium cottage cheese. Omit pickle and added salt.*

Mix together all ingredients; chill.

Total		Per Serving
230.8	Calories	57.7
17.0	Carbohydrate (g)	4.2
32.2	Protein (g)	8.0
2.2	Total Fat (g)	0.5
1.2	Saturated Fat (g)	0.3
19.4	Cholesterol (mg)	4.8
1177.3	Sodium (mg)	294.3

Hamburger Sausage Patties

Makes 16 patties

- 2 lb. lean beef round, trimmed of fat, ground
- 1/4 cup shaved or crushed ice
- 2 tsp. salt or garlic salt ● (optional)
- 1 tsp. poultry seasoning
- 1/4 tsp. coarsely ground pepper

● *HIGH SODIUM ALERT — Omit added salt or garlic salt.*

Combine all ingredients. Mix lightly. Shape into 16 patties. (If not to be used immediately, wrap, label and store in freezer.) Fry in nonstick skillet or broil until done as desired.

Total		Per Patty
1624.0	Calories	101.5
0.0	Carbohydrate (g)	0.0
187.8	Protein (g)	11.7
90.8	Total Fat (g)	5.7
43.6	Saturated Fat (g)	2.7
590.0	Cholesterol (mg)	36.9
658.0	Sodium (mg)	41.1

1 tsp. = 5 mL   1 tbsp. = 15 mL   1 cup = 250 mL   1 oz. = 30 g

Savory Pork Sausage

Makes 8 patties

1 lb. lean boneless fresh ham, trimmed of fat, ground
2 egg whites
1/4 cup shaved or crushed ice
2 tsp. instant minced onion
1 tsp. salt ● (optional)
1/2 tsp. poultry seasoning
1/4 tsp. coarsely ground pepper
1/4 tsp. liquid smoke seasoning ● (optional)
1/8 tsp. garlic powder

● *HIGH SODIUM ALERT — Omit added salt and smoke seasoning.*

Combine all ingredients; mix lightly. Shape the ham mixture into 8 patties. Spray nonstick skillet with cooking spray. Fry patties in skillet over moderate heat, turning once, until brown on both sides and cooked through, with no trace of pinkness remaining.

   WARNING: Do not taste raw or undercooked pork sausage for seasoning. If you would like to taste-test before completing the seasoning, fry a small sample.

Total		Per Patty
917.1	Calories	114.6
1.7	Carbohydrate (g)	0.2
102.8	Protein (g)	12.8
45.4	Total Fat (g)	5.7
16.3	Saturated Fat (g)	2.0
280.0	Cholesterol (mg)	35.0
348.8	Sodium (mg)	43.6

Cumin Sausage

Makes 8 patties

1 lb. lean beef, lamb or pork, trimmed of fat, ground
1 small onion, minced
1 egg, lightly beaten ■
2 tbsp. chopped fresh parsley
1 tbsp. cumin seeds
1 tsp. salt ● (optional)
1/2 tsp. curry powder
2 or 3 drops liquid smoke seasoning ● (optional)

● *HIGH SODIUM ALERT — Omit added salt and smoke seasoning.*

■ *HIGH CHOLESTEROL ALERT — Use 2 egg whites or 1/4 cup liquid egg substitute.*

Combine all ingredients; mix lightly. Shape into 8 patties. Fry in nonstick skillet (sprayed with cooking spray) over moderate heat, or broil or grill close to heat turning once, until brown on both sides. (If using pork, be sure sausage is completely cooked through.)

   WARNING: Do not taste raw or undercooked pork sausage for seasoning. If you would like to taste-test before completing the seasoning, fry a small sample.

Total		Per Patty
926.0	Calories	115.7
8.1	Carbohydrate (g)	1.0
101.6	Protein (g)	12.7
51.4	Total Fat (g)	6.4
23.8	Saturated Fat (g)	3.0
547.0	Cholesterol (mg)	68.4
402.2	Sodium (mg)	50.3

Fried Sausage and Apples

Makes 4 servings

1 lb. homemade low-fat sausage patties (any of the sausage recipes in this chapter)
2 apples, pared, cored and sectioned (or thickly sliced)
1/4 cup water
Ground cinnamon or caraway seed (optional)

Defrost sausage patties, if frozen. Spray large nonstick skillet with cooking spray. Fry the sausage patties in skillet over moderate heat, turning once, until brown on both sides (pork patties must be completely cooked through, with no pinkness remaining). Remove from skillet; keep warm. Pour off fat from skillet.

   Arrange apple sections in skillet in a single layer; add water. Cook uncovered, turning once, until water evaporates and apples are browned but still crisp. (Don't overcook.) Serve sausage patties topped with apples. Sprinkle with cinnamon or caraway.

Total		Per Serving
1057.1	Calories	264.3
37.7	Carbohydrate (g)	9.4
102.8	Protein (g)	25.7
45.4	Total Fat (g)	11.4
16.3	Saturated Fat (g)	4.1
280.0	Cholesterol (mg)	70.0
352.8	Sodium (mg)	88.2

Alert Symbols: ● Sodium   ■ Cholesterol   ▲ Sugar

Company-Pleasing
Appetizers

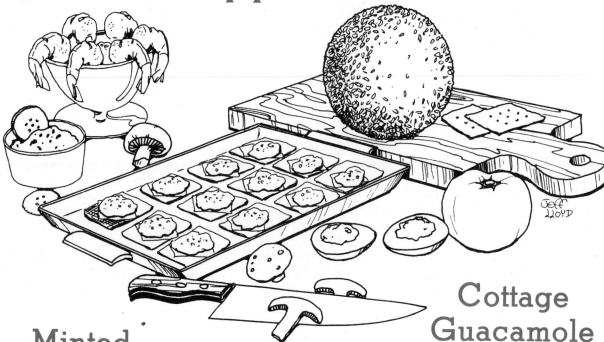

Minted Nectarine Fruit Cocktail

Makes 8 servings

3 or 4 fresh mint sprigs
2 tbsp. defrosted undiluted frozen unsweetened orange juice concentrate
4 large ripe unpeeled nectarines or peeled peaches, thinly sliced
Fresh mint sprigs (optional)

Crush 3 or 4 mint sprigs with the juice concentrate; combine concentrate with the nectarines. Stir gently to coat. Spoon into stemmed glasses; garnish with additional fresh mint, if desired.

Total		Per Serving
352.0	Calories	44.0
90.5	Carbohydrate (g)	11.3
4.8	Protein (g)	0.6
0.0	Total Fat (g)	0.0
0.0	Saturated Fat (g)	0.0
0.0	Cholesterol (mg)	0.0
28.6	Sodium (mg)	3.6

Ambrosia Fruit Cocktail

Makes 4 servings

1 ripe banana, sliced
2 oranges, seeded, cut into chunks
8-oz. can juice-packed pineapple chunks, undrained
1 tbsp. defrosted undiluted frozen unsweetened pineapple juice concentrate
4 tsp. flaked coconut

Combine fruits and juice concentrate. Spoon into 4 stemmed glasses. Sprinkle with coconut.

Total		Per Serving
436.1	Calories	109.0
105.6	Carbohydrate (g)	26.4
4.5	Protein (g)	1.1
2.4	Total Fat (g)	0.6
2.0	Saturated Fat (g)	0.5
0.0	Cholesterol (mg)	0.0
11.0	Sodium (mg)	2.7

Cottage Guacamole Dip

Makes about 2 cups

1 ripe avocado, halved, pitted
8 oz. low-fat cottage cheese ●
1/4 cup chopped fresh parsley
1 small onion, quartered
1 tbsp. fresh or reconstituted lime juice
1 tsp. garlic salt ●

● *HIGH SODIUM ALERT — Use low-sodium cottage cheese. Substitute garlic powder to taste for garlic salt.*

Scoop out avocado pulp; discard skin. Combine pulp with remaining ingredients in blender or food processor, using the steel blade. Process until smooth. Cover and chill until serving time. (Serve surrounded with raw red and green bell pepper squares to be used for dipping, if desired.)

Total		Per Tablespoon
580.6	Calories	18.1
26.7	Carbohydrate (g)	0.8
36.7	Protein (g)	1.2
39.1	Total Fat (g)	1.2
8.2	Saturated Fat (g)	0.3
19.4	Cholesterol (mg)	0.6
2878.4	Sodium (mg)	90.0

1 tsp. = 5 mL   1 tbsp. = 15 mL   1 cup = 250 mL   1 oz. = 30 g

Tuna Stuffed Mushrooms or Celery

Makes 20 appetizers
2 cans (7 oz. each) water-packed white-meat tuna, drained ●
4 small stalks celery, cut into chunks ●
1 small onion, quartered, or 1 tbsp. onion flakes
3 tbsp. low-calorie low-fat mayonnaise ●
2 tbsp. lemon juice
3 or 4 sprigs fresh parsley
Salt ● and pepper to taste (optional)
20 mushroom caps or 2-inch lengths of celery ●
Paprika (optional)
Minced parsley (optional)

● *HIGH SODIUM ALERT — Use unsalted tuna and mayonnaise. Omit celery and added salt.*

Combine tuna, 4 small stalks celery, onion, mayonnaise, lemon juice, parsley sprigs, salt and pepper in blender or food processor, using the steel blade. Process until smooth. Spoon into mushroom caps or lengths of celery. Sprinkle with paprika and minced parsley, if desired.

Total		Per Serving
637.3	Calories	31.8
21.8	Carbohydrate (g)	1.1
115.2	Protein (g)	5.8
10.0	Total Fat (g)	0.5
0.0	Saturated Fat (g)	0.0
276.0	Cholesterol (mg)	13.8
3625.2	Sodium (mg)	181.3

Franks and Apples on Skewers•

Makes 32
1 lb. low-fat turkey or chicken frankfurters
4 firm red unpared apples

● *HIGH SODIUM ALERT — Not recommended for low-sodium diets.*

Slice the franks into 1-inch lengths. Use an apple sectioner or sharp knife to core and section each apple into 8 wedges. Arrange an apple wedge and a hot dog chunk on each of 32 small wooden skewers. Broil

just until franks are browned and apples are tender-firm.

Total		Per Serving
1331.0	Calories	41.6
88.0	Carbohydrate (g)	2.8
48.0	Protein (g)	1.5
88.2	Total Fat (g)	2.8
23.8	Saturated Fat (g)	0.7
235.0	Cholesterol (mg)	7.3
3908.0	Sodium (mg)	122.1

Broiled Grapefruit

Makes 4 first-course servings
2 seedless grapefruits, halved
2 tbsp. defrosted undiluted frozen unsweetened pineapple juice concentrate
2 tsp. diet margarine, at room temperature ■

■ *HIGH CHOLESTEROL ALERT — Use polyunsaturated margarine.*

Use a grapefruit knife to loosen sections. Mix remaining ingredients together with the back of a spoon, then spread over grapefruit. Broil 3 to 4 inches from heat 6 to 8 minutes.

Total		Per Serving
277.3	Calories	69.3
63.9	Carbohydrate (g)	16.0
4.5	Protein (g)	1.1
4.0	Total Fat (g)	1.0
0.7	Saturated Fat (g)	0.2
0.0	Cholesterol (mg)	0.0
119.0	Sodium (mg)	29.7

Turkey Veronica

Makes 32 party servings
1 lb. unsliced cooked turkey breast
32 seedless green grapes
1 cup low-calorie low-fat Roquefort or creamy Caesar dressing ●

● *HIGH SODIUM ALERT — Use unsalted dressing.*

Cut turkey into 1-inch cubes. Arrange a cube of turkey and a green grape on frilled party picks. Arrange around a bowl of salad dressing, for dipping.

Total		Per Serving
1100.8	Calories	34.4
38.3	Carbohydrate (g)	1.2
157.9	Protein (g)	4.9
33.3	Total Fat (g)	1.1
12.9	Saturated Fat (g)	0.4
367.9	Cholesterol (mg)	11.5
3203.4	Sodium (mg)	100.1

Holiday Cheese and Pepper Dip

Makes 1 1/2 cups
6 slices low-calorie low-fat cheese, broken up ●
3/4 cup low-fat cottage cheese ●
2 tbsp. water
2 tsp. lemon juice
1/4 cup finely chopped green bell pepper
1/4 cup finely chopped red bell pepper
2 tbsp. finely chopped onion

● *HIGH SODIUM ALERT — Use low-sodium cheeses.*

Combine cheese, cottage cheese, water and lemon juice in blender or food processor. Cover; blend until smooth. Transfer to bowl and stir in peppers and onion. (Serve with fresh vegetables for dipping.)

Total		Per Tablespoon
321.1	Calories	13.4
16.2	Carbohydrate (g)	0.7
45.1	Protein (g)	1.9
7.5	Total Fat (g)	0.3
6.9	Saturated Fat (g)	0.3
44.6	Cholesterol (mg)	1.9
1908.2	Sodium (mg)	79.5

Ham and Melon on Party Picks•

Makes 16 party servings
1 ripe cantaloupe, halved, seeded
1/2 lb. lean ready-to-eat ham steak or unsliced Canadian bacon

● *HIGH SODIUM ALERT — Not recommended for low-sodium diets.*

Scoop melon with a melon baller, or quarter melon and slice into 1-inch cubes. Slice ham into 1-inch cubes. Arrange a cube of melon and a cube of ham on frilled party picks.

Total		Per Serving
596.0	Calories	37.3
28.0	Carbohydrate (g)	1.8
71.1	Protein (g)	4.4
21.3	Total Fat (g)	1.3
8.0	Saturated Fat (g)	0.5
199.5	Cholesterol (mg)	12.5
2140.2	Sodium (mg)	133.8

Alert Symbols: ● Sodium ■ Cholesterol ▲ Sugar

French Deviled Eggs ▪

Makes 2 dozen

1 dozen hard-cooked eggs, shelled
¼ cup low-calorie low-fat French dressing ●
1 tbsp. hot Dijon-style mustard or to taste ●
1 tsp. Worcestershire sauce ●
Paprika

● *HIGH SODIUM ALERT — Use unsalted dressing. Substitute dry mustard to taste for Dijon mustard. Omit Worcestershire.*

■ *HIGH CHOLESTEROL ALERT — Not recommended for low-cholesterol diets.*

Cut eggs lengthwise in half; remove yolks. Mash yolks with remaining ingredients, except paprika. Spoon yolk mixture into pastry bag with a decorative tip; pipe yolk mixture into whites. Sprinkle with paprika.

Total		Per Serving
976.7	Calories	40.7
2.1	Carbohydrate (g)	0.1
73.1	Protein (g)	3.0
73.0	Total Fat (g)	3.0
24.0	Saturated Fat (g)	1.0
3024.0	Cholesterol (mg)	126.0
1448.4	Sodium (mg)	60.3

Lean Deviled Eggs ▪

Makes 16

8 hard-cooked eggs, shelled
½ cup low-fat cottage cheese ●
1 tsp. prepared mustard ●
Dash of red pepper sauce
Salt or celery salt ● and pepper to taste (optional)

● *HIGH SODIUM ALERT — Use low-sodium cottage cheese. Substitute dry mustard to taste for prepared mustard. Omit added salt or celery salt.*

■ *HIGH CHOLESTEROL ALERT — Not recommended for low-cholesterol diets.*

Cut eggs lengthwise in half. Remove yolks. Mash yolks with remaining ingredients. Mound yolk mixture into whites.

Total		Per Serving
733.7	Calories	45.9
3.3	Carbohydrate (g)	0.2
63.3	Protein (g)	3.9
49.3	Total Fat (g)	3.1
16.6	Saturated Fat (g)	1.0
2025.7	Cholesterol (mg)	126.6
965.7	Sodium (mg)	60.4

Savory Pinwheels ▪

Makes 32 servings

8 oz. Neufchâtel or low-calorie low-fat cream cheese
¼ cup plain low-fat yogurt or skim milk
1 tbsp. prepared horseradish
12 stuffed green (Spanish) olives, finely chopped
Salt and pepper to taste (optional)
1 lb. lean boiled ham, sliced

● *HIGH SODIUM ALERT — Not recommended for low-sodium diets.*

Beat cream cheese, yogurt and horseradish together. Fold in olives. Sprinkle with salt and pepper. Spread on ham slices and roll up. Secure with toothpicks. Refrigerate several hours, until firm. Slice into pinwheels.

Total		Per Serving
1722.2	Calories	53.8
12.3	Carbohydrate (g)	0.4
106.0	Protein (g)	3.3
135.0	Total Fat (g)	4.2
64.5	Saturated Fat (g)	2.0
581.0	Cholesterol (mg)	18.2
7725.3	Sodium (mg)	241.4

Zesty Cream Cheese Dip

Makes 1 cup

8 oz. Neufchâtel or low-calorie low-fat cream cheese ●
4 or 5 tbsp. water
1 tbsp. lemon juice
2 tsp. celery seeds ●
1 tsp. Worcestershire sauce ●
½ tsp. garlic powder
¼ tsp. onion salt ● or ⅛ tsp. onion powder
Dash red pepper sauce or to taste ●

● *HIGH SODIUM ALERT — Use low-sodium cheese. Omit celery seeds, Worcestershire and pepper sauce. Use onion powder, not onion salt.*

Combine all ingredients in blender or food processor, using the steel blade. Process until smooth; add more water if a thinner dip is desired. (Serve with fresh vegetables for dipping.)

Total		Per Serving
565.7	Calories	35.4
10.3	Carbohydrate (g)	0.6
16.1	Protein (g)	1.0
48.0	Total Fat (g)	3.0
32.0	Saturated Fat (g)	2.0
168.0	Cholesterol (mg)	10.5
1466.7	Sodium (mg)	91.7

Lean "Liptauer" Cheese Spread

Makes 32 servings

1 cup low-fat cottage cheese ●
8 oz. Neufchâtel or low-calorie low-fat cream cheese ●
1 tbsp. caraway seeds
1 tbsp. minced onion or chives
1 tbsp. minced parsley
1 tbsp. capers ● (optional)
1 tbsp. paprika
1 tsp. dry mustard
1 tsp. Worcestershire sauce ●

● *HIGH SODIUM ALERT — Use low-sodium cheeses. Omit capers and Worcestershire.*

Combine all ingredients in blender or food processor, using the steel blade. Process until smooth. Spoon into large crock or shape into mound. Cover and chill.

Total		Per Serving
751.2	Calories	23.5
18.6	Carbohydrate (g)	0.6
46.5	Protein (g)	1.4
50.0	Total Fat (g)	1.6
33.2	Saturated Fat (g)	1.0
187.4	Cholesterol (mg)	5.9
1906.2	Sodium (mg)	59.6

Devil Dreams ▪

Makes about 32

1 lb. turkey bologna or turkey pastrami, unsliced
20-oz. can juice-packed pineapple chunks, drained, juice reserved
1 tbsp. hot mustard

● *HIGH SODIUM ALERT — Not recommended for low-sodium diets.*

Dice meat into 1-inch cubes. Thread the meat and pineapple, alternately on toothpicks or small wooden skewers. Combine mustard with 3 or 4 tbsp. of the reserved pineapple juice. Brush meat and pineapple lightly with this mustard mixture. Broil until hot.

Total		Per Tablespoon
1220.2	Calories	38.0
94.0	Carbohydrate (g)	2.9
67.2	Protein (g)	2.1
65.0	Total Fat (g)	2.0
8.7	Saturated Fat (g)	0.3
229.0	Cholesterol (mg)	7.2
2754.5	Sodium (mg)	86.1

1 tsp. = 5 mL   1 tbsp. = 15 mL   1 cup = 250 mL   1 oz. = 30 g

Sunshine Cheese Ball

Makes 32 servings

8-oz. can juice-packed crushed
   pineapple, well drained
2 packages (8 oz. each) Neufchâtel
   or low-calorie low-fat cream
   cheese, softened ●
6 tbsp. diced red or green bell
   pepper (or 3 tbsp. of each)
3 tbsp. minced purple onion
   Salt ● and pepper to taste
   (optional)
½ cup plus 1 tbsp. unsalted
   sunflower seeds

● *HIGH SODIUM ALERT — Use low-sodium
cheese. Omit added salt.*

Beat pineapple into cheese until
well blended. Fold in bell pepper
and onion. Sprinkle with salt and
pepper. Shape into a ball and roll in
sunflower seeds. Cover and chill
until serving time.

Total		Per Serving
1752.1	Calories	54.7
76.6	Carbohydrate (g)	2.4
53.8	Protein (g)	1.7
134.5	Total Fat (g)	4.2
64.0	Saturated Fat (g)	2.0
336.0	Cholesterol (mg)	10.5
1846.1	Sodium (mg)	57.7

Asparagus Tips in Blankets

Makes 32

32 fresh asparagus spears, or 2
   packages (10 oz. each) frozen
   asparagus spears, partly
   defrosted
8 slices high-fiber white bread,
   trimmed of crusts ●
1 tbsp. low-calorie low-fat
   mayonnaise ●
2 tbsp. grated extra-sharp Romano
   cheese ● ■
2 tsp. dried oregano
2 tbsp. safflower or corn oil
   Salt ● and pepper to taste
   (optional)
   Paprika

● *HIGH SODIUM ALERT — Use low-sodium
bread and unsalted mayonnaise. Use low-
sodium cheese, or omit. Omit added salt.*

■ *HIGH CHOLESTEROL ALERT — Use low-fat
cheese, or omit.*

Choose uniform asparagus; cut tips
into 3-inch lengths (reserve the rest
to slice and add to soup or stew).
Steam asparagus in a small amount
of water just until crisp-tender. Cool.

Meanwhile, flatten bread with a
rolling pin. Cut each slice into 4
equal squares. Lightly dab each
square with mayonnaise; sprinkle
lightly with cheese and oregano.
Arrange an asparagus tip diagonally
on each bread square and roll up.
Arrange seam-side down on a
nonstick baking sheet sprayed with
cooking spray. Brush tops very
lightly with oil. Sprinkle with salt,
pepper and paprika. Bake in a
preheated 425° oven until tops are
crisp and toasted. Serve warm.

Total		Per Serving
765.3	Calories	23.9
86.2	Carbohydrate (g)	2.7
29.2	Protein (g)	0.9
37.3	Total Fat (g)	1.2
4.6	Saturated Fat (g)	0.1
20.7	Cholesterol (mg)	0.7
1430.3	Sodium (mg)	44.7

Oriental Shrimp Cocktail Dip ●

Makes about 1 cup

1 cup low-calorie low-fat creamy
   French dressing
2 tbsp. soy sauce
2 tsp. minced or grated fresh
   gingerroot or 1 tsp. ground
   ginger
   Parsley sprigs

● *HIGH SODIUM ALERT — Not recommended
for low-sodium diets.*

■ *HIGH CHOLESTEROL ALERT — Shrimp are
not recommended for low-cholesterol diets.*

Stir together all ingredients and
pour into serving bowl. Garnish with
parsley. (Arrange cooked, deveined,
shelled shrimp ■ around bowl for
dipping.)

Total		Per Serving
272.9	Calories	17.1
4.5	Carbohydrate (g)	0.3
2.4	Protein (g)	0.2
0.0	Total Fat (g)	0.0
0.0	Saturated Fat (g)	0.0
0.0	Cholesterol (mg)	0.0
4087.6	Sodium (mg)	255.5

Hawaiian Shrimp Cocktail ●■

Makes 4 servings

½ lb. cooked, shelled shrimp, chilled
8-oz. can juice-packed pineapple
   chunks, drained
1 cup Oriental Shrimp Cocktail Dip
   (recipe in this chapter)
   Red-leaf lettuce

● *HIGH SODIUM ALERT — Not recommended
for low-sodium diets.*

■ *HIGH CHOLESTEROL ALERT — Not
recommended for low-cholesterol diets.*

Combine shrimp and pineapple.
For each cocktail, arrange
approximately ½ cup of the shrimp-
pineapple mixture on lettuce. Top
with ¼ cup Oriental Shrimp
Cocktail Dip.

Total		Per Serving
627.2	Calories	156.8
47.2	Carbohydrate (g)	11.8
43.6	Protein (g)	10.9
3.2	Total Fat (g)	0.8
0.0	Saturated Fat (g)	0.0
338.0	Cholesterol (mg)	84.5
4404.8	Sodium (mg)	1101.2

Alert Symbols: ● Sodium ■ Cholesterol ▲ Sugar

From The Soup Kettle

"Cream" of Turkey Mushroom Soup

Makes 6 servings

- 1 small meaty turkey carcass
- 1 qt. water
- 1 onion, sliced
- 2 tbsp. sherry
- Pinch nutmeg
- 1/2 lb. fresh mushrooms, finely chopped
- 2 tsp. safflower or corn oil
- 13-oz. can evaporated skim milk
- 1 tbsp. flour
- Parsley flakes
- Salt ● and pepper to taste (optional)

● *HIGH SODIUM ALERT — Omit added salt.*

Combine turkey carcass, water, onion, sherry and nutmeg in kettle. Simmer covered 2 hours. Strain broth; cool to room temperature.

Refrigerate until fat hardens; remove and discard fat. Separate meat from bones; reserve meat. Discard bones and skin.

Brown mushrooms in oil in large nonstick skillet. Add reserved turkey meat and broth. Heat to boiling. Mix together milk and flour; stir into skillet. Cook and stir over moderate heat until hot and bubbling. Sprinkle with parsley, salt and pepper.

Total		Per Serving
770.5	Calories	128.4
73.7	Carbohydrate (g)	12.3
77.4	Protein (g)	12.9
16.0	Total Fat (g)	2.7
2.7	Saturated Fat (g)	0.5
206.0	Cholesterol (mg)	34.3
631.2	Sodium (mg)	105.2

Fat-Skimmed Scotch Broth

Makes 8 servings

- Meaty lamb bones
- 2 qt. water
- 2 onions, chopped
- 3 small carrots, sliced
- 3 stalks celery, sliced ●
- 3 tbsp. pearl barley
- 2 bay leaves
- 2 tsp. monosodium glutamate ● (optional)
- Salt ● and pepper to taste (optional)

● *HIGH SODIUM ALERT — Omit celery, monosodium glutamate and added salt.*

Combine lamb bones with water in kettle. Simmer covered 1 1/2 to 2 hours. Strain broth; cool to room temperature. Refrigerate broth until fat hardens; remove and discard fat. Separate meat from bones; discard bones. Wrap and refrigerate meat. Stir remaining ingredients into broth. Simmer covered 50 to 60 minutes. Stir in reserved meat and heat through. Remove bay leaves.

Total		Per Serving
520.9	Calories	65.1
70.6	Carbohydrate (g)	8.8
30.1	Protein (g)	3.8
16.4	Total Fat (g)	2.1
9.0	Saturated Fat (g)	1.1
83.0	Cholesterol (mg)	10.4
305.1	Sodium (mg)	38.1

1 tsp. = 5 mL   1 tbsp. = 15 mL   1 cup = 250 mL   1 oz. = 30 g

Trim Turkey Soup

Makes 6 servings

1 small meaty turkey carcass
6 cups water
1 bay leaf
1 tsp. monosodium glutamate ●
   (optional)
1/8 tsp. ground nutmeg
   Salt ● and pepper to taste
   (optional)
3 small carrots, diced or sliced
4 stalks celery, diced or sliced ●
2 onions, sliced

● *HIGH SODIUM ALERT — Omit monosodium glutamate, added salt and celery.*

Combine turkey carcass, water, bay leaf, monosodium glutamate, nutmeg, salt and pepper in kettle. Heat to boiling; reduce heat. Simmer covered about 2 hours. Strain broth; cool to room temperature. Refrigerate broth until fat hardens; remove and discard fat. Separate meat from bones; reserve meat. Discard bones and skin. Stir meat and vegetables into broth. Simmer covered 25 to 30 minutes or until vegetables are tender.

Total		Per Serving
350.0	Calories	58.3
43.0	Carbohydrate (g)	7.2
39.0	Protein (g)	6.5
6.0	Total Fat (g)	1.0
2.0	Saturated Fat (g)	0.3
89.0	Cholesterol (mg)	14.8
424.0	Sodium (mg)	70.7

Spanish Chicken Soup

Makes 8 meal-size servings

2 1/2 lb. frying chicken, cut up
6 cups water
16-oz. can tomatoes, well broken up,
   undrained ●
1 onion, sliced
3 small carrots, sliced
3 stalks celery, sliced ●
1 bay leaf
   Salt ● and pepper to taste
   (optional)
1 small zucchini, diced
1 red or green bell pepper, sliced

● *HIGH SODIUM ALERT — Use unsalted tomatoes. Omit celery and added salt.*

Combine chicken and water in kettle. Simmer covered 1 hour or until chicken is tender. Remove chicken from broth; reserve. Skim fat from broth. Stir tomatoes, onion, carrots, celery, bay leaf, salt and pepper into broth. Simmer covered about 30 minutes, or until carrots are tender. When chicken is cool, remove and discard skin and bones. Cube chicken meat. Stir chicken, zucchini and red pepper into broth. Simmer covered 6 to 8 minutes, or until zucchini is tender. Remove bay leaf.

Total		Per Serving
1289.8	Calories	161.2
60.3	Carbohydrate (g)	7.5
191.7	Protein (g)	24.0
28.9	Total Fat (g)	3.6
9.0	Saturated Fat (g)	1.1
603.0	Cholesterol (mg)	75.4
1317.9	Sodium (mg)	164.7

Main-Course Minestrone

Makes 4 meal-size servings

10-oz. package frozen mixed
   vegetables
2 cups tomato juice ●
1 1/2 cups fat-skimmed chicken or beef
   broth, canned or homemade ●
1 cup minced celery ●
1/2 cup chopped onion
1 clove garlic, minced
1 tsp. dried oregano
   Pinch thyme or poultry seasoning
   Salt ● and pepper to taste
   (optional)
2 cups diced cooked poultry or
   leftover lean roast beef,
   trimmed of fat

● *HIGH SODIUM ALERT — Use unsalted tomato juice and broth. Omit celery and added salt.*

Combine all ingredients except meat in large saucepan. Heat to boiling; reduce heat. Simmer covered 10 minutes. Stir in meat. Simmer covered 10 minutes, or until heated through.

Total		Per Serving
743.3	Calories	185.8
74.9	Carbohydrate (g)	18.7
86.4	Protein (g)	21.6
10.9	Total Fat (g)	2.7
3.3	Saturated Fat (g)	0.8
241.7	Cholesterol (mg)	60.4
2561.4	Sodium (mg)	640.4

Split-Pea Soup●

Makes 12 servings

1 ham hock
2 qt. water
2 cups dry split peas
1 cup finely chopped celery
1 cup finely chopped carrots
1 cup finely chopped onion

● *HIGH SODIUM ALERT — Not recommended for low-sodium diets.*

Combine ham hock with water in kettle. Simmer covered 1 1/2 hours. Strain broth; cool to room temperature. Refrigerate broth until fat hardens. Remove and discard fat. Separate meat from bone; discard bone. Stir remaining ingredients into broth. Simmer covered 2 hours. Stir in meat and heat through.

Total		Per Serving
2168.5	Calories	180.7
280.3	Carbohydrate (g)	23.4
149.6	Protein (g)	12.5
53.9	Total Fat (g)	4.5
18.1	Saturated Fat (g)	1.5
201.4	Cholesterol (mg)	16.8
2062.1	Sodium (mg)	171.8

"Cream" of Potato Soup

Makes 8 servings

3 potatoes, pared, sliced
1 onion, minced
2 cups fat-skimmed chicken broth,
   canned or homemade ●
1 1/2 cups water
13-oz. can evaporated skim milk
   Salt ● and white pepper to taste
   (optional)
3 tbsp. minced chives (optional)

● *HIGH SODIUM ALERT — Use unsalted broth. Omit added salt.*

Combine potatoes, onion, broth and water in saucepan. Simmer covered 35 minutes. Pour into blender. Cover; blend until smooth. Return to saucepan and heat to boiling. Stir in milk. Simmer covered 4 to 5 minutes. Sprinkle with salt and pepper. Garnish with chives, if desired.

Total		Per Serving
718.0	Calories	89.8
128.8	Carbohydrate (g)	16.1
45.7	Protein (g)	5.7
0.3	Total Fat (g)	0.0
0.0	Saturated Fat (g)	0.0
145.0	Cholesterol (mg)	18.1
1922.0	Sodium (mg)	240.2

Alert Symbols: ● Sodium   ■ Cholesterol   ▲ Sugar

Easy, Cheesy "Cream" of Tomato Soup

Makes 4 servings

- 1-lb. can tomatoes, undrained, well broken up ●
- 1½ cups water
- 1¼ cups fat-skimmed chicken or beef broth, canned or homemade ●
- 1 stalk celery, chopped ●
- 1 small onion, minced
- Salt ● and pepper to taste (optional)
- 1 cup nonfat dry milk powder
- ¼ cup grated extra-sharp Cheddar or Romano cheese ● ■

● *HIGH SODIUM ALERT — Use unsalted tomatoes and broth. Omit celery and added salt. Use low-sodium cheese, or omit.*

■ *HIGH CHOLESTEROL ALERT — Use low-fat cheese, or omit.*

Combine tomatoes, water, broth, celery, onion, salt and pepper in large saucepan. Simmer covered 20 minutes. Pour into blender. Add milk; cover. Blend until smooth. Sprinkle each serving with cheese. Serve immediately.

Total		Per Serving
683.5	Calories	170.8
66.5	Carbohydrate (g)	16.6
50.3	Protein (g)	12.6
24.7	Total Fat (g)	6.2
12.7	Saturated Fat (g)	3.2
103.3	Cholesterol (mg)	25.8
2401.9	Sodium (mg)	600.5

Jellied Gazpacho

Makes 8 servings

- 1 envelope unflavored gelatin
- 1½ cups fat-skimmed beef or chicken broth, canned or homemade ●
- 2 tbsp. vinegar
- 1 tsp. paprika
- ½ tsp. basil
- ¼ tsp. ground cloves
- ⅛ tsp. red pepper sauce
- 1 clove garlic, minced (optional)
- 1½ cups finely chopped tomatoes
- ½ cup finely chopped cucumber
- ½ cup finely chopped green pepper
- ¼ cup finely chopped celery
- 2 tbsp. finely chopped onion

● *HIGH SODIUM ALERT — Use unsalted broth.*

Sprinkle gelatin over ½ cup of the cold broth in saucepan. Cook over low heat, stirring constantly, until gelatin dissolves. Remove from heat; stir in remaining broth, the vinegar and seasonings. Chill until mixture is the consistency of unbeaten egg white. Fold in remaining ingredients. Turn into soup cups or serving bowl. Chill until firm.

Total		Per Serving
177.5	Calories	22.2
29.5	Carbohydrate (g)	3.7
18.6	Protein (g)	2.3
0.8	Total Fat (g)	0.1
0.0	Saturated Fat (g)	0.0
36.0	Cholesterol (mg)	4.5
1242.3	Sodium (mg)	155.3

Gringo Gazpacho

Makes 6 servings

- 4 ripe tomatoes, peeled, diced
- 1 large cucumber, pared, coarsely chopped
- 1 green pepper, coarsely chopped
- 1 medium onion, minced
- 1 clove garlic, minced
- 1 cup tomato juice or non-alcoholic Bloody Mary mix ●
- ¼ cup low-calorie low-fat Italian salad dressing ●

● *HIGH SODIUM ALERT — Use unsalted tomato juice or Bloody Mary mix and unsalted dressing.*

Mix together all ingredients. Chill several hours. Serve cold.

Total		Per Serving
325.0	Calories	54.2
69.0	Carbohydrate (g)	11.5
14.2	Protein (g)	2.4
2.8	Total Fat (g)	0.5
0.5	Saturated Fat (g)	0.1
0.0	Cholesterol (mg)	0.0
1016.2	Sodium (mg)	169.4

Lamb-Barley Soup

Makes 10 servings

- Meaty bone from roast leg of lamb
- 2 qt. water
- ¼ cup chopped fresh parsley
- Salt ● and pepper to taste (optional)
- 2 cups sliced carrots
- 2 cups sliced onions
- 2 cups sliced celery ●
- 16-oz. can tomatoes, well broken up, undrained ●
- 6 tbsp. medium pearl barley

● *HIGH SODIUM ALERT — Omit added salt and celery. Use unsalted tomatoes.*

Combine lamb bone, water, parsley, salt and pepper in kettle. Simmer covered 1 hour. Strain broth; cool to room temperature. Refrigerate until fat hardens; remove and discard fat. Separate meat from bones; discard bones. Wrap and refrigerate meat. Stir vegetables and barley into broth. Simmer covered 1½ hours, or until barley is tender. Stir in reserved meat and heat through.

Total		Per Serving
1041.3	Calories	104.1
129.3	Carbohydrate (g)	12.9
64.3	Protein (g)	6.4
33.7	Total Fat (g)	3.3
18.0	Saturated Fat (g)	1.8
166.0	Cholesterol (mg)	16.6
1141.0	Sodium (mg)	114.1

Easy Mushroom-Clam Chowder

Makes 4 servings

- 4-oz. can mushroom stems and pieces ●
- 1 tsp. safflower or corn oil
- 1 can (7 or 8 oz.) minced clams, undrained ●
- 1 stalk celery, chopped ●
- 1 small onion, chopped
- 1⅓ cups nonfat dry milk powder
- 1½ cups cold water
- 1 tbsp. cornstarch or arrowroot
- Salt ● and pepper to taste (optional)
- Pinch cayenne pepper
- 2 tbsp. minced fresh parsley

● *HIGH SODIUM ALERT — Use unsalted mushrooms and clams. Omit celery and added salt.*

Drain mushrooms; reserve liquid. Sauté mushrooms in oil in nonstick saucepan. Stir in reserved mushroom liquid, the clams, celery and onion. Simmer covered 5 minutes. Mix together milk powder, the water, cornstarch, salt and peppers; stir into saucepan. Cook and stir over low heat just until soup bubbles and thickens. Sprinkle with parsley before serving.

Total		Per Serving
569.4	Calories	142.3
71.4	Carbohydrate (g)	17.8
54.3	Protein (g)	13.6
7.0	Total Fat (g)	1.7
0.3	Saturated Fat (g)	0.1
83.0	Cholesterol (mg)	20.7
2594.3	Sodium (mg)	648.6

1 tsp. = 5 mL   1 tbsp. = 15 mL   1 cup = 250 mL   1 oz. = 30 g

Color-Me-Slim Photo Gallery I

Don't skip breakfast or skimp at lunch.
Start the day with a German Puff Pancake or French Breakfast Sausage Patties.
At lunch think lean with a Manicotti-Style Omelet
or Polynesian Shrimp-Stuffed Papaya. And you can enjoy appetizers, too;
dip into a Sunshine Cheese Ball or sample some Tuna-Stuffed Mushrooms.
Those are just a few of the colorful dishes you'll find on
the following pages.

Mushroom Vinaigrette Salad, page 37

◁Minestrone
with Meatballs,
page 34

Chicken or ▷
Turkey Salad
Hawaiian-Style,
page 38

△
**Asparagus Tips
in Blankets,**
page 29

**Tuna-Stuffed
Mushrooms,**
page 27

Blender-Jellied Tomato Consommé

Makes 4 servings
- 1 envelope unflavored gelatin
- 1¾ cups tomato juice ●
- 1 onion, chopped
- 2 tbsp. lemon juice
- 2 tsp. Worcestershire sauce ●
- Salt ● and pepper to taste (optional)
- Dash red pepper sauce (optional)

● *HIGH SODIUM ALERT — Use unsalted tomato juice. Omit Worcestershire and added salt.*

Sprinkle gelatin over ¼ cup of the tomato juice in blender container. Simmer remaining tomato juice and the onion in saucepan 5 minutes. Add to blender; cover. Blend on high speed. Stir in lemon juice, Worcestershire, salt, pepper and pepper sauce. Pour into individual molds or 2-cup mold. Chill until set.

Total		Per Serving
155.3	Calories	38.8
25.2	Carbohydrate (g)	6.3
11.8	Protein (g)	2.9
0.0	Total Fat (g)	0.0
0.0	Saturated Fat (g)	0.0
0.0	Cholesterol (mg)	0.0
980.3	Sodium (mg)	245.1

"Cream" of Mushroom Soup

Makes 6 servings
- 1 lb. fresh mushrooms
- 4 cups fat-skimmed chicken broth, canned or homemade ●
- 13-oz. can evaporated skim milk
- ½ cup cold water
- 3 tbsp. instant-blend flour
- Salt ● and pepper to taste (optional)
- Chopped fresh parsley (optional)

● *HIGH SODIUM ALERT — Use unsalted broth. Omit added salt.*

Remove and chop mushroom stems. Reserve caps. Combine chopped stems with broth in saucepan and simmer covered over very low heat 30 minutes. Strain broth; discard the stems. Return broth to saucepan; heat to boiling. Reduce heat; stir in the milk and heat until simmering. Mix water and flour into a smooth paste; stir into the simmering soup. Continue to cook and stir over low heat until soup is slightly thickened. Slice the reserved mushroom caps very thin; stir into soup. Simmer 6 to 8 minutes. Sprinkle with salt and pepper. Garnish with parsley, if desired.

Total		Per Serving
628.1	Calories	104.7
91.9	Carbohydrate (g)	15.3
56.0	Protein (g)	9.3
1.6	Total Fat (g)	0.3
0.0	Saturated Fat (g)	0.0
173.0	Cholesterol (mg)	28.8
3411.6	Sodium (mg)	568.6

Curried Chicken Gumbo Soup

Makes 4 servings
- 10¾-oz. can condensed chicken gumbo soup ●
- 1 soup can water
- ½ tsp. curry powder
- 1 unpared red apple, diced

● *HIGH SODIUM ALERT — Use unsalted soup.*

Combine all ingredients, except diced apple, in saucepan. Heat to boiling, stirring occasionally. Stir in diced apple before serving.

Total		Per Serving
207.0	Calories	51.8
36.2	Carbohydrate (g)	9.0
7.7	Protein (g)	1.9
3.9	Total Fat (g)	1.0
2.5	Saturated Fat (g)	0.6
42.0	Cholesterol (mg)	10.5
2362.0	Sodium (mg)	590.5

Asparagus Vichyssoise

Makes 6 servings
- 10½-oz. can cut asparagus spears, undrained ●
- 1 cup fat-skimmed chicken broth, canned or homemade ●
- ⅓ cup chopped onion
- ¾ cup instant potato flakes
- 1 cup evaporated skim milk
- Salt ● and pepper to taste (optional)
- Chopped chives

● *HIGH SODIUM ALERT — Use unsalted asparagus and broth. Omit added salt.*

Puree asparagus in blender; reserve. Combine broth and onion in saucepan. Heat to boiling. Reduce heat; simmer covered 5 minutes. Remove from heat; stir in potato flakes. Add pureed asparagus, milk, salt and pepper. Chill thoroughly. Sprinkle with chives before serving.

Total		Per Serving
420.6	Calories	70.1
71.9	Carbohydrate (g)	12.0
30.0	Protein (g)	5.0
1.2	Total Fat (g)	0.2
0.0	Saturated Fat (g)	0.0
86.0	Cholesterol (mg)	14.3
1740.7	Sodium (mg)	290.1

Tuna-Vegetable Soup Romano

Makes 4 meal-size servings
- 1 small onion, minced
- 1 clove garlic, minced (optional)
- 2 tsp. safflower or corn oil
- 2 cans (6½ or 7 oz. each) water-packed tuna, undrained, flaked ●
- 10-oz. package frozen mixed vegetables
- 1½ cups fat-skimmed chicken broth, canned or homemade ●
- 1½ cups tomato, tomato-clam or tomato-vegetable juice ●
- 1 stalk celery, minced ●
- 2 tbsp. minced fresh parsley or 2 tsp. parsley flakes
- 1 tsp. dried oregano or mixed Italian seasoning
- ¼ tsp. thyme
- Salt ● and pepper to taste (optional)
- 4 tsp. grated extra-sharp Romano cheese ● ■

● *HIGH SODIUM ALERT — Use unsalted tuna, broth and juice. Omit celery and added salt. Use low-sodium cheese, or omit.*

■ *HIGH CHOLESTEROL ALERT — Use low-fat cheese, or omit.*

Sauté onion and garlic in oil in nonstick saucepan until golden. Stir in remaining ingredients except cheese. Simmer covered 15 minutes. Sprinkle with cheese before serving.

Total		Per Serving
935.3	Calories	233.8
64.1	Carbohydrate (g)	16.0
132.6	Protein (g)	33.2
16.4	Total Fat (g)	4.1
2.4	Saturated Fat (g)	0.6
281.5	Cholesterol (mg)	70.4
5601.7	Sodium (mg)	1400.4

Alert Symbols: ● Sodium ■ Cholesterol ▲ Sugar

Minestrone with Meatballs

Makes 2 meal-size servings

½ lb. lean beef round, trimmed of fat, ground
    Garlic powder, salt ● and pepper to taste (optional)
2 onions, thinly sliced
10½-oz. can condensed minestrone soup ●
1 soup can water
½ tsp. dried oregano or mixed Italian seasoning
2 tbsp. grated extra-sharp Romano cheese ● ■

● *HIGH SODIUM ALERT — Omit added salt. Use unsalted soup. Use low-sodium cheese, or omit.*

■ *HIGH CHOLESTEROL ALERT — Use low-fat cheese, or omit.*

Sprinkle the meat with garlic powder, salt and pepper; mix lightly. Shape into 1-inch meatballs. Brown on all sides under broiler. Combine meatballs, onions, soup, water, and oregano in saucepan. Simmer covered until onions are tender. Pour into 2 soup bowls and sprinkle with cheese.

Total		Per Serving
798.3	Calories	399.2
55.8	Carbohydrate (g)	27.9
67.2	Protein (g)	33.6
34.5	Total Fat (g)	17.3
13.5	Saturated Fat (g)	6.8
215.6	Cholesterol (mg)	107.8
2813.8	Sodium (mg)	1406.9

Chilled Tomato Soup

Makes 6 servings

2-lb. can plum tomatoes, undrained ●
1½ cups sliced onions
1½ tsp. dried basil
1 tsp. minced fresh garlic
1 tsp. sugar ▲ (optional)
½ tsp. dried savory
    Salt ● and pepper to taste (optional)
2 tbsp. cornstarch
2½ cups fat-skimmed beef broth, canned or homemade ●
1½ cups water
1½ cups chopped seeded pared cucumber
1 tbsp. vinegar
6 tbsp. herb-seasoned croutons ●

● *HIGH SODIUM ALERT — Use unsalted tomatoes, broth and croutons. Omit added salt.*

▲ *HIGH SUGAR ALERT — Omit sugar or use sugar substitute.*

Combine tomatoes, onions, basil, garlic, sugar, savory, salt and pepper in large saucepan. Simmer covered 20 minutes. Blend cornstarch with ½ cup of the beef broth; stir into tomato mixture. Stir in remaining broth and the water. Heat to boiling, stirring constantly. Boil 2 minutes.

    Pour enough tomato mixture into blender to fill ⅔ full. Cover; blend until smooth. Repeat with remaining tomato mixture. Chill thoroughly. Stir in cucumber and vinegar before serving. Serve with croutons.

Total		Per Serving
541.6	Calories	90.3
107.3	Carbohydrate (g)	17.9
30.3	Protein (g)	5.0
4.8	Total Fat (g)	0.8
0.0	Saturated Fat (g)	0.0
60.0	Cholesterol (mg)	10.0
4028.9	Sodium (mg)	671.5

Chinese Egg Drop Soup

Makes 4 servings

10¾-oz. can condensed chicken broth ●
1 soup can water
1 tbsp. chopped green onion
1 egg, slightly beaten ■

● *HIGH SODIUM ALERT — Use unsalted broth.*

■ *HIGH CHOLESTEROL ALERT — Use ¼ cup liquid egg substitute.*

Combine broth, water and green onion in saucepan. Heat to boiling; reduce heat. Gradually pour egg into simmering soup, stirring gently until egg is set. Serve immediately.

Total		Per Serving
138.0	Calories	34.5
5.4	Carbohydrate (g)	1.4
14.5	Protein (g)	3.6
6.3	Total Fat (g)	1.6
2.0	Saturated Fat (g)	0.5
286.3	Cholesterol (mg)	71.6
1856.0	Sodium (mg)	464.0

Tuna Chowder

Makes 3 servings

10¾-oz. can condensed cream of potato soup ●
½ cup skim milk
½ cup water
7-oz. can water-packed tuna, undrained ●
2 tbsp. minced onion
    Salt ● and pepper to taste (optional)
    Dash Worcestershire sauce (optional)

● *HIGH SODIUM ALERT — Use unsalted soup and tuna. Omit added salt.*

Mix all ingredients in saucepan. Heat just to boiling.

Total		Per Serving
500.5	Calories	166.8
37.9	Carbohydrate (g)	12.6
65.2	Protein (g)	21.7
8.4	Total Fat (g)	2.8
5.5	Saturated Fat (g)	1.8
134.9	Cholesterol (mg)	45.0
3948.5	Sodium (mg)	1316.2

Onion Soup Elegante

Makes 4 servings

10½-oz. can condensed onion soup ●
1 soup can water
¼ cup sliced drained canned water chestnuts ●
2-oz. can sliced mushrooms, drained ●

● *HIGH SODIUM ALERT — Use unsalted soup and vegetables.*

Combine all ingredients in saucepan. Heat to boiling, stirring occasionally.

Total		Per Serving
240.0	Calories	60.0
30.9	Carbohydrate (g)	7.7
15.5	Protein (g)	3.9
6.5	Total Fat (g)	1.6
0.0	Saturated Fat (g)	0.0
59.5	Cholesterol (mg)	14.9
2869.5	Sodium (mg)	717.4

1 tsp. = 5 mL   1 tbsp. = 15 mL   1 cup = 250 mL   1 oz. = 30 g

Salads And Salad Dressings

Fruits and Vegetables—What Your Mother Never Told You!

She undoubtedly said they were good for you, thereby making them immediately suspect. She promised they'd put a curl in your hair or hair on your chest (depending on your gender).

What Mother never mentioned—probably because she didn't know—is that fresh fruits and vegetables are the most significant source of low-fat, low-calorie food fiber, an important element that's often missing in America's over-processed, refined foods.

Q. *What exactly is fiber?*

A. Fiber—or roughage—is the non-nutritive, indigestible residue found in most fruits and vegetables, seeds, nuts and whole grains. It contains no vitamins or minerals, no protein or fat and no calories. It's been virtually ignored until this decade. Food makers seldom bother to list fiber content on their labels, because it is, after all, non-nutritive. So little attention has been paid to it, that the true fiber content of most foods isn't really known.

Q. *If it's non-nutritive, what good is it?*

A. What fiber does is help to fill you up. That can reduce the likelihood of overeating. So eating a big salad along with your steak can mean you will be satisfied with a smaller steak.

But there's more. Since fiber speeds up the passage of material through your system, it minimizes constipation and all the discomforts and ills that result from sluggish bowels. And by speeding food through the system, fiber may also minimize the length of time that indigestible toxins and additives remain in the body.

That somewhat simplified explanation of the current thinking of the value of fiber is based on the recent research that supports the value of fiber in our diets. In some primitive societies where life expectancy is long and our modern diseases are unknown, people's natural diets consist of fruits and vegetables in abundance, but little meats and sweets.

Q. *How can fruits and vegetables help me be slim?*

A. Fruits and vegetables—in and of themselves—are filling. Fifty calories' worth of steak or cake barely makes a dent in your appetite. But there's not much room for overeating after you've put away a 50-calorie bowl of salad greens.

They take time to eat. The 50-calorie salad takes much longer to chew than a mouthful of meat or dessert, even though the calories are equal.

Fruits and vegetables are low in calories and fat. No other category of food is lower. Both are high in vitamins. They help you meet your daily requirements, naturally, without vitamin supplements—with fewer calories and less fat than any other type of food.

Food	Calories/Gram of Fiber*	Food	Calories/Gram of Fiber*	Food	Calories/Gram of Fiber*
Fresh Fruits		Pineapple	125	Winter squash	23
Guava	7	Prunes, dried	156	Asparagus	24
Blackberries	11	Damson plum	160	Lettuce	24
Red raspberries	15	Banana, peeled	166	Mushrooms	24
Rhubarb	19	Cherries	170	Celery	25
Strawberries	25	**Fresh Vegetables**		Cucumber	30
Blueberries	37	Green pepper	11	Peas	32
Nectarine	39	Beet greens	13	Carrots	34
Pear	39	Eggplant	17	Spinach	35
Apple, unpeeled	58	Cauliflower	18	Bean sprouts	36
Apricot, unpeeled	81	Brussels sprouts	19	Beets	40
Peach	81	Cabbage	19	Tomato	40
Watermelon	83	Broccoli	20	Lima beans	58
Tangerine	88	Radishes	20	Onion	60
Cantaloupe	97	Summer squash	20	Potato	126
Grapes	112	Green beans	22	Corn	139

*The approximate number of calories contained in the amount of food you must eat to obtain 1 gram of fiber. For example, you must eat 7 calories' worth of guava to get 1 gram of fiber.

Q. *Which foods are high in fiber?*

A. Almost all vegetables, most fruits, nuts, beans, seeds and whole grain cereals, especially bran, contain substantial amounts of fiber. Try to choose foods with the most fiber and the fewest calories. Of these, vegetables are generally lower in calories and fat than the other types of foods. For example, you can get two grams of fiber from a cup of green beans—or from 16 Brazil nuts. But the beans have only 50 calories, while the nuts have 650 because of their high fat content.

Q. *How can I add more low-calorie low-fat fiber to my menus while cutting calories and fat?*

A. Some tips for boosting fiber intake while keeping calories low follow:

Breakfast: Serve bran-based cereal instead of presweetened, high-calorie, highly refined cereal products. Make whole-grain toast. Eat an orange or some grapefruit instead of drinking juice. Add fresh berries to cereal.

Lunch: Make sandwiches with whole-grain bread and lots of lettuce and tomatoes. Substitute a side order of cole slaw (made without high-calorie mayonnaise) for French fries, and pickles for potato chips. Or, make a chef's salad instead of a sandwich. Toss your ham and cheese with a bowlful of greenery and some diet dressing.

Dinner: Start every meal with salad. Serve less meat and more vegetables. Cook Chinese-style: stir-fry a little meat with lots of vegetables (seasoned with soy sauce if you are not on a sodium-restricted diet). Add shredded vegetables to a meatloaf. Slow-simmer vegetables with lean meat to make a flavorful stew or ragout.

Dessert: Skip the pastry, cakes and puddings, and opt for fruit instead. Fresh fruit is better than canned. An unpeeled apple is better than applesauce.

Snacks: Stick to raw nibbles such as celery, pepper rings and cauliflower.

Deli Marinated Salad

Makes 16 servings

1 head cabbage, shredded (1³/₄ to 2 lb.)
2 cucumbers, pared, sliced
1 large carrot, pared, sliced ●
2 small red or green bell peppers, seeded, halved, sliced (preferably 1 red and 1 green)
1 red onion, sliced into rings
1 cup cider vinegar
1 cup water
6-oz. can frozen apple or apple cider concentrate, defrosted, undiluted
¼ cup safflower or corn oil
3 tbsp. salt or to taste ●

● *HIGH SODIUM ALERT — Omit carrot and added salt.*

Combine ingredients in large crock or nonmetallic bowl. Refrigerate covered at least 24 hours before serving, stirring occasionally. Store in refrigerator.

Total		Per Serving
978.8	Calories	61.2
118.1	Carbohydrate (g)	7.4
17.5	Protein (g)	1.1
57.6	Total Fat (g)	3.6
4.0	Saturated Fat (g)	0.3
0.0	Cholesterol (mg)	0.0
19,424.3	Sodium (mg)	1214.0

Cottage-Style Tuna Salad

Makes 6 servings

½ cup low-fat cottage cheese ●
7-oz. can water-packed tuna, drained ●
½ small green pepper, diced
¼ cup diced celery ●
1 tbsp. minced chives
1 tsp. lemon juice
Salt ● and pepper to taste (optional)

● *HIGH SODIUM ALERT — Use unsalted cottage cheese and tuna. Omit celery and added salt; the quantity of green pepper can be doubled.*

1 tsp. = 5 mL   1 tbsp. = 15 mL   1 cup = 250 mL   1 oz. = 30 g

Combine ingredients; toss lightly to mix. (Serve on lettuce or in sandwiches.)

Total		Per Serving
367.3	Calories	61.2
8.3	Carbohydrate (g)	1.4
72.3	Protein (g)	12.0
3.0	Total Fat (g)	0.5
0.6	Saturated Fat (g)	0.1
135.7	Cholesterol (mg)	22.6
2195.8	Sodium (mg)	366.0

Pear Luncheon Salad

Makes 2 servings

1 cup low-fat cottage cheese ●
1/4 cup raisins
2 tbsp. low-calorie low-fat mayonnaise ●
8-oz. can juice-packed pear halves, drained
Lettuce
Cinnamon

● *HIGH SODIUM ALERT — Use unsalted cottage cheese and mayonnaise.*

Combine cottage cheese, raisins and mayonnaise. Slice each pear half into quarters. Arrange cottage cheese mixture and pear slices on lettuce. Sprinkle with cinnamon.

Total		Per Serving
397.8	Calories	198.9
54.8	Carbohydrate (g)	27.4
31.4	Protein (g)	15.7
6.6	Total Fat (g)	3.3
1.2	Saturated Fat (g)	0.6
35.4	Cholesterol (mg)	17.7
879.8	Sodium (mg)	439.9

Mushroom Vinaigrette Salad

Makes 6 servings

2 tbsp. safflower or corn oil
2 tbsp. vinegar
2 tbsp. water
2 tbsp. liquid pectin
1 tbsp. chopped fresh parsley
1/4 tsp. paprika
Salt ● and pepper to taste (optional)
1/2 lb. sliced fresh mushrooms
1 tbsp. capers ● (optional)
6 cups torn lettuce
1 tomato, cut in wedges
1 cup raw cauliflowerets

● *HIGH SODIUM ALERT — Omit added salt and capers.*

Beat together oil, vinegar, water, pectin, parsley, paprika, salt and pepper in small bowl. Add mushrooms and capers; stir well. Refrigerate several hours or overnight. Place lettuce in bowl; arrange tomato wedges and cauliflowerets in rings on top. Remove mushrooms from marinade and mound in center. When ready to serve pour marinade over salad and toss lightly to mix well.

Total		Per Serving
431.5	Calories	72.0
37.6	Carbohydrate (g)	6.3
14.2	Protein (g)	2.4
28.9	Total Fat (g)	4.8
2.0	Saturated Fat (g)	0.3
0.0	Cholesterol (mg)	0.0
85.0	Sodium (mg)	14.2

Quick Salade Nicoise

Makes 4 servings

2 cups potatoes, pared, cooked, sliced ●
2 cups cooked green beans (fresh or canned) ●
4 pitted black olives, sliced ●
1/3 cup olive liquid (from can) ●
1/4 cup wine vinegar
1 tbsp. safflower or corn oil
1 tsp. Worcestershire sauce ●
1/8 tsp. garlic powder
2 cans (7 oz. each) water-packed tuna, undrained, flaked ●
4 small tomatoes, sliced
2 red or green bell peppers, sliced
1 red onion, thinly sliced
Salt ● and pepper to taste (optional)
Lettuce

● *HIGH SODIUM ALERT — Cook potatoes without salt. Use unsalted green beans and tuna. Omit olives, olive liquid, Worcestershire and added salt.*

Combine potatoes, green beans, olives, olive liquid, vinegar, oil, Worcestershire and garlic. Cover and chill at least 2 hours. Add tuna (including liquid), tomatoes, peppers, onion, salt and pepper. Toss lightly to mix. Serve on lettuce.

Total		Per Serving
1117.2	Calories	279.3
107.5	Carbohydrate (g)	26.9
131.9	Protein (g)	33.0
21.2	Total Fat (g)	5.3
1.0	Saturated Fat (g)	0.3
252.0	Cholesterol (mg)	63.0
7090.9	Sodium (mg)	1772.7

Chef's Salad Mold

Makes 6 servings

2 envelopes unflavored gelatin
2 1/2 cups cold water
1/2 cup sugar ▲
1 tsp. salt ● or to taste (optional)
1/2 cup cider vinegar
2 tbsp. lemon juice
1 cup shredded Swiss cheese ● ■
1 cup finely diced cooked ham ●
3/4 cup diced green pepper
3/4 cup thinly sliced celery ●
Lettuce (optional)

● *HIGH SODIUM ALERT — Omit added salt. Use low-sodium cheese. Substitute diced turkey for ham. Substitute cucumber for celery.*

■ *HIGH CHOLESTEROL ALERT — Use low-fat Swiss-style processed cheese.*

▲ *HIGH SUGAR ALERT — Omit sugar or use sugar substitute.*

Sprinkle gelatin over 1 cup of the cold water in saucepan. After 1 minute add sugar. Place over low heat; cook, stirring constantly, until gelatin dissolves. Remove from heat. Stir in salt. Add remaining 1 1/2 cups cold water. Stir in vinegar and lemon juice. Chill until mixture is slightly thickened. Fold in remaining ingredients, except lettuce. Turn into 6-cup mold or individual molds. Chill until firm. Unmold on lettuce, if desired.

Total		Per Serving
1187.7	Calories	198.0
119.9	Carbohydrate (g)	20.0
81.4	Protein (g)	13.6
44.5	Total Fat (g)	7.4
22.1	Saturated Fat (g)	3.7
240.1	Cholesterol (mg)	40.0
2225.8	Sodium (mg)	371.0

Alert Symbols: ● Sodium ■ Cholesterol ▲ Sugar

Marinated Cucumbers

Makes 4 servings

1/2 cup plain low-fat yogurt
2 tbsp. lemon juice
1 tsp. sugar ▲ (optional)
    Salt ● and pepper to taste
    (optional)
2 cucumbers, pared, thinly sliced

● *HIGH SODIUM ALERT — Omit added salt.*

▲ *HIGH SUGAR ALERT — Omit sugar or use sugar substitute.*

Combine yogurt, lemon juice, sugar, salt and pepper. Toss with cucumber; chill.

Total		Per Serving
130.5	Calories	32.6
22.9	Carbohydrate (g)	5.7
6.2	Protein (g)	1.6
2.0	Total Fat (g)	0.5
1.0	Saturated Fat (g)	0.3
10.0	Cholesterol (mg)	2.5
86.5	Sodium (mg)	21.6

Beef Stroganoff Salad

Makes 6 servings

1 lb. leftover lean broiled beef round steak or roast beef
1/4 cup dry white wine
3 tbsp. white vinegar
2 tbsp. catsup ● ▲
1 tsp. dry mustard
4 potatoes, pared, cooked, diced ●
2 cups sliced fresh mushrooms
3/4 cup plain low-fat yogurt
1 red onion, halved, thinly sliced

● *HIGH SODIUM ALERT — Use unsalted catsup. Cook potatoes without salt.*

▲ *HIGH SUGAR ALERT — Use sugarless catsup.*

Trim all fat from meat. Slice meat thinly against the grain into bite-size chunks. Combine meat with wine, vinegar, catsup and mustard. Marinate at least 1 hour in refrigerator. Stir in remaining ingredients and chill.

Total		Per Serving
1478.4	Calories	246.4
117.5	Carbohydrate (g)	19.6
162.2	Protein (g)	27.0
30.5	Total Fat (g)	5.1
14.8	Saturated Fat (g)	2.5
428.3	Cholesterol (mg)	71.4
2678.8	Sodium (mg)	446.5

Chicken or Turkey Salad Hawaiian-Style

Makes 4 servings

2 cups diced cooked white-meat chicken or turkey
1 cup chopped celery ●
1 cup juice-packed pineapple chunks, drained
1/4 cup pineapple juice (from can)
1/4 cup low-calorie low-fat mayonnaise ●
    Salt ● and pepper to taste (optional)
    Lettuce (optional)

● *HIGH SODIUM ALERT — Substitute diced cucumber for celery. Use unsalted mayonnaise. Omit added salt.*

Combine all ingredients, except lettuce and toss lightly. Chill well. Serve on lettuce, if desired.

Total		Per Serving
748.8	Calories	187.2
56.2	Carbohydrate (g)	14.0
90.8	Protein (g)	22.7
17.6	Total Fat (g)	4.4
3.0	Saturated Fat (g)	0.7
253.0	Cholesterol (mg)	63.2
410.5	Sodium (mg)	102.6

Chicken or Turkey Salad Mold

Makes 4 servings

2 envelopes unflavored gelatin
1 cup cold water
10 1/2-oz. can condensed cream of chicken soup ●
1 tbsp. lemon juice
1/8 tsp. pepper
2 cups diced cooked white-meat chicken or turkey
1 cup chopped celery ●
1/4 cup chopped green pepper
2 tbsp. diced red bell pepper or canned pimiento ●
1 tbsp. minced onion

● *HIGH SODIUM ALERT — Use unsalted soup. Substitute diced cucumber for celery. Use red pepper, not canned pimiento.*

Sprinkle gelatin over 1/2 cup of the cold water in saucepan. After 1 minute place over low heat. Cook, stirring constantly, until gelatin dissolves. Remove from heat. Blend in soup. Stir in remaining 1/2 cup water, the lemon juice and pepper. Refrigerate until mixture is slightly thickened. Fold in remaining ingredients. Turn into 6-cup mold or 4 individual molds. Refrigerate until firm.

Total		Per Serving
791.2	Calories	197.8
29.9	Carbohydrate (g)	7.5
110.0	Protein (g)	27.5
23.9	Total Fat (g)	6.0
5.5	Saturated Fat (g)	1.4
245.7	Cholesterol (mg)	61.4
2760.0	Sodium (mg)	690.0

Crab Louisiana

Makes 4 servings

1 medium head iceberg lettuce
2 stalks celery, sliced (about 1 cup) ●
1 carrot, shredded
1/2 onion, chopped
5 or 6 radishes, sliced
5 tbsp. low-calorie low-fat mayonnaise ●
2 1/2 tbsp. catsup ● ▲
1/2 tsp. horseradish
1/8 tsp. dry mustard
    Salt to taste ● (optional)
2 cans (7 1/2 oz. each) Alaskan king crab, drained, or 2 packages (6 oz. each) frozen Alaskan king crab, defrosted, drained ●

● *HIGH SODIUM ALERT — Use unsalted mayonnaise and catsup. Omit celery and added salt. Substitute unsalted water-packed tuna for crab.*

▲ *HIGH SUGAR ALERT — Use sugarless catsup.*

Core, rinse and thoroughly drain lettuce; refrigerate in disposable plastic bag or plastic crisper. Chill other vegetables. Combine mayonnaise, catsup, horseradish, mustard and salt. Slice crab. Shred lettuce and combine with vegetables and crab meat in salad bowl. Add dressing; toss 3 to 5 minutes, or until ingredients are moist and well coated.

Total		Per Serving
616.5	Calories	154.1
47.0	Carbohydrate (g)	11.8
68.9	Protein (g)	17.2
19.0	Total Fat (g)	4.7
0.0	Saturated Fat (g)	0.0
441.3	Cholesterol (mg)	110.3
4261.8	Sodium (mg)	1065.5

1 tsp. = 5 mL   1 tbsp. = 15 mL   1 cup = 250 mL   1 oz. = 30 g

Greek Salad

Makes 8 servings

- 1 large head lettuce, torn
- 4 tomatoes, cut into chunks
- 1 cucumber, thinly sliced
- 1/4 cup sliced pitted ripe olives ●
- 6-oz. jar marinated artichoke hearts, well drained ● (optional)
- 1/4 lb. feta cheese, crumbled ● ■
- 3 tbsp. lemon juice
- 1 tsp. dried mint leaves
  Salt ● and pepper to taste (optional)

● *HIGH SODIUM ALERT — Omit olives and artichokes. Use low-sodium cheese. Omit added salt.*

■ *HIGH CHOLESTEROL ALERT — Use low-fat cheese.*

Arrange lettuce on a large platter or individual serving plates. Top with tomatoes, cucumber, olives, artichoke hearts and cheese. Sprinkle with lemon juice, mint, salt and pepper.

Total		Per Serving
639.0	Calories	79.9
68.6	Carbohydrate (g)	8.6
30.8	Protein (g)	3.9
30.9	Total Fat (g)	3.9
20.0	Saturated Fat (g)	2.5
100.0	Cholesterol (mg)	12.5
1767.9	Sodium (mg)	221.0

Spinach Caesar Salad•

Makes 8 servings

- 10-oz. package fresh spinach, torn
- 1/4 cup minced onion
- 1 clove garlic, minced
- 1/4 cup low-calorie low-fat mayonnaise
- 1/4 cup low-calorie low-fat Italian salad dressing
- 1 tbsp. lemon juice
  Salt and pepper to taste (optional)
- 3 slices high-fiber bread, toasted, cubed
- 2 tbsp. plus 2 tsp. grated Parmesan cheese ■

● *HIGH SODIUM ALERT — Not recommended for low-sodium diets.*

■ *HIGH CHOLESTEROL ALERT — Use low-fat cheese or omit.*

Discard any tough ribs from spinach. Combine spinach with onion and garlic in salad bowl. Combine mayonnaise, dressing,

lemon juice, salt and pepper and pour over spinach. Toss warm bread cubes with Parmesan cheese. Sprinkle over salad.

Total		Per Serving
423.3	Calories	52.9
52.6	Carbohydrate (g)	6.6
23.9	Protein (g)	3.0
17.1	Total Fat (g)	2.1
2.8	Saturated Fat (g)	0.4
44.1	Cholesterol (mg)	5.5
1426.7	Sodium (mg)	178.3

Crab and Mushroom Salad

Makes 2 servings

- 1/2 head iceberg lettuce, torn
- 1 cup (5 to 6 oz.) fresh (cooked, drained), frozen (defrosted, drained) or canned (drained) Alaskan king crab ●
- 1/4 lb. fresh mushrooms, quartered (about 1 1/2 cups)
- 1 large tomato, cut into wedges
- 1 tbsp. lemon juice
- 2 tsp. safflower or corn oil
  Salt ● and pepper to taste (optional)

● *HIGH SODIUM ALERT — Substitute unsalted water-packed tuna for crab. Omit added salt.*

Arrange lettuce in 2 large bowls. Combine remaining ingredients; divide between bowls. Toss lightly.

Total		Per Serving
316.9	Calories	158.5
19.8	Carbohydrate (g)	9.9
32.6	Protein (g)	16.3
13.0	Total Fat (g)	6.5
0.7	Saturated Fat (g)	0.4
155.6	Cholesterol (mg)	77.8
358.4	Sodium (mg)	179.2

Polynesian Shrimp-Stuffed Papaya

Makes 2 servings

- 1 ripe fresh papaya
- 1/2 lb. fresh shrimp, cooked, shelled, deveined ● ■
- 1/4 cup low-calorie low-fat mayonnaise ●
- 2 tbsp. finely chopped green onion
- 2 tbsp. plain low-fat yogurt
- 1 tbsp. lemon juice

● *HIGH SODIUM ALERT — Use unsalted mayonnaise. Substitute cooked diced white-meat chicken or turkey for the shrimp.*

■ *HIGH CHOLESTEROL ALERT — Substitute cooked diced white-meat chicken or turkey for the shrimp.*

Slice papaya lengthwise in half. Scoop out and discard seeds. Combine remaining ingredients and mix well. Chill. At serving time, mound shrimp mixture in papaya halves.

Total		Per Serving
427.4	Calories	213.7
40.9	Carbohydrate (g)	20.5
43.1	Protein (g)	21.6
11.5	Total Fat (g)	5.8
0.3	Saturated Fat (g)	0.1
375.7	Cholesterol (mg)	187.9
417.9	Sodium (mg)	209.0

Yogurt Egg Salad

Makes 2 servings

- 2 hard-cooked eggs, chopped ■
- 2 tbsp. plain low-fat yogurt
- 2 or 3 drops lemon juice
- 1/2 tsp. prepared mustard ●
  Salt or celery salt ● and pepper to taste (optional)

● *HIGH SODIUM ALERT — Substitute dry mustard to taste for prepared mustard. Omit salt or celery salt.*

■ *HIGH CHOLESTEROL ALERT — Use 1/2 cup liquid egg substitute, cooked and chopped.*

Combine all ingredients and fork-blend lightly. Chill. (Serve on lettuce or in sandwiches.)

Total		Per Serving
177.4	Calories	88.7
1.8	Carbohydrate (g)	0.9
13.2	Protein (g)	6.6
12.7	Total Fat (g)	6.3
4.3	Saturated Fat (g)	2.2
506.5	Cholesterol (mg)	253.3
168.9	Sodium (mg)	84.4

Alert Symbols:　● Sodium　■ Cholesterol　▲ Sugar

Tuna Salad Florentine•

Makes 1 luncheon-size serving

- 2 cups torn fresh spinach
- 2 plum tomatoes, sliced
- 2 tbsp. chopped onion
- 3¾-oz. can water-packed tuna, undrained
- 2 tbsp. low-calorie low-fat Italian salad dressing

● *HIGH SODIUM ALERT — Not recommended for low-sodium diets.*

Combine spinach, tomatoes and onion in large salad bowl. Flake tuna (including liquid) on top. Add dressing and toss lightly to mix.

Total		Per Serving
259.0	Calories	259.0
24.6	Carbohydrate (g)	24.6
36.0	Protein (g)	36.0
3.4	Total Fat (g)	3.4
0.3	Saturated Fat (g)	0.3
63.0	Cholesterol (mg)	63.0
1194.1	Sodium (mg)	1194.1

Mushroom and Turkey Club Salad

Makes 1 serving

- 3 or 4 lettuce leaves
- ½ cup diced turkey
- 4 fresh mushrooms, sliced
- ½ cup cooked green beans ●
- 4 cherry tomatoes, cut into halves
- 5 slices cucumber
- 1 tbsp. cocktail vegetable juice ●
- 1 tbsp. lemon juice
- 1 tsp. safflower or corn oil
- Salt to taste ● (optional)
- Dash red pepper sauce

● *HIGH SODIUM ALERT — Cook green beans without salt. Use unsalted vegetable juice. Omit added salt.*

Line bowl with lettuce leaves. Place turkey in center of bowl; surround with separate clusters of each of the vegetables. Combine vegetable juice, lemon juice, oil, salt and red pepper sauce; pour over salad.

Total		Per Serving
220.7	Calories	220.7
11.0	Carbohydrate (g)	11.0
25.0	Protein (g)	25.0
8.9	Total Fat (g)	8.9
1.6	Saturated Fat (g)	1.6
62.3	Cholesterol (mg)	62.3
275.4	Sodium (mg)	275.4

No-Lettuce Mushroom Salad

Makes 4 servings

- 1 cup sliced fresh mushrooms
- 1 cup diced celery ●
- 1 cup diced green pepper
- ¼ cup coarsely chopped onion
- 2 tbsp. safflower or corn oil
- 2 tbsp. lemon juice
- 1 tbsp. wine vinegar
- Salt ● and pepper to taste (optional)

● *HIGH SODIUM ALERT — Substitute diced cucumber for celery. Omit added salt.*

Combine mushrooms, celery, green pepper and onion in large bowl. Mix together remaining ingredients; pour over vegetables.

Total		Per Serving
349.2	Calories	87.3
22.0	Carbohydrate (g)	5.5
5.7	Protein (g)	1.4
28.2	Total Fat (g)	7.1
2.0	Saturated Fat (g)	0.5
0.0	Cholesterol (mg)	0.0
186.5	Sodium (mg)	46.6

Mushroom Zucchini Salad

Makes 4 servings

- 1 cup sliced fresh mushrooms
- 2 cups thinly sliced zucchini
- 1 tomato, diced
- 6 green onions, sliced
- ½ cup low-calorie, low-fat Italian dressing ●

● *HIGH SODIUM ALERT — Use unsalted dressing.*

Combine mushrooms, zucchini, tomato and onions in large bowl. Add dressing and toss to mix.

Total		Per Serving
184.0	Calories	46.0
29.6	Carbohydrate (g)	7.4
8.4	Protein (g)	2.1
6.1	Total Fat (g)	1.5
1.0	Saturated Fat (g)	0.3
0.0	Cholesterol (mg)	0.0
966.5	Sodium (mg)	241.6

Orange Dressing

Makes ¾ cup

- ½ cup fresh orange juice
- ¼ cup fresh lemon juice
- ½ tsp. paprika
- 1 tsp. garlic salt ● (optional)
- ⅛ tsp. pepper

● *HIGH SODIUM ALERT — Substitute garlic powder to taste for garlic salt.*

Combine all ingredients in jar. Cover and shake well. Store in refrigerator.

Total		Per Tablespoon
70.0	Calories	5.8
18.0	Carbohydrate (g)	1.5
1.3	Protein (g)	0.1
0.5	Total Fat (g)	0.0
0.0	Saturated Fat (g)	0.0
0.0	Cholesterol (mg)	0.0
1.5	Sodium (mg)	0.1

Deviled Dressing

Makes about ¾ cup

- 6-oz. can cocktail vegetable juice ●
- 1 tbsp. safflower or corn oil
- 1 tbsp. vinegar
- ½ tsp. prepared mustard ●
- ½ tsp. Worcestershire sauce ●
- Dash red pepper sauce (optional)

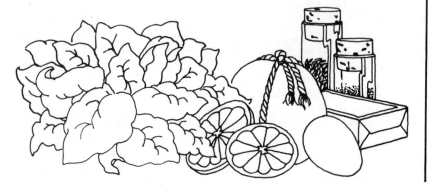

1 tsp. = 5 mL   1 tbsp. = 15 mL   1 cup = 250 mL   1 oz. = 30 g

● HIGH SODIUM ALERT — Use unsalted vegetable juice. Substitute dry mustard to taste for prepared mustard. Omit Worcestershire.

Combine all ingredients in jar. Cover and shake well; chill. Store in refrigerator.

Total		Per Tablespoon
159.7	Calories	13.3
8.4	Carbohydrate (g)	0.7
1.8	Protein (g)	0.2
14.4	Total Fat (g)	1.2
1.0	Saturated Fat (g)	0.1
0.0	Cholesterol (mg)	0.0
423.5	Sodium (mg)	35.3

Savory Salad Dressing

Makes 2/3 cup

1/2 cup plain tomato sauce (check label for no added oil) ●
3 tbsp. lemon juice
2 tbsp. chopped onion
1/2 tsp. salt ● (optional)
1/2 tsp. sugar ▲ (optional)
1/2 tsp. steak sauce ●
1/4 tsp. monosodium glutamate ● (optional)
1/4 tsp. caraway seed

● HIGH SODIUM ALERT — Use unsalted tomato sauce. Omit added salt, steak sauce and monosodium glutamate.

▲ HIGH SUGAR ALERT — Use sugar substitute, or omit.

Combine all ingredients in jar. Cover and shake well; chill. Store in refrigerator.

Total		Per Tablespoon
58.3	Calories	5.5
14.7	Carbohydrate (g)	1.4
2.3	Protein (g)	0.2
0.2	Total Fal (g)	0.0
0.0	Saturated Fat (g)	0.0
0.0	Cholesterol (mg)	0.0
885.7	Sodium (mg)	83.0

Cottage Cheese Sundae Salads

Pineapple-Peach

Makes 1 serving

1/3 cup low-fat cottage cheese ●
1 peeled fresh peach or unpeeled nectarine, pitted, sliced
1 tbsp. defrosted undiluted, unsweetened frozen pineapple juice concentrate

● HIGH SODIUM ALERT — Use unsalted cottage cheese.

Place mound of cottage cheese on salad plate; surround with peach slices. Top with juice concentrate.

Total		Per Serving
126.9	Calories	126.9
20.0	Carbohydrate (g)	20.0
11.3	Protein (g)	11.3
0.7	Total Fat (g)	0.7
0.4	Saturated Fat (g)	0.4
6.5	Cholesterol (mg)	6.5
278.2	Sodium (mg)	278.2

Banana Split

Makes 1 serving

1 small ripe banana
1/3 cup low-fat cottage cheese ●
1 tbsp. defrosted undiluted, unsweetened frozen orange juice concentrate

● HIGH SODIUM ALERT — Use unsalted cottage cheese.

Split banana; place halves in shallow dish. Add scoop of cottage cheese and top with juice concentrate.

Total		Per Serving
189.9	Calories	189.9
35.3	Carbohydrate (g)	35.3
11.4	Protein (g)	11.4
0.7	Total Fat (g)	0.7
0.4	Saturated Fat (g)	0.4
6.5	Cholesterol (mg)	6.5
279.0	Sodium (mg)	279.0

Strawberry-Orange

Makes 1 serving

1/3 cup low-fat cottage cheese ●
5 or 6 fresh strawberries, hulled, sliced
1 tbsp. defrosted undiluted, unsweetened frozen orange juice concentrate

● HIGH SODIUM ALERT — Use unsalted cottage cheese.

Place scoop of cottage cheese on salad plate; surround with strawberries. Top with juice concentrate.

Total		Per Serving
117.4	Calories	117.4
15.8	Carbohydrate (g)	15.8
10.9	Protein (g)	10.9
1.2	Total Fat (g)	1.2
0.4	Saturated Fat (g)	0.4
6.5	Cholesterol (mg)	6.5
277.5	Sodium (mg)	277.5

Apple-Raisin

Makes 1 serving

1/3 cup low-fat cottage cheese ●
1 tbsp. raisins
1 tbsp. defrosted undiluted, unsweetened frozen apple juice concentrate
Apple-pie spice or cinnamon (optional)

● HIGH SODIUM ALERT — Use unsalted cottage cheese.

Mix cottage cheese with raisins; mound in a dessert dish. Top with juice concentrate. Sprinkle with apple-pie spice or cinnamon, if desired.

Total		Per Serving
94.0	Calories	94.0
11.1	Carbohydrate (g)	11.1
10.0	Protein (g)	10.0
0.7	Total Fat (g)	0.7
0.4	Saturated Fat (g)	0.4
6.5	Cholesterol (mg)	6.5
279.4	Sodium (mg)	279.4

Blueberry-Pineapple

Makes 1 serving

1/3 cup low-fat cottage cheese ●
1/4 cup fresh blueberries
1 tbsp. defrosted undiluted, unsweetened frozen pineapple juice concentrate

● HIGH SODIUM ALERT — Use unsalted cottage cheese.

Place scoop of cottage cheese on salad plate; surround with blueberries. Top with juice concentrate.

Total		Per Serving
113.1	Calories	113.1
15.3	Carbohydrate (g)	15.3
10.6	Protein (g)	10.6
1.0	Total Fat (g)	1.0
0.4	Saturated Fat (g)	0.4
6.5	Cholesterol (mg)	6.5
277.5	Sodium (mg)	277.5

Alert Symbols: ● Sodium ■ Cholesterol ▲ Sugar

Creamy Caesar Salad Dressing

Makes ³/4 cup

- ¹/3 cup low-calorie low-fat mayonnaise ●
- ¹/4 cup lemon juice
- ¹/4 cup water
- 2 tbsp. grated Parmesan cheese ● ■ (optional)
- 1 clove garlic, finely chopped
- Dash Worcestershire sauce
- Salt ● and pepper to taste (optional)

● *HIGH SODIUM ALERT — Use unsalted mayonnaise. Use low-sodium cheese, or omit. Omit added salt.*

■ *HIGH CHOLESTEROL ALERT Use low-fat cheese, or omit.*

Combine all ingredients in jar; cover and shake well. (Or combine ingredients in bowl; beat until well blended.) Store in refrigerator.

Total		Per Tablespoon
125.7	Calories	10.5
11.2	Carbohydrate (g)	0.9
0.5	Protein (g)	0.0
10.7	Total Fat (g)	0.9
0.0	Saturated Fat (g)	0.0
42.7	Cholesterol (mg)	3.6
109.9	Sodium (mg)	9.2

Creamy Salad Dressing

Makes ³/4 cup

- ¹/4 cup low-calorie low-fat mayonnaise ●
- ¹/4 cup white or cider vinegar
- ¹/4 cup cold water

● *HIGH SODIUM ALERT — Use unsalted mayonnaise.*

Combine all ingredients in jar. Cover and shake well. Store in refrigerator. (For an Italian version of this recipe, add ¹/2 tsp. dried oregano and pinch onion powder or garlic powder.)

Total		Per Tablespoon
84.0	Calories	7.0
8.0	Carbohydrate (g)	0.7
0.0	Protein (g)	0.0
8.0	Total Fat (g)	0.7
0.0	Saturated Fat (g)	0.0
32.0	Cholesterol (mg)	2.7
76.0	Sodium (mg)	6.3

"Shake and Make" Oil and Vinegar Dressing

Makes about 1 cup

- ¹/3 cup water
- ¹/4 cup white or cider vinegar
- ¹/4 cup liquid pectin
- 2 tbsp. safflower or corn oil
- 2 tbsp. liquid from can of ripe olives ●
- 1 clove garlic, finely chopped or ¹/8 to ¹/4 tsp. garlic powder
- 1 tsp. dried oregano, mixed Italian seasoning or other dried herbs (optional)
- Salt ● and pepper to taste (optional)

● *HIGH SODIUM ALERT — Omit olive liquid; increase water by 2 tablespoons. Omit added salt.*

Combine all ingredients in jar. Cover and shake well. Store in refrigerator.

Total		Per Tablespoon
266.0	Calories	16.6
8.9	Carbohydrate (g)	0.6
0.2	Protein (g)	0.0
28.0	Total Fat (g)	1.8
2.0	Saturated Fat (g)	0.1
0.0	Cholesterol (mg)	0.0
776.0	Sodium (mg)	48.5

Chianti Dressing

Makes about ³/4 cup

- ³/4 cup Chianti or other dry red wine
- ³/4 tsp. safflower or corn oil
- ³/4 tsp. vinegar
- 1 small clove garlic, minced
- 1 tsp. dried oregano
- Salt ● and pepper to taste (optional)

● *HIGH SODIUM ALERT — Omit added salt.*

Combine all ingredients in jar. Cover and shake well. Store in refrigerator.

Total		Per Tablespoon
355.5	Calories	29.6
15.6	Carbohydrate (g)	1.3
0.2	Protein (g)	0.0
3.5	Total Fat (g)	0.3
0.3	Saturated Fat (g)	0.0
0.0	Cholesterol (mg)	0.0
13.0	Sodium (mg)	1.1

Celery Seed Dressing I

Makes 1¹/2 cups

- ³/4 cup water
- ¹/2 cup cider vinegar
- ¹/4 cup safflower or corn oil
- 2 tbsp. celery seed
- 2 tbsp. sugar ▲ (optional)
- 2 tsp. paprika
- 1 tsp. onion powder
- ¹/2 tsp. prepared mustard ●
- Salt ● and pepper to taste (optional)

● *HIGH SODIUM ALERT — Replace prepared mustard with dry mustard to taste. Omit added salt.*

▲ *HIGH SUGAR ALERT — Omit sugar, or replace with sugar substitute.*

Combine all ingredients; heat to boiling. Reduce heat; simmer and stir 1 minute. Chill before serving. Store covered in refrigerator.

Total		Per Tablespoon
513.4	Calories	21.4
9.0	Carbohydrate (g)	0.4
0.3	Protein (g)	0.0
56.2	Total Fat (g)	2.3
4.0	Saturated Fat (g)	0.2
0.0	Cholesterol (mg)	0.0
56.8	Sodium (g)	2.4

Celery Seed Dressing II

Makes 1¹/4 cups

- ²/3 cup water
- ¹/2 cup lemon juice
- 2 tbsp. safflower or corn oil
- 2 tsp. cornstarch or arrowroot
- 2 tsp. celery seed
- 1 tsp. prepared mustard ●
- 1 tsp. paprika
- Salt ● and pepper to taste (optional)

● *HIGH SODIUM ALERT — Substitute dry mustard to taste for prepared mustard. Omit added salt.*

Combine all ingredients; heat to boiling. Reduce heat; simmer and stir until thickened. Chill before serving. Store covered in refrigerator.

Total		Per Tablespoon
303.0	Calories	25.3
15.0	Carbohyrate (g)	1.3
0.8	Protein (g)	0.1
28.3	Total Fat (g)	2.4
2.0	Saturated Fat (g)	0.2
0.0	Cholesterol (mg)	0.0
71.9	Sodium (mg)	6.0

1 tsp. = 5 mL   1 tbsp. = 15 mL   1 cup = 250 mL   1 oz. = 30 g

Fruit Juice Dressing

Makes 1 1/4 cups

1/2 cup unsweetened orange or
   pineapple juice
1/4 cup liquid pectin
1/4 cup safflower or corn oil
3 tbsp. lemon juice
1 tsp. prepared mustard ●
3/4 tsp. salt ● (optional)
1/2 tsp. paprika
   Pinch pepper

● *HIGH SODIUM ALERT — Substitute dry
mustard to taste for prepared mustard. Omit
added salt.*

Combine all ingredients in jar.
Cover and shake well. Store in
refrigerator.

Total		Per Tablespoon
578.0	Calories	28.9
21.2	Carbohydrate (g)	1.1
1.5	Protein (g)	0.1
56.8	Total Fat (g)	2.8
4.0	Saturated Fat (g)	0.2
0.0	Cholesterol (mg)	0.0
64 1	Sodium (mg)	3.2

Quickie Tomato French Dressing●

Makes about 1 cup

3/4 cup tomato juice or liquid
   nonalcoholic Bloody Mary mix
1/4 cup vinegar
1 envelope French-style salad
   dressing mix

● *HIGH SODIUM ALERT — Not recommended
for low-sodium diets.*

Combine all ingredients in jar.
Cover and shake well. Store in
refrigerator.

Total		Per Tablespoon
71.6	Calories	4.5
16.9	Carbohydrate (g)	1.1
3.3	Protein (g)	0.2
0.6	Total Fat (g)	0.0
0.0	Saturated Fat (g)	0.0
0.0	Cholesterol (mg)	0.0
1912.5	Sodium (mg)	119.5

Thousand Island Dressing●

Makes about 1 1/4 cups

1/3 cup low-calorie low-fat
   mayonnaise
1/3 cup cider vinegar
1/3 cup tomato juice
2 tbsp. chopped stuffed green
   (Spanish) olives
2 tbsp. chopped dill pickle
1/2 tsp. chili powder
1/4 tsp. paprika
1/4 tsp. dry mustard

● *HIGH SODIUM ALERT — Not recommended
for low-sodium diets.*

Combine all ingredients in jar.
Cover and shake well. Store in
refrigerator.

Total		Per Tablespoon
149.1	Calories	7.5
19.5	Carbohydrate (g)	1.0
0.9	Protein (g)	0.0
12.7	Total Fat (g)	0.6
0.0	Saturated Fat (g)	0.0
42.7	Cholesterol (mg)	2.1
802.0	Sodium (mg)	40.1

Lemon Sweet-and-Sour Dressing

Makes 1 1/4 cups

1/4 cup boiling water
2 tbsp. sugar ▲
1/2 cup fresh lemon juice
1/4 cup safflower or corn oil
1/4 cup liquid pectin
1 tsp. prepared mustard ●
1 tsp. grated lemon rind
1/4 tsp. Worcestershire sauce
1/8 tsp. garlic powder
   Salt ● and pepper to taste
   (optional)

● *HIGH SODIUM ALERT — Substitute dry
mustard to taste for prepared mustard. Omit
added salt.*

▲ *HIGH SUGAR ALERT — Use sugar
substitute, or omit.*

Combine boiling water and sugar.
Stir until sugar is dissolved. Stir in
remaining ingredients; mix well.
Store in covered jar in refrigerator.
Shake before using.

Total		Per Tablespoon
627.2	Calories	31.4
34.7	Carbohydrate (g)	1.7
0.8	Protein (g)	0.0
56.3	Total Fat (g)	2.8
4.0	Saturated Fat (g)	0.2
0.0	Cholesterol (mg)	0.0
78.1	Sodium (mg)	3.9

Blender Blue Cheese Dressing●

Makes 1 1/2 cups

1 cup low-fat cottage cheese
1 envelope blue cheese flavor salad
   dressing mix
1/4 cup cider vinegar
1/4 cup water

● *HIGH SODIUM ALERT — Not recommended
for low-sodium diets.*

Combine all ingredients in blender.
Cover and blend until smooth. Store
in covered container in refrigerator.

Total		Per Tablespoon
256.0	Calories	10.7
17.8	Carbohydrate (g)	0.7
33.8	Protein (g)	1.4
4.9	Total Fat (g)	0.2
1.2	Saturated Fat (g)	0.1
49.4	Cholesterol (mg)	2.1
2545.0	Sodium (mg)	106.0

Alert Symbols: ● Sodium   ■ Cholesterol   ▲ Sugar

Cooked Oil and Vinegar Dressing

Makes about 1 1/4 cups

- 1 cup water
- 1/4 cup cider vinegar or white wine vinegar
- 2 tbsp. safflower or corn oil
- 1 tbsp. cornstarch
- 3/4 tsp. paprika
- 1 clove garlic, minced
- Salt ● and pepper to taste (optional)

● *HIGH SODIUM ALERT — Omit added salt.*

Combine all ingredients in saucepan. Cook and stir over moderate heat until mixture simmers and thickens. Cool. Pour into jar. Store covered in refrigerator.

Total		Per Tablespoon
287.0	Calories	14.4
11.9	Carbohydrate (g)	0.6
0.2	Protein (g)	0.0
28.0	Total Fat (g)	1.4
2.0	Saturated Fat (g)	0.1
0.0	Cholesterol (mg)	0.0
1.0	Sodium (mg)	0.1

Old-Fashioned Potato Salad Dressing

Makes about 1 cup

- 3/4 cup evaporated skim milk
- 2 tbsp. all-purpose flour
- 2 tsp. sugar ▲
- 2 tsp. safflower or corn oil
- 1 egg, beaten ■
- 2 tbsp. cider vinegar
- 1 tsp. dry mustard
- Salt ● and pepper to taste (optional)

● *HIGH SODIUM ALERT — Omit added salt.*

■ *HIGH CHOLESTEROL ALERT — Use 1/4 cup liquid egg substitute.*

▲ *HIGH SUGAR ALERT — Use sugar substitute, or omit.*

Mix milk, flour, sugar and oil in saucepan. Cook and stir over moderate heat until mixture thickens slightly. Remove from heat. Gradually add egg, vinegar, mustard, salt and pepper. Stir until well blended; cool. Store covered in refrigerator.

Total		Per Serving
404.3	Calories	50.5
43.2	Carbohydrate (g)	5.4
21.1	Protein (g)	2.6
15.4	Total Fat (g)	1.9
2.7	Saturated Fat (g)	0.3
306.0	Cholesterol (mg)	38.3
271.5	Sodium (mg)	33.9

Easy Creamy Italian Dressing●

Makes about 1 1/4 cups

- 1 cup part-skim ricotta cheese ■
- 1/4 cup cider or white vinegar
- 1 envelope Italian salad dressing mix

● *HIGH SODIUM ALERT — Not recommended for low-sodium diets.*

■ *HIGH CHOLESTEROL ALERT — Use low-fat cottage cheese.*

Combine all ingredients in blender. Cover and blend until smooth. Scrape down container with rubber spatula. Store in covered container in refrigerator.

Total		Per Tablespoon
450.7	Calories	22.5
37.0	Carbohydrate (g)	1.9
31.3	Protein (g)	1.6
20.5	Total Fat (g)	1.0
12.1	Saturated Fat (g)	0.6
77.0	Cholesterol (mg)	3.9
2247.0	Sodium (mg)	112.4

Banana Dressing▲

Makes about 2 cups

- 1 ripe medium banana, cut into chunks
- 1/2 cup low-fat lemon yogurt
- 1/2 cup low-fat cottage cheese ●
- 4 to 5 tbsp. skim milk
- 1 tbsp. honey (optional)

● *HIGH SODIUM ALERT — Use unsalted cottage cheese.*

▲ *HIGH SUGAR ALERT — Not recommended for low-sugar diets.*

Combine all ingredients in blender. Cover and blend until smooth. Scrape down container with rubber spatula. (Add more milk if thinner consistency is desired.) Store in covered container in refrigerator. (Serve with cottage cheese or fruit salads.)

Total		Per Tablespoon
312.5	Calories	9.8
48.0	Carbohydrate (g)	1.5
24.3	Protein (g)	0.8
2.5	Total Fat (g)	0.1
1.4	Saturated Fat (g)	0.0
17.0	Cholesterol (mg)	0.5
316.3	Sodium (mg)	9.9

Mock Mayonnaise

Makes 1 cup

- 1 cup low-fat cottage cheese ●
- 1/4 cup liquid egg substitute
- 1 tbsp. vinegar or lemon juice
- 2 tsp. sugar ▲
- 1/2 tsp. salt ● (optional)
- 1/2 tsp. dry mustard
- 1/2 tsp. paprika
- Pinch pepper

● *HIGH SODIUM ALERT — Use unsalted cottage cheese. Omit added salt.*

▲ *HIGH SUGAR ALERT — Use sugar substitute, or omit.*

Combine all ingredients in blender. Cover and blend on medium speed until smooth. Scrape down container with rubber spatula. Store in covered container in refrigerator.

Total		Per Tablespoon
253.1	Calories	15.8
18.3	Carbohydrate (g)	1.1
37.0	Protein (g)	2.3
2.0	Total Fat (g)	0.1
1.2	Saturated Fat (g)	0.1
19.4	Cholesterol (mg)	1.2
960.1	Sodium (mg)	60.0

1 tsp. = 5 mL   1 tbsp. = 15 mL   1 cup = 250 mL   1 oz. = 30 g

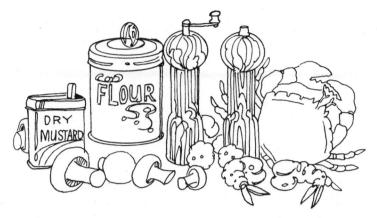

Easy Yogurt Dressings

Yogurt Dressing

Makes 1 1/4 cups

1 cup plain low-fat yogurt
3 tbsp. lemon juice
1/8 tsp. dry mustard
    Salt ● and pepper to taste
    (optional)
    Pinch garlic powder (optional)

● *HIGH SODIUM ALERT—Omit added salt.*

Combine all ingredients in jar. Cover and shake well. Store in refrigerator.

Total		Per Tablespoon
136.4	Calories	6.8
16.9	Carbohydrate (g)	0.9
8.3	Protein (g)	0.4
4.0	Total Fat (g)	0.2
2.0	Saturated Fat (g)	0.1
20.0	Cholesterol (mg)	1.0
125.3	Sodium (mg)	6.3

Green Goddess Dressing ●

Makes 1 cup

1 cup plain low-fat yogurt
2 tbsp. lemon juice
1 envelope Green Goddess salad
    dressing mix

● *HIGH SODIUM ALERT—Not recommended for low-sodium diets.*

Combine all ingredients in jar. Cover and shake well. Store in refrigerator.

Total		Per Tablespoon
166.4	Calories	10.4
21.0	Carbohydrate (g)	1.3
10.1	Protein (g)	0.6
4.6	Total Fat (g)	0.3
2.0	Saturated Fat (g)	0.1
20.0	Cholesterol (mg)	1.3
1673.2	Sodium (mg)	104.6

Parsley Dressing

Makes 1 cup

1 cup plain low-fat yogurt
3 tbsp. minced fresh parsley
1 tsp. dillweed
1/4 tsp. garlic salt ● (optional)

● *HIGH SODIUM ALERT—Substitute garlic powder to taste for garlic salt.*

Combine all ingredients; mix well. Store in refrigerator.

Total		Per Tablespoon
128.0	Calories	8.0
13.0	Carbohydrate (g)	0.8
8.0	Protein (g)	0.5
4.0	Total Fat (g)	0.3
2.0	Saturated Fat (g)	0.1
20.0	Cholesterol (mg)	1.3
131.0	Sodium (mg)	8.2

Curried Fruit Dressing

Makes 1 1/4 cups

1 cup plain low-fat yogurt
3 tbsp. golden raisins
2 tbsp. defrosted undiluted,
    unsweetened frozen pineapple
    juice concentrate
1/2 tsp. grated lemon rind
1/2 tsp. curry powder
1/4 tsp. cinnamon

Combine all ingredients; mix well. Store in refrigerator.

Total		Per Tablespoon
269.1	Calories	13.5
50.9	Carbohydrate (g)	2.5
8.5	Protein (g)	0.4
4.0	Total Fat (g)	0.2
2.0	Saturated Fat (g)	0.1
20.0	Cholesterol (mg)	1.0
134.0	Sodium (mg)	6.7

Russian Dressing

Makes 2 cups

1 cup plain low-fat yogurt
1 cup low-calorie low-fat Russian
    salad dressing ●
2 tbsp. catsup ● ▲

● *HIGH SODIUM ALERT—Use unsalted dressing and catsup.*

▲ *HIGH SUGAR ALERT—Use sugarless catsup.*

Combine all ingredients in large jar. Cover and shake well. Store in refrigerator.

Total		Per Tablespoon
635.0	Calories	19.8
85.0	Carbohydrate (g)	2.7
8.0	Protein (g)	0.3
20.0	Total Fat (g)	0.6
2.0	Saturated Fat (g)	0.1
20.0	Cholesterol (mg)	0.6
3557.0	Sodium (mg)	111.2

Seafood Dressing

Makes 2 3/4 cups

1 cup plain low-fat yogurt
1 cup low calorie low-fat
    mayonnaise ●
1/2 cup hot chili sauce ● ▲
2 tbsp. lemon juice
1 tbsp. minced onion
1 tbsp. prepared horseradish
    Pinch tarragon
    Salt ● and pepper to taste
    (optional)

● *HIGH SODIUM ALERT—Use unsalted mayonnaise. Substitute tomato paste with chili powder to taste for chili sauce. Omit added salt.*

▲ *HIGH SUGAR ALERT—Use sugarless chili sauce.*

Combine all ingredients; mix well. Store in refrigerator.

Total		Per Tablespoon
597.2	Calories	13.6
67.0	Carbohydrate (g)	1.5
8.4	Protein (g)	0.2
36.0	Total Fat (g)	0.8
2.0	Saturated Fat (g)	0.0
148.0	Cholesterol (mg)	3.4
2054.0	Sodium (mg)	46.7

Yogurt Tartar Sauce ●

Makes 2 1/2 cups

1 cup plain low-fat yogurt
1 cup low-calorie low-fat
    mayonnaise
1/2 cup pickle relish
1 tbsp. prepared mustard

● *HIGH SODIUM ALERT—Not recommended for low-sodium diets.*

Combine all ingredients; mix well. Store in refrigerator.

Total		Per Tablespoon
627.4	Calories	15.7
73.9	Carbohydrate (g)	1.9
9.3	Protein (g)	0.2
37.0	Total Fat (g)	0.9
2.0	Saturated Fat (g)	0.1
148.0	Cholesterol (mg)	3.7
1473.3	Sodium (mg)	36.8

Alert Symbols: ● Sodium ■ Cholesterol ▲ Sugar

Seven Saucy Ways With Mayonnaise

Mock Hollandaise
Makes ¾ cup

½ cup low-calorie low-fat
  mayonnaise ●
2 tbsp. lemon juice
2 to 3 tbsp. hot water

● HIGH SODIUM ALERT — Use unsalted
mayonnaise.

Combine mayonnaise and lemon
juice. Stir in enough hot water to
obtain desired consistency. Serve
immediately (over cooked green
vegetables).

Total		Per Tablespoon
167.6	Calories	14.0
10.6	Carbohydrate (g)	0.9
0.1	Protein (g)	0.0
16.0	Total Fat (g)	1.3
0.0	Saturated Fat (g)	0.0
64.0	Cholesterol (mg)	5.3
152.3	Sodium (mg)	12.7

Savory Mayonnaise
Makes 1 cup

½ cup low-calorie low-fat
  mayonnaise ●
½ cup plain low-fat yogurt
1 tsp. prepared mustard ●
  Pinch paprika
  Dash Worcestershire sauce

● HIGH SODIUM ALERT — Use unsalted
mayonnaise. Substitute dry mustard to taste for
prepared mustard.

Combine all ingredients; mix well.
(Serve with vegetable, meat or
seafood salads.)

Total		Per Tablespoon
226.2	Calories	14.1
14.8	Carbohydrate (g)	0.9
4.3	Protein (g)	0.3
18.3	Total Fat (g)	1.1
1.0	Saturated Fat (g)	0.1
74.0	Cholesterol (mg)	4.6
277.2	Sodium (mg)	17.3

Fruit Dressing ▲
Makes 1 cup

½ cup low-calorie low-fat
  mayonnaise ●
½ cup lemon low-fat yogurt
  Pinch cinnamon or apple-pie spice

● HIGH SODIUM ALERT — Use unsalted
mayonnaise.

▲ HIGH SUGAR ALERT — Not recommended
for low-sugar diets.

Combine all ingredients. (Serve
with fruit salads.)

Total		Per Tablespoon
260.0	Calories	16.3
24.0	Carbohydrate (g)	1.5
6.3	Protein (g)	0.4
17.5	Total Fat (g)	1.1
0.8	Saturated Fat (g)	0.1
70.0	Cholesterol (mg)	4.4
227.0	Sodium (mg)	14.2

Curry Dressing
Makes 1 cup

½ cup low-calorie low-fat
  mayonnaise ●
⅓ cup plain low-fat yogurt
1 tbsp. soy sauce ●
1 tbsp. defrosted, undiluted frozen
  unsweetened pineapple juice
  concentrate
½ tsp. curry powder, or to taste

● HIGH SODIUM ALERT — Use unsalted
mayonnaise. Omit soy sauce.

Combine all ingredients; mix well.
(Serve with fruit or cold seafood or
poultry salads.)

Total		Per Tablespoon
243.5	Calories	15.2
21.1	Carbohydrate (g)	1.3
3.1	Protein (g)	0.2
17.3	Total Fat (g)	1.1
0.7	Saturated Fat (g)	0.0
70.7	Cholesterol (mg)	4.4
1293.2	Sodium (mg)	80.8

Island Dressing
Makes 1 cup

½ cup low-calorie low-fat
  mayonnaise ●
2 tbsp. chili sauce ● ▲
½ tbsp. catsup ● ▲
1 tbsp. chopped chives
1 tbsp. chopped green pepper
1 tbsp. chopped pimiento
  Pinch paprika

● HIGH SODIUM ALERT — Use unsalted
mayonnaise. Use 2½ tbsp. unsalted tomato
sauce plus chili powder to taste for total chili
sauce and catsup.

▲ HIGH SUGAR ALERT — Use sugarless chili
sauce and catsup.

Combine all ingredients; mix well.
(Serve with vegetable salads.)

Total		Per Tablespoon
206.8	Calories	12.9
20.4	Carbohydrate (g)	1.3
0.3	Protein (g)	0.0
16.1	Total Fat (g)	1.0
0.0	Saturated Fat (g)	0.0
64.0	Cholesterol (mg)	4.0
636.7	Sodium (mg)	39.8

Horseradish Sauce
Makes 1 cup

½ cup low-calorie low-fat
  mayonnaise ●
⅓ cup plain low-fat yogurt
2 tbsp. prepared horseradish
1 tsp. prepared mustard ●

● HIGH SODIUM ALERT — Use unsalted
mayonnaise. Substitute dry mustard to taste for
prepared mustard.

Combine all ingredients; mix well.
(Serve with roast beef.)

Total		Per Tablespoon
217.4	Calories	13.6
14.6	Carbohydrate (g)	0.9
3.0	Protein (g)	0.2
17.6	Total Fat (g)	1.1
1.2	Saturated Fat (g)	0.1
70.7	Cholesterol (mg)	4.4
284.4	Sodium (mg)	17.8

Pimiento-Mustard Dressing
Makes ¾ cup

½ cup low-calorie low-fat
  mayonnaise ●
2 tbsp. minced pimiento
¼ tsp. dry mustard
  Salt ● and pepper to taste
  (optional)
  Pinch paprika
1 tsp. vinegar
  Evaporated skim milk

● HIGH SODIUM ALERT — Use unsalted
mayonnaise. Omit added salt.

Combine all ingredients except
skim milk; mix well. Stir in skim
milk, a teaspoonful at a time, until
desired consistency. (Serve with
meat or vegetable salads.)

Total		Per Tablespoon
192.6	Calories	16.1
14.0	Carbohydrate (g)	1.2
2.5	Protein (g)	0.2
16.2	Total Fat (g)	1.4
0.0	Saturated Fat (g)	0.0
73.0	Cholesterol (mg)	6.1
193.1	Sodium (mg)	16.1

1 tsp. = 5 mL   1 tbsp. = 15 mL   1 cup = 250 mL   1 oz. = 30 g

Meaty Main Dishes

The meat counter is the place, the shopping experts tell us, that we can do the most to stretch our food-buying dollar. Since meat eats up a lion's share of our food budget, sharp shopping amid the roasts and chops will do the most to keep costs down. The same is true of calories.

The Average American Eats More Than His Own Weight in Red Meat Every Year. Of an average of 189 pounds of meat consumed per person annually, most of it is from the fatty cuts that cost the most in calories as well as cash. Today 70 percent of our protein comes from animal foods, compared with only 50 percent in 1910. By eating so much meat, and such fattening meat, the average American consumes nearly double the amount of protein he or she really needs and perhaps triple the necessary fat.

You can cut calories simply by cutting down on the quantity of meat served. It's not necessary or even desirable to serve meat at every meal, and portions can be smaller. Everyone will be healthier and better fed if you offer a wider choice of other foods as side dishes: soups, salads, a variety of interesting vegetables, potatoes, pasta or rice prepared in nonfattening ways, breads, and fresh-fruit desserts. Even a seven-course banquet can add up to fewer calories if a variety of foods take the place of second and third helpings of meat.

But even if you don't cut down on the quantity of meat, choosing meat for its protein quality (low-fat content) can mean dramatic savings in calories. Here we are using the word quality in its nutritional context, rather than in the familiar terms of price.

Everything You Wanted to Know about Meat, but Didn't Know Whom to Ask

Q. *To get better quality meat should I look for meat marked prime?*

A. Not if you are trying to cut down on fat and calories. The most expensive meat—beef graded Prime—is also the highest in fat. There are three U.S. Department of Agriculture grades of meat available to the public: Prime, Choice and Good. Prime is the most expensive and usually only available in specialty butcher shops and some supermarkets. The most widely available grade of beef is marked Choice. Meat graded Good is found in some supermarkets and discount meat stores. (There are three lesser grades of meat, but these don't usually reach the retail market.)

A number of factors go into determining the grade of a cut of beef, but the main consideration is fatty marbling—veins of fat running all through the meat. When a butcher or retauranteur speaks of high quality meat, he or she is usually referring to meat with heavy fatty marbling. The more fat there is in meat, the more calories and the less protein it contains. So, the highest quality, most expensive meat is likely to be the least nutritious and most fattening from a nutritional viewpoint. The more nutritious cuts and grades of meat, with more protein, less fat and fewer calories can be prepared and served in ways that enhance their taste and tenderness. And they cost less money.

Q. *Which meats are the most fattening, and which are the leanest?*

A. It's inaccurate and an oversimplification to say that beef is more fattening than veal or that ham is more fattening than lamb. Although veal is generally leaner than beef, some cuts of veal do contain more fat and calories than some cuts of beef. And some cuts of pork are leaner than some cuts of beef or lamb. If you know the best cuts of each meat to choose, and the best ways to cook them, you needn't limit your choices to any one kind of meat.

Q. *Are there any simple rules for choosing the leanest and least fattening meats and poultry?*

A. Yes. Following are a few simple rules to remember. Check them against the chart of Fat Fighter's Choice Cuts of Meat, and you'll see that they apply in most cases.

1. Younger Is Leaner Than Older. Animals, like people, tend to add fat as they age. For that reason, a veal or lamb rib chop is less fattening than a beef or pork rib chop, because it comes from young animals. Young frying chickens are markedly less fattening than older fowl. Smaller, younger turkeys are lower in calories than larger, older birds.

2. The Leaner and Least Fattening Tender Cuts of Meat Come from the Rear—from the Leg. This applies to meat animals—beef, veal, lamb, pork, ham—not poultry. A leg cut of beef is called beef round. In veal, it is called veal round. In lamb, it's a leg steak or leg chop, and in pork it's called a fresh ham slice. (The word ham refers to a leg cut of pork and has nothing to do with whether it's cured or smoked. A cured ham slice would be called a smoked ham slice.)

3. The Most Fattening Tender Cuts Come from the Middle—from the Rib. Rib steaks and rib chops of all meat animals are generally the ones with the highest fat content and the most calories.

4. The Less Fattening, Less Tender Cuts Come from the Front End—from the Arm and Shoulder. Of these, the cuts from the arm or foreshank are less fattening than the shoulder. Beef cuts from this area are known as chuck. In pork, it's sometimes called picnic.

5. The Most Fattening, Least Tender Cuts Come from the Underbelly. This includes beef brisket and short plate, from which corned beef and pastrami are usually made. Also avoid breast of veal and lamb, pork spareribs and bacon. One big exception, beef flank steak, an exceedingly lean and tender steak, is cut from the underbelly of beef. It's virtually fat-free. It's also the leanest and least fattening of all beef cuts—a real find for fat-fighters.

Q. *What cut should I choose if I want a really tender, luxury steak or roast, if cost is no object, but calories are?*

A. Your best bet is the tenderloin, the long thin, lean-but-tender, fat-trimmed boneless center of beef loin. The steaks from this cut are called filet mignon. (You can also ask the butcher for a tenderloin roast of pork, or loin roasts of lamb or veal.)

Q. *How should I buy hamburger?*

A. According to federal law, hamburger may contain up to 30 percent fat. State and local laws sometimes impose a 25-percent fat content limit. That still represents a lot of fat. And unfortunately, the ground meat you take home may even exceed the legal limit; stores are occasionally cited for such infractions. Many grocery chains offer premium-priced lean, or diet lean hamburger, but the fat content is usually at least 10 percent, sometimes 15 percent or more.

The safest way for a fat-fighter to buy hamburger is to select a lean bottom round or chuck roast, have it trimmed of fat and ground to order. It will be fresher, less fattening, and usually no more expensive than the ready-ground premium-lean meats. Bottom round is leaner and more expensive than chuck, but the calorie savings are worth it.

What really counts most is your own eyeball inspection of the meat you choose for grinding. You may get lucky and find a bargain-priced chuck that's actually leaner than a bottom round steak. Because all packaged roasts contain some fat, look for a roast where the fat can be trimmed,—situated around the meat, not marbled all through it.

Q. *Are the fat and calorie savings really worth the bother of having hamburger ground to order?*

A. Decide for yourself: regular hamburger with 30 percent fat content has approximately 1,600 calories a pound. Regular ground chuck or lean hamburger with 20 percent fat content has about 1,200 calories. A boneless chuck roast, trimmed of fat and ground to order will contain only 7 to 8 percent fat and about 750 calories. Fat-trimmed bottom round with less than 5 percent fat can have as few as 600 calories a pound. If you eat 50 pounds of hamburger a year and save 1,000 calories on every pound, that's a 50,000-calorie savings!

Q. *I never asked a supermarket to custom-grind hamburger. Will they do it?*

A. If they don't, shop at a market that will. You can also grind fat-trimmed hamburger at home with an electric meat grinder, an attachment to your standing mixer or an old-fashioned hand grinder. The new food processors grind meat as well. You can custom-order porkburger, vealburger, and lamburger, as well as turkeyburger, or grind it yourself.

Q. *My store sells turkeyburger in frozen one-pound packages. What can I do with it?*

A. Anything you'd do with beefburger, and more: Turkeyburger has only about 750 calories per pound. You can shape it into burgers for the skillet, broiler or barbecue, make it into meatballs, use it in casseroles, soups or chili, turn it into seasoned sausage patties or shape it into meatloaf.

Q. *How much meat should I allow for a serving?*

A. According to U.S. Department of Agriculture data, one pound of lean, boneless meat (no waste) is adequate for four servings. A pound of lean fat-trimmed hamburger, flank steak, liver, chicken-breast fillets, boneless fish or roast turkey breast all provide between 80 and 100 grams of protein, or about 20 to 25 grams per quarter-pound serving. Your main-course meat, seafood or poultry should provide one-third of your daily protein needs and you only need 50 to 60 grams of protein a day.

In buying meat, fish or poultry with a lot of bones and waste to be trimmed, you will have to allow more. As a general rule, a two-pound young chicken serves four amply. Young turkey offers about three servings per pound.

Q. *I always have my meat custom cut and trimmed, but I hate to see all that fat and bones go to waste. After all, I paid for them! What can I do with them?*

A. Don't waste them. Put the bones (the fat, too) in a big stockpot, and cover them with water. Simmer for 2 to 3 hours. Strain out broth and reserve; discard the bones. Chill broth until the fat rises to the surface and hardens. Lift off and discard hardened fat. Spoon the broth into freezer containers or jars, then label and freeze. The broth is pure flavor, a valuable ingredient in soups, sauces, glazes, stews and vegetables that has many other uses as well.

	CHOOSE			AVOID		
	Steaks and Chops[1]	**Roasts**[2]	**Potroasts, Stews and Ragouts**[3]	**Steaks and Chops**[1]	**Roasts**[2]	**Potroasts, Stews and Ragouts**[3]
Beef	flank steak; top round; fat-trimmed tenderloin and sirloin steaks	fat-trimmed tenderloin; top round; eye of round; rump; sirloin	rolled flank; fat-trimmed bottom round; chuck arm or shank	rib; club; porterhouse; T-bone steaks	rib roast	shoulder; chuck blade; short ribs; brisket; short plate
Veal	round steak; loin chops or cutlets	round; rump; sirloin	shoulder; arm; shank	rib chops	shoulder; rib; breast	breast
Lamb	centerbone leg steaks; fat-trimmed loin chops	fat-trimmed leg of lamb	shank	rib chops	rib; loin; shoulder	shoulder; breast
Pork and Ham	fresh or cured ham slice (pork leg steak); center-cut pork chops or loin cutlets; all fat-trimmed	fat-trimmed fresh or smoked ham; tenderloin; center-cut loin	fat-trimmed fresh or smoked bottom or rump; arm or picnic; cured ham	rib chops; spareribs; bacon	picnic; shoulder; rib-end roasts	shoulder; blade; ribs; hocks; jowl; feet

[1] For quick-cooking, high heat (pan-fry, broil or charcoal grill)
[2] For oven roasting, dry heat or cooking on a rotisserie
[3] For slow-cooking, braising, simmering in liquids

The Best Of Beef

Chinatown Pot Roast•

Makes 12 servings

3½ lb. lean boneless chuck arm roast, trimmed of fat
1 cup dry sherry
½ cup water
¼ cup soy sauce
2 tsp. fresh or dried chopped gingerroot or 1 tsp. ground ginger
¼ tsp. garlic powder (optional)
1 tsp. monosodium glutamate (optional)
2 onions, sliced
1 red or green bell pepper, sliced
2 stalks celery, sliced diagonally

● HIGH SODIUM ALERT — Not recommended for low-sodium diets.

Brown meat on all sides under broiler. Transfer to heavy Dutch oven. Stir in sherry, water, soy sauce, ginger, garlic and monosodium glutamate. Simmer covered over very low heat 3 hours, or until meat is tender. Cool to room temperature.

Refrigerate overnight.

Remove and discard hardened fat. Simmer covered 20 minutes, or until meat is heated through. Remove meat to serving platter; keep warm. Add vegetables to liquid in pan. Simmer sauce uncovered 10 to 15 minutes or until vegetables are crisp-tender and sauce has reduced to desired thickness. Serve meat with sauce and vegetables.

Total		Per Serving
3508.0	Calories	292.3
51.2	Carbohydrate (g)	4.3
364.1	Protein (g)	30.3
163.7	Total Fat (g)	13.6
76.3	Saturated Fat (g)	6.4
1052.5	Cholesterol (mg)	87.7
1572.5	Sodium (mg)	131.0

German Meatballs

Makes 8 servings

1½ lb. lean beef round, trimmed of fat, ground
1 slice high-fiber bread, cut into small pieces ●
2 eggs, well beaten ■
¼ cup minced fresh parsley or 1 tbsp. parsley flakes
1 small onion, minced
2 tbsp. pickle relish ●
1 tbsp. lemon juice
1 tbsp. Worcestershire sauce ●
2 tsp. paprika
½ tsp. grated lemon peel
Salt ● and pepper to taste (optional)

● HIGH SODIUM ALERT—Use low-sodium bread and unsalted relish. Omit Worcestershire and added salt.
■ HIGH CHOLESTEROL ALERT — Use ½ cup liquid egg substitute.

Mix all ingredients thoroughly. Shape into 8 large or 16 small meatballs. Arrange in single layer in shallow baking dish. Bake in a preheated 350° oven 25 to 30 minutes, turning once.

Total		Per Serving
1513.6	Calories	189.2
33.1	Carbohydrate (g)	4.1
157.8	Protein (g)	19.7
80.7	Total Fat (g)	10.1
36.7	Saturated Fat (g)	4.6
946.5	Cholesterol (mg)	118.3
1171.3	Sodium (mg)	146.4

Alert Symbols: ● Sodium   ■ Cholesterol   ▲ Sugar

Greek-Style Hamburgers

Makes 4 servings

- 2 slices stale high-fiber bread ●
- 1 lb. lean beef round, trimmed of fat, ground
- 1 egg, lightly beaten ■
- 1/4 cup tomato juice ●
- 2 tbsp. chopped fresh or 2 tsp. dried mint or parsley
- 1 clove garlic, minced, or 1/8 tsp. garlic powder
- 1/8 tsp. ground nutmeg
- 1/8 tsp. ground cumin
- Dash red pepper sauce ●
- Lemon wedges (optional)

● HIGH SODIUM ALERT—Use unsalted tomato juice and low-sodium bread.

■ HIGH CHOLESTEROL ALERT — Use 2 egg whites or 1/4 cup liquid egg substitute.

Crush the bread into crumbs; mix thoroughly with remaining ingredients, except lemon. Shape into 4 patties. Broil or grill 4 inches from heat about 5 minutes on each side or until done as desired. Garnish with lemon wedges, if desired.

Total		Per Serving
1009.3	Calories	252.3
22.4	Carbohydrate (g)	5.6
105.6	Protein (g)	26.4
52.4	Total Fat (g)	13.1
23.8	Saturated Fat (g)	6.0
547.0	Cholesterol (mg)	136.8
829.5	Sodium (mg)	207.4

Steak Stroganoff

Makes 6 servings

- 1 1/2 lb. lean boneless round steak, trimmed of fat
- 1 tbsp. safflower or corn oil
- 1/2 lb. fresh mushrooms, thinly sliced
- 1 onion, thinly sliced
- Salt ● and pepper to taste (optional)
- 1 tbsp. instant-blend flour
- 1/2 cup plain low-fat yogurt
- 1/4 cup sherry

● HIGH SODIUM ALERT — Omit added salt.

Cut steak into thin slices. Spray large nonstick skillet with cooking spray. Combine meat, oil, mushrooms, onion, salt and pepper in skillet. Cook over moderate heat until meat is well browned. Mix flour with yogurt; stir into meat mixture. Cook, stirring constantly, until thickened. Add sherry; simmer 3 minutes.

Total		Per Serving
1619.4	Calories	269.9
37.2	Carbohydrate (g)	6.2
154.0	Protein (g)	25.7
84.9	Total Fat (g)	14.2
34.7	Saturated Fat (g)	5.8
452.5	Cholesterol (mg)	75.4
603.2	Sodium (mg)	100.5

Eggplant Chili

Makes 4 servings

- 1 lb. lean round steak, trimmed of fat, cut into 1-inch cubes
- Salt ● and pepper to taste (optional)
- 2 cans (6 oz. each) tomato paste
- 2 cups fat-skimmed beef broth, canned or homemade ●
- 1 medium eggplant, pared, diced
- 1 large onion, chopped
- 1 green pepper, sliced
- 2 cloves garlic, minced
- 1 1/2 tsp. chili powder, or to taste
- 1 tsp. dried oregano
- 1/2 tsp. ground cumin
- 1/4 cup shredded sharp Cheddar cheese ● ■

● HIGH SODIUM ALERT — Omit added salt. Use unsalted broth. Use low-sodium cheese, or omit.

■ HIGH CHOLESTEROL ALERT — Use low-fat cheese, or omit.

Spray large nonstick skillet with cooking spray. Brown meat in skillet over moderate heat, stirring frequently. Sprinkle with salt and pepper. Mix tomato paste with beef broth and stir into skillet. Stir in remaining ingredients except cheese. Simmer covered 30 minutes. Uncover and continue to simmer, stirring occasionally, until most of the liquid has evaporated and the mixture is very thick. Spoon into 4 serving bowls and sprinkle with cheese.

Total		Per Serving
1389.5	Calories	347.4
99.4	Carbohydrate (g)	24.9
129.2	Protein (g)	32.3
55.1	Total Fat (g)	13.8
26.8	Saturated Fat (g)	6.7
371.0	Cholesterol (mg)	92.8
2251.8	Sodium (mg)	563.0

Red Wine Round Roast

Makes 12 servings

- 3 1/2 lb. lean bottom round roast, trimmed of fat, boned and tied
- 1/2 tsp. poultry seasoning
- 1/2 tsp. pumpkin pie spice
- Pinch garlic powder
- Salt ● and pepper to taste (optional)
- 1/2 cup dry red table wine
- 1/2 cup water
- 1 bay leaf
- 2 cups fresh, frozen or drained canned small white onions ●
- 2 cups fresh or drained canned sliced mushrooms ●
- 2 tbsp. instant-blend flour
- 1/4 cup cold water

● HIGH SODIUM ALERT — Omit added salt. Use fresh, frozen or unsalted canned vegetables.

Brown meat on all sides under broiler. Transfer meat to heavy Dutch oven. Sprinkle with seasonings; add wine, 1/2 cup water and the bay leaf. Simmer covered over low heat 3 hours, or until meat is very tender. Drain pan juices into heat-resistant container; skim surface fat carefully with bulb-type baster. Return fat-skimmed broth to pot. Stir in vegetables and simmer covered until onions are tender (or just until heated through, if using canned vegetables). Remove meat to serving platter. Remove vegetables with slotted spoon and place around meat. Keep warm. Mix flour and 1/4 cup cold water; stir into simmering liquid. Cook, stirring constantly, until sauce thickens and bubbles. Serve meat and vegetables with sauce.

Total		Per Serving
3128.8	Calories	260.7
43.3	Carbohydrate (g)	3.6
337.6	Protein (g)	28.1
159.7	Total Fat (g)	13.3
76.3	Saturated Fat (g)	6.4
1032.5	Cholesterol (mg)	86.0
1151.5	Sodium (mg)	96.0

1 tsp. = 5 mL   1 tbsp. = 15 mL   1 cup = 250 mL   1 oz. = 30 g

Italian Flank Steak

Makes 6 servings

1½ lb. lean flank steak
1 cup sliced fresh or canned
    mushrooms ●
1 small onion, thinly sliced
½ cup lemon juice
2 tsp. sugar ▲ (optional)
1 tsp. dried oregano
1 tsp. grated lemon peel
1 small clove garlic, minced, or
    pinch garlic powder (optional)
    Salt ● and pepper to taste
    (optional)

● *HIGH SODIUM ALERT — Use fresh or unsalted canned mushrooms. Omit added salt.*

▲ *HIGH SUGAR ALERT — Omit sugar or use sugar substitute.*

Score steak ⅛ inch deep on both sides in diamond design with sharp knife. Place steak in baking dish or heavy-duty plastic bag. Combine remaining ingredients and pour over steak. Refrigerate covered several hours, turning steak several times. Pour off marinade, including mushrooms and onions; reserve. Broil or grill steak 3 inches from heat 4 to 6 minutes on each side, or until done as desired. Meanwhile, heat mushrooms and onion in reserved marinade in tightly covered skillet 1 to 2 minutes. To serve, slice steak very thinly against the grain; top with onion and mushrooms.

Total		Per Serving
1060.0	Calories	176.7
20.7	Carbohydrate (g)	3.5
151.0	Protein (g)	25.2
39.4	Total Fat (g)	6.6
18.6	Saturated Fat (g)	3.1
442.5	Cholesterol (mg)	73.8
534.8	Sodium (mg)	89.1

Boeufburgers

Makes 8 servings

2 lb. lean beef round, trimmed of fat,
    ground
½ cup cracked ice
2 tbsp. minced onion
2 tsp. garlic salt ● (optional)
    Pinch pepper
8-oz. can mushroom stems and
    pieces ●
¾ cup dry red wine
¼ cup cold water
2 tbsp. instant-blend flour
½ tsp. poultry seasoning

● *HIGH SODIUM ALERT — Substitute garlic powder to taste for garlic salt or omit. Use unsalted mushrooms.*

Mix meat, ice, onion, garlic salt and pepper thoroughly. Shape into 8 patties. Spray large nonstick skillet with cooking spray. Brown burgers in skillet quickly on both sides over high heat. Reduce heat; continue cooking just until burgers are rare. Remove burgers to platter. Pour off any fat. Drain mushrooms, reserving liquid. Combine mushroom liquid, wine, water, flour and seasoning. Blend well. Add to skillet. Cook over moderate heat, stirring constantly, until thick and bubbling. Add mushrooms and cook until mushrooms are heated through, about 5 minutes. Add burgers; cook until meat is heated through.

Total		Per Serving
1880.8	Calories	235.1
27.3	Carbohydrate (g)	3.4
194.9	Protein (g)	24.4
91.0	Total Fat (g)	11.4
43.6	Saturated Fat (g)	5.5
590.0	Cholesterol (mg)	73.8
1642.4	Sodium (mg)	205.3

Skewered Indian Steak

Makes 6 servings

2 lb. lean round steak, trimmed of
    fat, cut into 1½-inch cubes

Marinade
⅓ cup plain low-fat yogurt
¼ cup instant minced onion
2 tsp. ground coriander seeds
2 tsp. curry powder
2 tsp. ground turmeric
1 tsp. ground ginger

Vegetables
6 onions, quartered
3 small tomatoes, quartered
2 red or green bell peppers, cut into
    2-inch squares

Combine meat with marinade ingredients and mix well to coat. Marinate covered 1 hour at room temperature or several hours in refrigerator. Thread meat and vegetables alternately on skewers. Broil or grill 10 minutes, turning frequently.

Total		Per Serving
2033.7	Calories	339.0
92.9	Carbohydrate (g)	15.5
209.1	Protein (g)	34.9
92.3	Total Fat (g)	15.4
44.3	Saturated Fat (g)	7.4
596.7	Cholesterol (mg)	99.5
801.7	Sodium (mg)	133.6

Oriental Beef and Asparagus ●

Makes 5 servings

2 tsp. safflower or corn oil
1¼ lb. lean flank steak
1 lb. fresh asparagus
2 large onions
¼ cup dry white wine
    Monosodium glutamate (optional)
3 tbsp. soy sauce
1 tsp. cornstarch or arrowroot
½ tsp. sugar ▲ (optional)

● *HIGH SODIUM ALERT — Not recommended for low-sodium diets.*

▲ *HIGH SUGAR ALERT — Use sugar substitute or omit.*

Spray nonstick skillet with cooking spray. Heat the oil in the skillet and add meat. Brown meat quickly on both sides over high heat; remove from skillet. Slice against the grain in very thin strips; reserve. Break off the tough bottom stems of asparagus and discard. Cut asparagus spears into 1-inch lengths. Cut onions into thick slices. Combine asparagus, onions, wine and monosodium glutamate in skillet. Cook covered over moderately high heat 2 minutes. Separate the onion slices into rings. Stir soy sauce, cornstarch, and sugar together and add to skillet. Cook and stir over moderate heat until liquid has reduced to a sauce. Stir in reserved steak strips. Cook only until heated through to desired doneness. Meat should be rare, and vegetables should be crisp-tender.

Total		Per Serving
1206.2	Calories	241.2
55.2	Carbohydrate (g)	11.0
141.8	Protein (g)	28.4
42.6	Total Fat (g)	8.5
16.2	Saturated Fat (g)	3.2
368.8	Cholesterol (mg)	73.8
3764.3	Sodium (mg)	752.9

Alert Symbols: ● Sodium   ■ Cholesterol   ▲ Sugar

Savory Meatloaf

Makes 8 servings

2 lb. lean beef round, trimmed of fat, ground
6-oz. can tomato paste
2 eggs, lightly beaten ■
1/2 cup chopped onion
1/2 cup minced celery ●
2 medium carrots, grated ●
1 medium green pepper, chopped
2 tbsp. minced fresh parsley
1 tbsp. prepared horseradish
1 tbsp. prepared mustard ●
1 tbsp. Worcestershire sauce ●
1 tsp. garlic salt ● (optional)
1/4 tsp. coarsely ground pepper

●*HIGH SODIUM ALERT — Omit celery, carrots and Worcestershire. Substitute dry mustard to taste for prepared mustard. Substitute garlic powder to taste for garlic salt or omit.*

■*HIGH CHOLESTEROL ALERT — Use 4 egg whites or 1/2 cup liquid egg substitute.*

Mix all ingredients thoroughly. Shape into a loaf. Place on rack in baking pan. Bake in a preheated 350° oven 1 hour.

Total		Per Serving
2045.7	Calories	255.7
60.3	Carbohydrate (g)	7.5
211.6	Protein (g)	26.5
104.9	Total Fat (g)	13.1
47.6	Saturated Fat (g)	6.0
1094.0	Cholesterol (mg)	136.8
1362.2	Sodium (mg)	170.3

Speedy Moussaka

Makes 4 servings

1 lb. lean beef round, trimmed of fat, ground
2 cups plain tomato sauce (check label for no added oil) ●
1 small onion, minced
2 tsp. garlic salt ● (optional)
1/2 tsp. dried oregano
1/8 tsp. cinnamon
1/8 tsp. ground nutmeg
1 eggplant (about 1 1/4 lb.), pared, diced
2 oz. part-skim feta cheese, crumbled ● (optional)

●*HIGH SODIUM ALERT — Use unsalted tomato sauce. Substitute garlic powder to taste for garlic salt or omit. Use a low-sodium cheese.*

Break meat into chunks in baking pan; broil meat until browned. Pour off fat. For sauce combine tomato sauce, onion, garlic salt, oregano, cinnamon and nutmeg. Layer meat, sauce and eggplant in ovenproof casserole. Sprinkle with cheese. Bake in a preheated 350° oven 45 minutes.

Total		Per Serving
1140.1	Calories	285.0
75.2	Carbohydrate (g)	18.8
109.7	Protein (g)	27.4
47.3	Total Fat (g)	11.8
21.8	Saturated Fat (g)	5.5
295.0	Cholesterol (mg)	73.8
3698.1	Sodium (mg)	924.5

Yankee Corned Beef Boiled Dinner●

Makes 8 servings

3 lb. corned beef round (not brisket), trimmed of fat
Boiling water
8 carrots, cut into chunks
3 cups diced white turnips
4 potatoes, pared
4 onions
1 head cabbage, cut into 8 wedges

●*HIGH SODIUM ALERT — Not recommended for low-sodium diets.*

Place meat in large pot or Dutch oven; add boiling water to cover. Simmer covered 2 to 3 hours, or until tender. Stir in carrots, turnips, potatoes and onions. Simmer covered 30 to 45 minutes. Add cabbage wedges. Cook until cabbage is just crisp-tender, 12 to 15 minutes. Remove meat and slice very thin against the grain. Serve on platter surrounded by drained vegetables.

Total		Per Serving
4933.0	Calories	616.6
220.9	Csrbohydrate (g)	27.6
251.2	Protein (g)	31.4
341.5	Total Fat (g)	42.7
163.2	Saturated Fat (g)	20.4
1279.8	Cholesterol (mg)	160.0
18193.0	Sodium (mg)	2274.1

Simple Sauerbraten

Makes 12 servings

3 1/2 lb. lean round steak, trimmed of fat
1 tbsp. safflower or corn oil
1 1/2 cups tomato juice ●
5 tbsp. wine vinegar or cider vinegar
2 tbsp. mixed pickling spice
1/2 tsp. ground ginger
Salt ● and pepper to taste (optional)
2 onions, sliced
1 1/2 tbsp. cornstarch or arrowroot
1/4 cup cold water

●*HIGH SODIUM ALERT — Use unsalted tomato juice. Omit added salt.*

1 tsp. = 5 mL   1 tbsp. = 15 mL   1 cup = 250 mL   1 oz. = 30 g

Brown meat in oil in heavy nonstick skillet or Dutch oven over high heat. Pour off oil. Add tomato juice, vinegar, pickling spice, ginger, salt and pepper. Simmer covered over very low heat 3 hours, or until meat is tender. Cool to room temperature. Refrigerate overnight.

Remove and discard hardened fat. Heat to boiling. Add onions. Simmer covered over low heat 30 minutes, or until meat is heated through and onions are tender. Remove meat to serving platter; keep warm. Mix cornstarch with cold water; stir into simmering liquid. Cook and stir until sauce thickens and bubbles. Serve meat with sauce.

Total		Per Serving
3163.3	Calories	263.6
49.4	Carbohydrate (g)	4.1
335.7	Protein (g)	28.0
172.9	Total Fat (g)	14.4
77.3	Saturated Fat (g)	6.4
1032.5	Cholesterol (mg)	86.0
1902.5	Sodium (mg)	158.5

Meatballs Italiano

Makes 4 servings

Meatballs
- 1 slice dry whole-wheat, high-protein or high-fiber bread, broken into pieces ●
- 1 tbsp. water
- 1 lb. lean beef round, trimmed of fat, ground
- 1/4 cup chopped fresh parsley
- 1 small onion, minced, or 3 tbsp. onion flakes
- 1 egg, lightly beaten ■
- 2 tsp. dried oregano
- 1 small clove garlic, minced, or pinch garlic powder (optional)
- Salt ● and pepper to taste (optional)

Sauce
- 3 cups tomato juice ●
- 1 tsp. dried oregano
- 1 small clove garlic, minced, or pinch garlic powder

●*HIGH SODIUM ALERT — Use low-sodium bread. Omit added salt. Use unsalted tomato juice.*

■*HIGH CHOLESTEROL ALERT — Use 2 egg whites or 1/4 cup liquid egg substitute.*

Moisten bread with water. Mix thoroughly with remaining meatball ingredients. Shape into 4 large, 8 medium or 16 small meatballs.

Brown meatballs on all sides under broiler. Combine sauce ingredients in large saucepan. Heat to boiling. Add meatballs. Simmer uncovered until tomato juice has reduced to a thick sauce, about 1 hour. Skim any fat from the sauce before serving. (Serve on crusty Italian bread, or as a main course with a side dish of 1/2 cup tender-cooked protein-enriched spaghetti per person, if desired.)

Total		Per Serving
1128.0	Calories	282.0
51.3	Carbohydrate (g)	12.8
110.0	Protein (g)	27.5
52.0	Total Fat (g)	13.0
23.9	Saturated Fat (g)	6.0
547.7	Cholesterol (mg)	137.0
2012.3	Sodium (mg)	503.1

Flank Bracciole

Makes 6 servings

- 1 1/2 lb. lean flank steak
- 3 tbsp. grated extra-sharp Romano cheese ● ■ (optional)
- 1 clove garlic, minced or 1/8 tsp. garlic powder (optional)
- 2 tsp. dried oregano or mixed Italian seasoning
- Salt ● and pepper to taste (optional)

- 16-oz. can Italian tomatoes, chopped (undrained) ●
- 1 cup water
- 1 onion, chopped
- 1 stalk celery, minced ●

●*HIGH SODIUM ALERT — Use low-sodium cheese or omit. Omit celery and added salt. Use unsalted tomatoes.*

■*HIGH CHOLESTEROL ALERT — Use low-fat cheese or omit.*

Score steak 1/8 inch deep on 1 side in diamond design with sharp knife. Sprinkle unscored side with cheese, garlic and 1 tsp. of the oregano, and the salt and pepper. Roll up lengthwise and tie in several places. Spray heavy nonstick skillet or Dutch oven with cooking spray. Brown rolled steak on all sides. Pour off any fat. Add tomatoes, water, onion, celery and remaining 1 tsp. oregano. Simmer covered over very low heat 1 1/2 to 2 hours, or until meat is tender. Remove meat to serving platter; keep warm. Simmer tomato sauce uncovered until thickened. To serve, untie and slice meat very thin against the grain; top with sauce.

Total		Per Serving
1119.5	Calories	186.6
31.5	Carbohydrate (g)	5.3
153.5	Protein (g)	25.6
39.8	Total Fat (g)	6.6
18.6	Saturated Fat (g)	3.1
442.5	Cholesterol (mg)	73.8
1165.5	Sodium (mg)	194.3

Alert Symbols: ● Sodium   ■ Cholesterol   ▲ Sugar

Hungarian Steak Sausage

Makes 20 mini-sausages.
1 lb. lean beef round, trimmed of fat, ground
1 onion, minced
1 egg, lightly beaten ■
1 tsp. red Hungarian sweet paprika
Salt ● and pepper to taste (optional)

●*HIGH SODIUM ALERT — Omit added salt.*

■*HIGH CHOLESTEROL ALERT — Use 2 egg whites or ¹/₄ cup liquid egg substitute.*

Mix all ingredients lightly. Shape by tablespoonful into balls, then roll into mini-sausages 2 inches long. Broil or grill until done as desired.

Total		Per Serving
932.0	Calories	46.6
10.0	Carbohydrate (g)	0.5
101.9	Protein (g)	5.1
51.4	Total Fat (g)	2.6
23.8	Saturated Fat (g)	1.2
547.0	Cholesterol (mg)	27.4
401.0	Sodium (mg)	20.1

High-Protein Burgers

Makes 4 servings
1 lb. lean beef round, trimmed of fat, ground
1 cup high-protein cereal
¹/₂ cup skim milk
1 egg, lightly beaten ■
2 tsp. instant beef bouillon ● (optional)
3 tbsp. instant minced onion
Salt ● and pepper to taste (optional)

●*HIGH SODIUM ALERT — Use unsalted bouillon. Omit added salt.*

■*HIGH CHOLESTEROL ALERT — Use 2 egg whites or ¹/₄ cup liquid egg substitute.*

Mix all ingredients thoroughly. Shape into 4 patties. Broil or grill 4 inches from heat about 5 minutes on each side, or until done as desired.

Total		Per Serving
1057.1	Calories	264.3
30.3	Carbohydrate (g)	7.6
110.1	Protein (g)	27.5
51.4	Total Fat (g)	12.9
23.8	Saturated Fat (g)	6.0
549.5	Cholesterol (mg)	137.4
636.0	Sodium (mg)	159.0

Hamburger Sauerbraten

Makes 6 servings
1¹/₂ lb. lean beef round, trimmed of fat, ground
1 egg, lightly beaten ■
2 tbsp. minced onion
Salt ● and pepper to taste (optional)
Pinch thyme
1 cup cold water
1 tbsp. instant-blend flour
2 tbsp. catsup ● ▲
1 tbsp. brown sugar ▲
1 tbsp. cider vinegar
1 bay leaf
¹/₄ tsp. ground ginger
¹/₄ tsp. ground cloves

●*HIGH SODIUM ALERT — Omit added salt. Use unsalted catsup.*

■*HIGH CHOLESTEROL ALERT — Substitute 2 egg whites or ¹/₄ cup liquid egg substitute.*

▲*HIGH SUGAR ALERT — Use sugarless catsup and brown sugar substitute.*

Mix meat, egg, onion, salt, pepper and thyme thoroughly. Shape into 6 patties. Spray large nonstick skillet with cooking spray. Brown burgers in skillet quickly on both sides over high heat. Remove burgers to platter. Pour off any fat. Mix water with flour and add to skillet. Stir in remaining ingredients. Heat to boiling, stirring constantly. Reduce heat; add burgers. Simmer uncovered 20 minutes.

Total		Per Serving
1417.7	Calories	236.3
30.3	Carbohydrate (g)	5.0
148.2	Protein (g)	24.7
74.2	Total Fat (g)	12.4
34.7	Saturated Fat (g)	5.8
694.5	Cholesterol (mg)	115.8
872.8	Sodium (mg)	145.5

French Provincial Pot Roast

Makes 10 servings
3 lb. lean round steak, trimmed of fat
1¹/₄ cups fat-skimmed beef broth, canned or homemade ●
6-oz. can tomato paste
¹/₂ cup dry red wine
1 bay leaf
Salt ● and pepper to taste (optional)
¹/₄ tsp. garlic powder, or to taste (optional)
1 cup shredded carrot
¹/₂ cup finely chopped onion

●*HIGH SODIUM ALERT — Omit added salt and carrots. Use unsalted broth.*

Brown meat on all sides under broiler. Drain off any fat. Transfer meat to heavy Dutch oven. Combine broth, tomato paste, wine, bay leaf, salt, pepper and garlic powder; mix well. Pour over meat. Simmer covered over very low heat about 3 hours, or until meat is tender. Remove and discard bay leaf. Cool to room temperature. Refrigerate several hours or overnight.

Remove and discard hardened fat. Heat to boiling, add carrots and onion. Simmer covered over low heat 30 minutes, or until meat is heated through. Uncover and simmer until sauce thickens. Serve meat with sauce.

Total		Per Serving
2791.0	Calories	279.1
58.3	Carbohydrate (g)	5.8
296.2	Protein (g)	29.6
137.2	Total Fat (g)	13.7
65.4	Saturated Fat (g)	6.5
915.0	Cholesterol (mg)	91.5
2094.0	Sodium (mg)	209.4

1 tsp. = 5 mL   1 tbsp. = 15 mL   1 cup = 250 mL   1 oz. = 30 g

Lemon Seasoned Steak

Makes 6 servings

1½ lb. lean chuck steak, trimmed of fat
Juice of 1 lemon
1 clove garlic, minced, or ⅛ tsp. garlic powder
½ tsp. crumbled dried savory, or other herbs to taste (optional)
Coarsely ground pepper

Moisten steak with lemon juice; sprinkle liberally with garlic, herbs, and pepper. Puncture repeatedly with fork. Cover with plastic wrap or waxed paper; let stand 30 minutes at room temperature or several hours in refrigerator. (If refrigerated, allow to reach room temperature before broiling.) Sprinkle with pepper. Broil or grill 4 inches from heat, turning once until done as desired. Best if served rare or medium-rare.

Total		Per Serving
1323.0	Calories	220.5
6.9	Carbohydrate (g)	1.2
139.4	Protein (g)	23.2
78.9	Total Fat (g)	13.2
37.8	Saturated Fat (g)	6.3
442.5	Cholesterol (mg)	73.8
486.0	Sodium (mg)	81.0

Skillet-Barbecued Steaks

Makes 8 servings

8 minute steaks (cubed round steaks), ¼ lb. each
1 cup plain tomato sauce (check label for no added oil) ●
½ cup chopped green pepper
¼ cup unsweetened pineapple juice
2 tbsp. instant minced onion
2 tbsp. Worcestershire sauce ●
1 tbsp. prepared mustard ●
2 or 3 drops smoke seasoning ● (optional)
Salt ● and pepper to taste (optional)

●*HIGH SODIUM ALERT — Use unsalted tomato sauce. Substitute dry mustard to taste for prepared mustard. Omit Worcestershire, smoke seasoning and added salt.*

Spray large nonstick skillet with cooking spray. Brown steaks on both sides in skillet. Pour off any fat. Stir in remaining ingredients. Cook and stir uncovered until sauce is thick.

Total		Per Serving
1795.1	Calories	224.4
42.8	Carbohydrate (g)	5.3
194.5	Protein (g)	24.3
92.5	Total Fat (g)	11.6
43.6	Saturated Fat (g)	5.5
590.0	Cholesterol (mg)	73.8
2875.3	Sodium (mg)	359.4

Beef-Pork-Veal Loaf

Makes 8 servings

1 lb. lean beef round, trimmed of fat, ground
½ lb. lean pork, trimmed of fat, ground
½ lb. lean veal, ground
16-oz. can tomatoes, drained, chopped ●
1 green pepper, chopped
1 onion, chopped
2 tbsp. chopped fresh parsley
2 tbsp. dried oregano or mixed Italian seasoning
1 tbsp. lemon juice
1 tsp. fennel seeds
Garlic salt ● and pepper to taste (optional)

●*HIGH SODIUM ALERT — Use unsalted tomatoes. Substitute garlic powder to taste for garlic salt or omit.*

Mix all ingredients thoroughly. Shape into a loaf. Place on rack in baking pan. Bake in a preheated 350° oven 1 hour.

Total		Per Serving
1704.9	Calories	213.1
33.5	Carbohydrate (g)	4.2
193.3	Protein (g)	24.2
80.8	Total Fat (g)	10.1
35.3	Saturated Fat (g)	4.4
595.0	Cholesterol (mg)	74.4
1275.3	Sodium (mg)	159.4

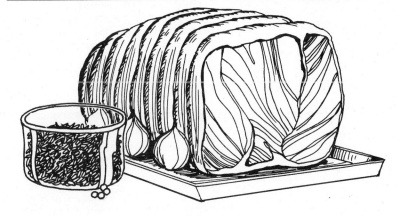

Belgian Beef Pot Roast

Makes 12 servings

1 tbsp. safflower or corn oil
3½ lb. lean bottom round roast, trimmed of fat, boned and tied
12 oz. low-calorie low-carbohydrate beer
1 tsp. honey ▲
½ tsp. thyme leaves, crumbled
2 bay leaves
¼ tsp. garlic powder
Salt ● and pepper to taste (optional)
2 medium onions, sliced

●*HIGH SODIUM ALERT — Omit added salt.*

▲*HIGH SUGAR ALERT — Use liquid sugar substitute; stir into sauce just before serving.*

Heat oil in heavy nonstick skillet or Dutch oven; brown meat on all sides over high heat. Pour off any remaining oil. Add beer, honey, thyme, bay leaves, garlic powder, salt and pepper. Simmer covered over very low heat 3 hours, or until meat is very tender. Remove and discard bay leaves. Cool to room temperature. Refrigerate several hours or overnight.

Remove and discard hardened fat. Heat to boiling; add onions. Simmer covered over low heat 20 minutes, or until meat is heated through. Uncover and simmer until onions are tender and most of the liquid has evaporated. Serve meat with sauce.

Total		Per Serving
3208.0	Calories	267.3
39.8	Carbohydrate (g)	3.3
333.6	Protein (g)	27.8
172.9	Total Fat (g)	14.4
77.3	Saturated Fat (g)	6.4
1032.5	Cholesterol (mg)	86.0
1177.5	Sodium (mg)	98.1

Alert Symbols: ● Sodium   ■ Cholesterol   ▲ Sugar

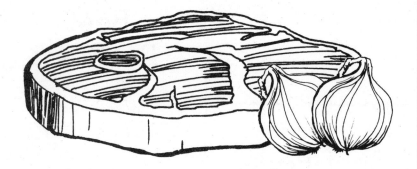

Sweet-and-Sour Stuffed Cabbage

Makes 8 servings

1 large head cabbage
Boiling water
1¹/₂ lb. lean beef round, trimmed of fat, ground
³/₄ cup uncooked rice
2 medium onions, chopped
2 eggs, lightly beaten ■
Salt ● and pepper to taste (optional)
3 cups tomato juice ●
¹/₄ cup brown sugar ▲
1¹/₂ tbsp. lemon juice

● HIGH SODIUM ALERT — Omit added salt. Use unsalted tomato juice.

■ HIGH CHOLESTEROL ALERT — Use 4 egg whites or ¹/₂ cup liquid egg substitute.

▲ HIGH SUGAR ALERT — Use brown sugar substitute; stir into sauce after cooking is completed.

Core cabbage. Cook cabbage in boiling water to cover 3 minutes. Drain cabbage and peel off individual leaves. Combine the meat, rice, onions, eggs, salt and pepper. Place a small mound of the mixture on each individual cabbage leaf; fold in the sides and roll up. Place rolls seam-side down in large skillet or Dutch oven. Combine tomato juice, brown sugar (unless using sugar substitute) and lemon juice; pour over cabbage rolls. Simmer covered 2 hours.

Total		Per Serving
2388.5	Calories	298.6
234.7	Carbohydrate (g)	29.3
176.6	Protein (g)	22.1
81.8	Total Fat (g)	10.2
36.7	Saturated Fat (g)	4.6
946.5	Cholesterol (mg)	118.3
2177.8	Sodium (mg)	272.2

Hamburger Stroganoff

Makes 8 servings

2 lb. lean beef round, trimmed of fat, ground
2 eggs, beaten ■
1 small onion, minced
¹/₂ cup crushed ice
1 tbsp. instant-blend flour
1 cup fat-skimmed beef broth, canned or homemade ●
2 tbsp. chopped fresh parsley
2 tbsp. catsup ● ▲
1 tsp. prepared mustard ●
Salt ● and pepper to taste (optional)
8-oz. can mushroom stems and pieces, drained ●
1 cup plain low-fat yogurt

● HIGH SODIUM ALERT — Use unsalted broth, catsup and mushrooms. Substitute dry mustard to taste for prepared mustard. Omit added salt.

■ HIGH CHOLESTEROL ALERT — Use 4 egg whites or ¹/₂ cup liquid egg substitute.

▲ HIGH SUGAR ALERT — Use sugarless catsup.

Mix meat, eggs, onion and ice thoroughly. Shape into 16 meatballs. Brown on all sides under broiler. Stir flour into beef broth in large saucepan. Heat to boiling, stirring constantly. Add parsley, catsup, mustard, salt and pepper. Reduce heat; add meatballs a few at a time. Simmer covered over low heat 10 minutes. Uncover; add mushrooms; heat to boiling. Stir in yogurt. Heat through, but do not boil.

Total		Per Serving
2074.1	Calories	259.3
44.0	Carbohydrate (g)	5.5
220.5	Protein (g)	27.6
107.2	Total Fat (g)	13.4
47.6	Saturated Fat (g)	6.0
1138.0	Cholesterol (mg)	142.3
2974.6	Sodium (mg)	371.9

Pineapple-Tenderized Steak

Makes 8 servings

2 lb. lean flank steak or top round steak, trimmed of fat
3 oz. undiluted defrosted frozen unsweetened pineapple juice concentrate

If using flank steak, score ¹/₈ inch deep on both sides in diamond design with sharp knife. Spread both sides with pineapple concentrate. If using round steak, place in shallow bowl and spread both sides with pineapple concentrate; puncture repeatedly with fork. Refrigerate covered several hours. Allow to reach room temperature before broiling. Broil or grill 4 inches from heat, turning once, until done as desired.

Total		Per Serving
1496.5	Calories	187.1
47.0	Carbohydrate (g)	5.9
197.5	Protein (g)	24.7
51.8	Total Fat (g)	6.5
24.8	Saturated Fat (g)	3.1
590.0	Cholesterol (mg)	73.8
689.0	Sodium (mg)	86.1

Oriental Meatballs ●

Makes 8 servings

Meatballs

2 lb. lean beef round, trimmed of fat, ground
1 cup chopped fresh or well-drained canned bean sprouts
1 small onion, chopped
2 egg whites

Sauce

2 cups tomato juice
¹/₃ cup dry sherry
3 tbsp. soy sauce
1 small onion, minced
1 small red or green bell pepper, minced
¹/₄ tsp. ground ginger

● HIGH SODIUM ALERT — Not recommended for low-sodium diets.

Mix meatball ingredients thoroughly. Shape into 8 large, 16 medium or 32 small meatballs.

1 tsp. = 5 mL   1 tbsp. = 15 mL   1 cup = 250 mL   1 oz. = 30 g

Color-Me-Slim
Photo Gallery 2

The *Lean Cuisine* approach cuts the calories—but
not the flavor—in Oriental Beef and Asparagus,
Veal Romanoff, Pineapple Pork Roast, Chicken
Cordon Bleu, Salmon Paysanne, Red Cabbage with
Apples, and lots more delicious entrees and side
dishes temptingly portrayed on the following pages.

Salmon Paysanne,
page 85

◁Mexican Stuffed
Green Peppers,
page 57

Oriental Beef▷
and Asparagus,
page 51

△ Savory Yankee
Chuck Roast,
page 59

Pacific Veal ▷
on Skewers,
page 61

◁ Veal Romanoff,
page 62

Greek Broiled▷
Lamb Chops,
page 63

◁Pineapple
Pork Roast,
page 66

Cornish Hens▷
with Cherries,
page 75

◁Chicken
Cordon Bleu,
page 76

△
Chicken
Portugaise,
page 77

◁Striped Bass with
Low-Cal Stuffing,
page 84

Chilled Shrimp▷
and Mushroom
Kebabs,
page 85

◁**Red Cabbage with Apples,** page 94

Stir-Fried▷ **Peppers and Onions,** page 99

Orange-Spiked
Zucchini and Carrots,
page 99

Brown on all sides under broiler. Combine sauce ingredients in large saucepan. Heat to boiling. Add meatballs a few at a time. Simmer uncovered until most of the liquid has evaporated and meatballs are well coated with a thick sauce.

Total		Per Serving
1997.0	Calories	250.0
55.1	Carbohydrate (g)	6.9
210.0	Protein (g)	26.3
90.9	Total Fat (g)	11.4
43.6	Saturated Fat (g)	5.5
590.0	Cholesterol (mg)	73.8
5057.3	Sodium (mg)	632.2

Mexican Stuffed Green Peppers

Makes 8 servings

- 8 large green peppers
  Boiling water
- 2 lb. lean beef round, trimmed of fat, ground
- 6-oz. can tomato paste
- 2 cloves garlic, minced
- 1 to 2 tbsp. chili powder
  Salt ● and pepper to taste (optional)
- 8 tsp. Italian-seasoned bread crumbs ●

●*HIGH SODIUM ALERT — Omit added salt. Use plain low-sodium bread crumbs.*

Cut a thin slice from the stem ends of peppers; discard ends. Remove and discard seeds and white pulp. Cook peppers in boiling water to cover 5 minutes. Drain. Spray large nonstick skillet with cooking spray. Brown meat in skillet over moderate heat. Pour off fat. Break meat into chunks. Add tomato paste, garlic, chili powder, salt and pepper. Cook over low heat 5 minutes. Spoon meat mixture into peppers. Sprinkle tops with bread crumbs. Place in shallow baking pan and add ½ inch water. Bake in a preheated 350° oven 30 minutes.

Total		Per Servings
1999.5	Calories	249.9
81.7	Carbohydrate (g)	10.2
205.7	Protein (g)	25.7
93.0	Total Fat (g)	11.6
43.6	Saturated Fat (g)	5.5
590.0	Cholesterol (mg)	73.8
1335.2	Sodium (mg)	166.9

Steak and Peppers

Makes 8 servings

- 2 lb. lean round steak, trimmed of fat
- 1 tbsp. safflower or corn oil
- 28-oz. can tomatoes, drained, chopped ●
- 2 medium onions, sliced
- ¼ cup Chianti or other dry red wine
- 1 clove garlic, minced
- ½ tsp. dried basil
  Salt ● and pepper to taste (optional)
- 2 red or green bell peppers (or 1 of each), cut into strips

●*HIGH SODIUM ALERT — Use unsalted tomatoes. Omit added salt.*

Cut meat into 8 equal pieces. Spray nonstick skillet with cooking spray. Heat the oil in the skillet and add meat. Brown quickly over high heat. Pour off fat. Stir in remaining ingredients except pepper strips. Simmer covered until meat is tender, 1 hour or more. Add pepper strips. Simmer uncovered until pepper is tender and liquid has reduced to a thick sauce.

Total		Per Serving
2082.0	Calories	260.2
64.4	Carbohydrate (g)	8.1
201.7	Protein (g)	25.2
108.3	Total Fat (g)	13.5
44.6	Saturated Fat (g)	5.6
590.0	Cholesterol (mg)	73.8
1735.0	Sodium (mg)	216.9

London Broil

Makes 8 servings

- 2 lb. lean flank steak
- 1 or 2 cloves garlic, minced, or ⅛ to ¼ tsp. garlic powder
  Meat tenderizer ● (optional)
  Monosodium glutamate ● (optional)
  Coarsely ground pepper

●*HIGH SODIUM ALERT — Omit meat tenderizer and monosodium glutamate.*

With sharp knife, score steak ⅛ inch deep on both sides in diamond design. Sprinkle both sides of steak with remaining ingredients. Roll up. Wrap with plastic wrap or waxed paper; let stand 30 minutes at room temperature or several hours in refrigerator. (If refrigerated, allow to reach room temperature before broiling.) Broil or grill 4 inches from heat, turning once, until done as desired (best if served rare or medium-rare). Or spray a large nonstick skillet with cooking spray and pan fry quickly on both sides over high heat. To serve, slice very thin against the grain.

Total		Per Serving
1310.0	Calories	163.8
0.9	Carbohydrate (g)	0.1
196.2	Protein (g)	24.5
51.8	Total Fat (g)	6.5
24.8	Saturated Fat (g)	3.1
590.0	Cholesterol (mg)	73.8
687.0	Sodium (mg)	85.9

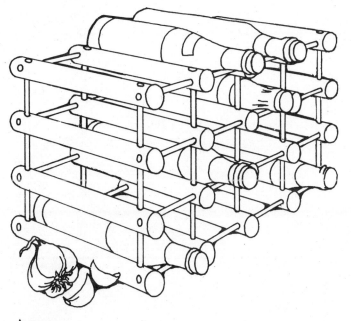

Alert Symbols: ● Sodium ■ Cholesterol ▲ Sugar

Boiled Beef with Horseradish

Makes 12 servings
3½ lb. lean boneless bottom round roast, trimmed of fat
    Salt to taste ● (optional)
    Boiling water
1 cup chopped fresh parsley
1 tsp. ground cloves
1 tsp. whole peppercorns
1 bay leaf
½ tsp. thyme
4 potatoes, pared, quartered
8 carrots, sliced ●
12 small white onions
1 cup plain low-fat yogurt
2 or 3 tbsp. prepared horseradish

●*HIGH SODIUM ALERT — Omit carrots and added salt.*

Place meat in Dutch oven; add salted boiling water to cover. Stir in parsley, cloves, peppercorns, bay leaf, and thyme. Simmer covered 2 to 3 hours, or until meat is tender. Stir in potatoes, carrots and onions; cook covered 30 minutes. Remove meat and slice very thin against the grain. Serve on platter surrounded by drained vegetables. Combine yogurt and horseradish and serve on the side.

Total		Per Serving
3697.0	Calories	308.1
182.5	Carbohydrate (g)	15.2
364.1	Protein (g)	30.3
163.7	Total Fat (g)	13.6
76.3	Saturated Fat (g)	6.4
1052.5	Cholesterol (mg)	87.7
1572.5	Sodium (mg)	131.0

Can-Do Stew for Two

Makes 2 servings
½ lb. lean boneless bottom round chuck arm or steak, trimmed of fat, cut into cubes
1 tsp. safflower or corn oil
¼ cup dry white wine or water
8-oz. can small white onions, drained, liquid reserved ●
8-oz. can sliced carrots, drained, liquid reserved ●
    Salt ● and pepper to taste (optional)
    Pinch garlic powder (optional)
2-oz. can mushroom stems, drained, liquid reserved ●

●*HIGH SODIUM ALERT — Omit carrots and added salt. Use unsalted onions and mushrooms.*

Brown meat in oil in nonstick skillet over high heat, stirring constantly. Pour off oil. Stir in wine, liquid from vegetables, salt, pepper and garlic powder. Simmer covered 1 hour, or until meat is tender. Cool to room temperature. Cover and refrigerate meat and vegetables separately overnight.

    Remove and discard hardened fat. Cover skillet and heat to boiling; stir in vegetables. Simmer uncovered over low heat, stirring frequently, until most of the liquid has evaporated.

Total		Per Serving
662.1	Calories	331.0
39.7	Carbohydrate (g)	19.9
53.1	Protein (g)	26.5
28.2	Total Fat (g)	14.1
11.2	Saturated Fat (g)	5.6
147.5	Cholesterol (mg)	73.7
1486.0	Sodium (mg)	743.0

Baked Spanish Meatballs●

Makes 8 servings
2 lb. lean beef round, trimmed of fat, ground
1 cup chopped onion
¼ cup chopped stuffed green (Spanish) olives
2 eggs, lightly beaten ■
    Salt and pepper to taste (optional)
    Lemon juice

●*HIGH SODIUM ALERT — Not recommended for low-sodium diets.*

■*HIGH CHOLESTEROL ALERT — Use 4 egg whites or ½ cup liquid egg substitute.*

Mix thoroughly all ingredients except lemon juice. Shape into 16 meatballs. Arrange in single layer in shallow baking dish. Bake in a preheated 350° oven 20 to 25 minutes, turning once. Brush meatballs frequently with lemon juice while they are baking.

Total		Per Serving
1894.0	Calories	236.8
14.8	Carbohydrate (g)	1.9
202.4	Protein (g)	25.3
109.0	Total Fat (g)	13.6
47.6	Saturated Fat (g)	6.0
1094.0	Cholesterol (mg)	136.8
1949.0	Sodium (mg)	243.6

Shoyu London Broil●

Makes 6 servings
1½ lb. lean flank steak
¼ cup soy sauce
¼ cup dry sherry or rice wine
1 or 2 cloves garlic, minced, or ⅛ to ¼ tsp. garlic powder (optional)

●*HIGH SODIUM ALERT — Not recommended for low-sodium diets.*

Score steak ⅛ inch deep on both sides in diamond design with sharp knife. Place steak in baking dish or heavy-duty plastic bag. Combine remaining ingredients and pour over steak. Refrigerate covered several hours, all day, or overnight, turning steak several times. Allow to reach room temperature before broiling. Broil or grill 4 inches from heat, turning once, until done as desired (best if served rare or

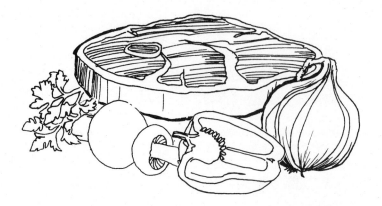

1 tsp. = 5 mL   1 tbsp. = 15 mL   1 cup = 250 mL   1 oz. = 30 g

medium-rare). Or spray a large nonstick skillet with cooking spray and pan fry quickly on both sides. To serve, slice very thin against the grain.

Total		Per Serving
1100.5	Calories	183.4
8.5	Carbohydrate (g)	1.1
151.1	Protein (g)	25.2
38.9	Total Fat (g)	6.5
18.6	Saturated Fat (g)	3.1
442.5	Cholesterol (mg)	73.8
4912.5	Sodium (mg)	818.8

Savory Yankee Chuck Roast•

Makes 12 servings

3½ lb. lean boneless chuck arm roast, trimmed of fat
3 cups water
1 tsp. dried savory
1 bay leaf
Salt and pepper to taste (optional)
1 lb. carrots, sliced
1 lb. white turnips, pared, sliced
2 cups small white onions or 16-oz. can, drained
2 stalks celery, sliced
2 tbsp. instant-blend flour
¼ cup cold water

●*HIGH SODIUM ALERT — Not recommended for low-sodium diets.*

Brown meat on all sides under broiler. Place meat in Dutch oven; add 3 cups water, the savory, bay leaf, salt and pepper. Simmer covered over very low heat 3 hours, or until meat is tender. Remove and discard bay leaf. Cool to room temperature. Refrigerate overnight.

Remove and discard hardened fat. Heat to boiling; stir in carrots, turnips, onions and celery. Simmer covered over low heat 20 to 30 minutes, or until vegetables are tender. Remove meat to serving platter; remove vegetables with slotted spoon and place around meat. Keep warm. Combine flour and ¼ cup cold water; stir into simmering liquid. Cook, stirring constantly, until sauce is thick. Serve meat and vegetables with sauce.

Total		Per Serving
3482.8	Calories	290.2
102.5	Carbohydrate (g)	8.5
336.1	Protein (g)	28.0
186.3	Total Fat (g)	15.5
88.2	Saturated Fat (g)	7.4
1032.5	Cholesterol (mg)	86.0
1618.4	Sodium (mg)	134.9

Spicy Indian Hamburgers

Makes 4 servings

1 lb. lean beef round, trimmed of fat, ground
¼ cup plain low-fat yogurt
2 tbsp. minced onion
½ tsp. ground cumin
½ tsp. ground turmeric
¼ tsp. ground ginger
⅛ tsp. garlic powder
Salt ● and pepper to taste (optional)

●*HIGH SODIUM ALERT — Omit added salt.*

Mix all ingredients thoroughly. Shape into 4 patties. Broil or grill 4 inches from heat about 5 minutes on each side, or until done as desired.

Total		Per Serving
851.3	Calories	212.8
5.1	Carbohydrate (g)	1.3
96.3	Protein (g)	24.1
46.4	Total Fat (g)	11.6
22.3	Saturated Fat (g)	5.6
300.0	Cholesterol (mg)	75.0
362.3	Sodium (mg)	90.6

Mexican Steak

Makes 4 servings

1 lb. lean top round steak, trimmed of fat
1 cup tomato juice ●
1 large onion, thinly sliced
1 clove garlic, minced (optional)
1 tsp. chili powder, or to taste
½ tsp. dried oregano
Pinch ground cumin (optional)
Salt ● and pepper to taste (optional)

●*HIGH SODIUM ALERT — Use unsalted tomato juice. Omit added salt.*

Spray large nonstick skillet or electric frypan with cooking spray. Add steak and brown quickly on both sides over high heat. Pour off any fat. Add remaining ingredients. Simmer uncovered until onions are tender and sauce is thick. Steak should be pink in the middle.

Total		Per Serving
921.0	Calories	230.3
25.9	Carbohydrate (g)	6.5
99.1	Protein (g)	24.8
45.4	Total Fat (g)	11.4
21.8	Saturated Fat (g)	5.5
295.0	Cholesterol (mg)	73.8
832.5	Sodium (mg)	208.1

Meatloaf Italian Style

Makes 8 servings

16-oz. can tomatoes ●
2 lb. lean beef round, trimmed of fat, ground
2 onions, chopped
½ to 1 clove garlic, minced, or ⅛ tsp. garlic powder
1 tsp. salt ● (optional)
2 tsp. dried oregano

●*HIGH SODIUM ALERT — Use unsalted tomatoes. Omit added salt.*

Drain tomatoes, reserving liquid. Chop tomatoes; mix thoroughly with remaining ingredients. Shape into a loaf. Place on rack in baking pan. Bake in a preheated 350° oven 1 hour, basting frequently with reserved tomato juice.

Total		Per Serving
1803.0	Calories	225.4
40.4	Carbohydrate (g)	5.1
196.5	Protein (g)	24.6
91.7	Total Fat (g)	11.5
43.6	Saturated Fat (g)	5.5
590.0	Cholesterol (mg)	73.8
1271.0	Sodium (mg)	158.9

Appleburgers Teriyaki

Makes 4 servings

1 lb. lean beef round, trimmed of fat, ground
½ cup unsweetened applesauce
½ cup water
3 tbsp. Japanese soy sauce ●
1 onion, chopped
1 clove garlic, minced or ⅛ tsp. garlic powder

●*HIGH SODIUM ALERT — Omit soy sauce.*

Spray nonstick skillet with cooking spray. Shape meat into 4 patties; brown in skillet quickly on both sides over high heat. Pour off any fat. Combine remaining ingredients; pour over burgers. Simmer uncovered, turning and stirring frequently until liquid reduces to a thick sauce. (Serve with cooked brown rice, if desired.)

Total		Per Serving
936.0	Calories	234.0
26.9	Carbohydrate (g)	6.7
99.6	Protein (g)	24.9
45.4	Total Fat (g)	11.4
21.8	Saturated Fat (g)	5.5
295.0	Cholesterol (mg)	73.8
3640.5	Sodium (mg)	910.1

Alert Symbols: ● Sodium ■ Cholesterol ▲ Sugar

Veal and Mushrooms in Wine

Makes 8 servings

2 lb. lean veal shoulder, trimmed of fat, cut into 1-inch cubes
1 tbsp. safflower or corn oil
1 onion, sliced
1 clove garlic, minced
Salt ● and pepper to taste (optional)
³/4 cup dry white wine
¹/2 lb. fresh mushrooms, sliced
2 tbsp. chopped fresh parsley

● *HIGH SODIUM ALERT—Omit added salt.*

Brown meat in oil in large nonstick skillet. Add onion, garlic, salt, pepper and wine. Simmer covered 45 minutes, or until meat is almost tender. Stir in mushrooms. Simmer covered 15 minutes. Sprinkle with parsley.

Total		Per Serving
1951.5	Calories	243.9
28.7	Carbohydrate (g)	3.6
184.1	Protein (g)	23.0
105.7	Total Fat (g)	13.2
44.8	Saturated Fat (g)	5.6
640.0	Cholesterol (mg)	80.0
615.0	Sodium (mg)	76.9

Italian Veal Sausage

Makes about 16 small links

1 lb. lean veal, trimmed of fat, ground
1 egg white
2 tbsp. Chianti
1 tbsp. finely chopped onion or 1 tsp. instant minced onion
2 tsp. dried oregano
1 tsp. fennel seeds
1 tsp. salt or to taste ● (optional)
¹/2 tsp. dried sage
¹/8 tsp. crushed dried red pepper or to taste
1 clove garlic, minced

● *HIGH SODIUM ALERT—Omit added salt.*

Combine all ingredients; mix lightly. Shape into sausage-shaped oblongs, or into small, flat patties. Fry sausage in nonstick skillet that has been sprayed with cooking spray or broil until done as desired. (Note: This is uncured sausage. Cook immediately, or wrap and freeze for later use.)

Total		Per Link
830.5	Calories	51.9
3.0	Carbohydrate (g)	0.2
92.2	Protein (g)	5.8
45.5	Total Fat (g)	2.8
21.9	Saturated Fat (g)	1.4
320.0	Cholesterol (mg)	20.0
355.5	Sodium (mg)	22.2

Veal and Spinach Meatballs●

Makes 4 servings

1 lb. lean veal, trimmed of fat, ground
10-oz. package frozen chopped spinach, defrosted, well drained
1 onion, minced
1 egg, lightly beaten ■
1 tsp. dried oregano or mixed Italian seasoning
1 tsp. garlic salt (optional)
Pinch cayenne pepper
16-oz. can plain tomato sauce (check label for no added oil)

● *HIGH SODIUM ALERT—Not recommended for low-sodium diets.*

■ *HIGH CHOLESTEROL ALERT—Use 2 egg whites or ¹/4 cup liquid egg substitute.*

Mix together all ingredients except tomato sauce. Shape into meatballs. Arrange in a single layer in a shallow baking dish; pour on the tomato sauce. Bake in a preheated 350° oven 30 minutes.

Total		Per Serving
1114.0	Calories	278.5
53.6	Carbohydrate (g)	13.4
110.9	Protein (g)	27.7
53.1	Total Fat (g)	13.3
23.9	Saturated Fat (g)	6.0
572.0	Cholesterol (mg)	143.0
3583.3	Sodium (mg)	895.8

Curried Veal Cabbage Rolls

Makes 6 servings

1 medium-size head cabbage
Cold water
2 cups ground or finely chopped roast lean veal
¹/2 cup chopped onion
¹/2 cup canned unsweetened applesauce
2 eggs, beaten ■
2 tbsp. golden raisins
1 tsp. curry powder
Salt ● and pepper to taste (optional)
1 cup fat-skimmed chicken broth, canned or homemade ●

● *HIGH SODIUM ALERT—Cook rice without salt. Omit added salt. Use unsalted broth.*

■ *HIGH CHOLESTEROL ALERT—Use 4 egg whites or ¹/2 cup liquid egg substitute.*

Remove core of cabbage; place cabbage in cold water to cover in saucepan. Heat to boiling. Boil until leaves separate easily. Drain. Remove 12 large leaves. Trim center vein of each leaf. Combine remaining ingredients except chicken broth in large bowl. Mix well; divide among leaves. Roll each leaf into a tight roll, tucking ends in to enclose filling. Arrange in a single layer in baking dish. Pour chicken broth over rolls. Bake in a preheated 350° oven 30 to 40 minutes.

Total		Per Serving
1128.3	Calories	188.1
1092.0	Carbohydrate (g)	182.0
81.3	Protein (g)	13.6
41.3	Total Fat (g)	6.9
17.7	Saturated Fat (g)	3.0
720.5	Cholesterol (mg)	120.1
1907.5	Sodium (mg)	317.9

1 tsp. = 5 mL   1 tbsp. = 15 mL   1 cup = 250 mL   1 oz. = 30 g

Sherried Veal with Peppers and Mushrooms

Makes 4 servings

- 1 lb. veal cutlets, thinly sliced
  Salt ● and pepper to taste (optional)
- 1 tbsp. safflower or corn oil
- 1/2 lb. fresh mushrooms, sliced
- 1/2 red or green bell pepper, cut into strips (optional)
- 1/4 cup sherry (optional)
- 1 tbsp. instant-blend flour
- 1 cup skim milk
- 2 tbsp. minced fresh parsley

● *HIGH SODIUM ALERT—Omit added salt.*

Cut veal into serving-size pieces. Sprinkle with salt and pepper; brown in oil in large nonstick skillet. Transfer veal to platter and keep warm. Brown mushrooms and bell pepper in skillet. Stir sherry into pan juices and cook 2 to 3 minutes. Mix flour and milk. Gradually stir into skillet; cook and stir until sauce thickens. Return veal to skillet and simmer in sauce until heated through. Sprinkle with parsley.

Total		Per Serving
1104.9	Calories	276.2
31.1	Carbohydrate (g)	7.8
104.4	Protein (g)	26.1
60.4	Total Fat (g)	15.1
22.9	Saturated Fat (g)	5.7
325.0	Cholesterol (mg)	81.3
472.7	Sodium (mg)	118.2

Oven-Fried Veal "Cutlets"

Makes 4 servings

- 1 egg, lightly beaten ■
- 1 tbsp. safflower or corn oil
- 6 tbsp. Italian-seasoned bread crumbs ●
- 1 lb. lean veal, trimmed of fat, ground
  Lemon wedges (optional)

● *HIGH SODIUM ALERT—Use low-sodium bread crumbs.*

■ *HIGH CHOLESTEROL ALERT—Use 2 egg whites or 1/4 cup liquid egg substitue.*

Stir egg and oil together in shallow dish. Sprinkle bread crumbs in another shallow dish. Shape meat into 4 oval "cutlets." Dip each cutlet in the egg-oil mixture, then press into the bread crumbs, coating lightly. Press to flatten. Spray shallow nonstick roasting pan with cooking spray. Arrange the cutlets in the pan so that they do not touch. Bake in a preheated 450° oven, turning once, 10 to 12 minutes, or until crisp and golden. Serve with lemon wedges, if desired.

Total		Per Serving
1141.6	Calories	285.4
30.0	Carbohydrate (g)	7.5
102.7	Protein (g)	25.7
66.6	Total Fat (g)	16.7
25.3	Saturated Fat (g)	6.3
572.0	Cholesterol (mg)	143.0
1516.4	Sodium (mg)	379.1

Veal Chausseur

Makes 4 servings

- 1 lb. lean stew veal, cut into 1 1/2-inch cubes
- 8 tbsp. dry white wine
- 1/2 lb. fresh mushrooms, sliced
- 8-oz. can stewed tomatoes, well broken up ●
- 1 small onion, chopped
- 1/4 tsp. dried tarragon (optional)
  Salt ● and coarsely ground pepper to taste (optional)

● *HIGH SODIUM ALERT—Use unsalted tomatoes. Omit added salt.*

Spray large nonstick skillet with cooking spray. Cook the veal and 1 tbsp. of the wine in skillet over high heat until wine has evaporated and veal begins to brown. Remove veal from skillet; reserve. Stir the mushrooms and 2 more tbsp. of the wine into the skillet. Cook uncovered, stirring frequently until wine has evaporated and mushrooms brown. Return veal to skillet; stir in remaining wine and remaining ingredients. Simmer covered, stirring occasionally, 1 1/2 to 2 hours, or until veal is tender. Uncover and continue to simmer until sauce is thick.

Total		Per Serving
1044.1	Calories	261.0
38.0	Carbohydrate (g)	9.5
97.2	Protein (g)	24.3
46.6	Total Fat (g)	11.7
21.9	Saturated Fat (g)	5.5
320.0	Cholesterol (mg)	80.0
1116.5	Sodium (mg)	279.1

Pacific Veal on Skewers

Makes 8 servings

- 1 tbsp. flour
- 1/2 tsp. dried marjoram
  Salt ● and pepper to taste (optional)
- 1 cup unsweetened pineapple juice
- 2 tbsp. soy sauce ● (optional)
- 1/4 cup chopped onion
- 1 clove garlic, minced
- 2 lb. boneless veal rump, cut into 1 1/4-inch cubes
- 3/4 cup juice-packed pineapple chunks, drained
- 2 bell peppers (1 red, 1 green), cut into squares
- 1 tbsp. safflower or corn oil

● *HIGH SODIUM ALERT—Omit added salt and soy sauce.*

Combine flour, marjoram, salt and pepper in saucepan; stir in pineapple juice, soy sauce, onion and garlic. Heat to boiling; reduce heat. Simmer 10 minutes, stirring occasionally. Cool. Pour marinade over cubed veal in large bowl. Refrigerate coverd 4 to 6 hours, or overnight. Drain veal, reserving marinade. Thread veal cubes on four 12-inch skewers alternately with pineapple and bell pepper. Broil or grill 5 to 6 inches from heat, brushing with oil and reserved marinade and turning frequently, 25 to 30 minutes, or until done as desired.

Total		Per Serving
1949.0	Calories	243.6
82.5	Carbohydrate (g)	10.3
182.4	Protein (g)	22.8
96.4	Total Fat (g)	12.1
40.4	Saturated Fat (g)	5.1
640.0	Cholesterol (mg)	80.0
634.8	Sodium (mg)	79.4

Alert Symbols:　● Sodium　　■ Cholesterol　　▲ Sugar

Easy Cheesy Chopped Veal•

Makes 4 servings

- 1 lb. lean veal, trimmed of fat, ground
- ¼ cup water
- 2 tbsp. minced fresh parsley or 2 tsp. parsley flakes
- 1½ tbsp. (½ envelope) cheese-flavored Italian salad dressing mix
- ¼ cup white wine (optional)

● *HIGH SODIUM ALERT—Not recommended for low-sodium diets.*

Lightly mix ingredients except wine. Shape into 4 oval "cutlets." Spray nonstick skillet with cooking spray. Brown the cutlets in skillet over moderate heat 4 or 5 minutes on each side. Remove to serving platter. If desired, stir ¼ cup white wine into skillet; cook over high heat, scraping pan well with spatula to loosen all crusty bits. Simmer and stir 1 minute; pour over cutlets.

Total		Per Serving
839.8	Calories	210.0
10.6	Carbohydrate (g)	2.6
89.6	Protein (g)	22.4
46.2	Total Fat (g)	11.6
21.9	Saturated Fat (g)	5.5
320.0	Cholesterol (mg)	80.0
1281.5	Sodium (mg)	320.4

Veal Romanoff

Makes 6 servings

- 1 tbsp. diet margarine ● ■
- 1½ lb. veal for scaloppine, cut into 1-inch strips
- ½ cup sliced onion
- ⅓ cup dry white wine
- ⅓ cup tomato juice ●
- 1 tsp. prepared mustard ●
- 2 tbsp. flour
- ½ cup plain low-fat yogurt
  Salt ● and pepper to taste (optional)
- 3 tbsp. grated extra-sharp Romano cheese ● ■
- 2 tbsp. minced fresh parsley
  Cooked rice or noodles ● (optional)

● *HIGH SODIUM ALERT—Use unsalted margarine and tomato juice. Substitute dry mustard to taste for prepared mustard. Omit added salt. Use low-sodium cheese, or omit. Cook rice or noodles without salt.*

■ *HIGH CHOLESTEROL ALERT—Use polyunsaturated margarine. Use low-fat cheese, or omit.*

Melt margarine in large nonstick skillet. Add veal strips and brown quickly over high heat, stirring constantly. Add onion, wine, tomato juice and mustard; simmer covered 10 minutes, or until onion is tender. Mix together flour and yogurt; stir into simmering liquid. Cook and stir until sauce is thick. Season to taste with salt and pepper. Sprinkle with cheese and garnish with parsley. Serve from the skillet (over rice or noodles, if desired).

Total		Per Serving
1524.8	Calories	254.1
31.9	Carbohydrate (g)	5.3
145.3	Protein (g)	24.2
81.7	Total Fat (g)	13.6
38.7	Saturated Fat (g)	6.4
508.9	Cholesterol (mg)	84.8
980.3	Sodium (mg)	163.4

Veal and Peppers Italian-Style

Makes 8 servings

- 2 lb. lean veal, cut into cubes
- 1 tbsp. olive oil ■
- 16-oz. can tomatoes, broken up ●
- 2 onions, sliced
- ½ cup dry white wine
- 2 tsp. dried oregano
- 1 tsp. fennel seeds (optional)
- 1 clove garlic, minced
  Salt ● and pepper to taste (optional)
- 3 green bell peppers, sliced

● *HIGH SODIUM ALERT—Use unsalted tomatoes. Omit added salt.*

■ *HIGH CHOLESTEROL ALERT—Substitute safflower or corn oil for olive oil.*

Brown veal in oil in large heavy skillet. Remove veal from skillet; blot. Pour off fat; return veal to skillet. Add remaining ingredients except green peppers to skillet. Simmer covered 1 hour or until meat is tender. Add green peppers. Simmer uncovered, stirring occasionally, until peppers are tender and sauce is reduced.

Total		Per Serving
2017.0	Calories	252.1
55.7	Carbohydrate (g)	7.0
187.0	Protein (g)	23.4
106.2	Total Fat (g)	13.3
45.8	Saturated Fat (g)	5.7
640.0	Cholesterol (mg)	80.0
1262.0	Sodium (mg)	157.8

Italian Veal Sausage and Peppers

Makes 4 servings

- 1 lb. Italian Veal Sausage (recipe in this chapter)
- 16-oz. can Italian plum tomatoes, broken up ●
- 8-oz. can Spanish-style tomato sauce (check label for no added oil) ●
- 3 red or green bell peppers, sliced
- 1 large onion, sliced
- 1 clove garlic, minced (optional)
- 2 tsp. mixed Italian seasoning
  Crushed red pepper (optional)
  Salt ● and pepper to taste (optional)

● *HIGH SODIUM ALERT—Use unsalted tomatoes and tomato sauce. Omit added salt.*

Combine all ingredients in large nonstick skillet or electric frypan. Simmer covered 10 minutes. Uncover and continue to simmer until sauce is very thick.

Total		Per Serving
1096.5	Calories	274.1
62.0	Carbohydrate (g)	15.5
105.0	Protein (g)	26.3
47.1	Total Fat (g)	11.8
21.9	Saturated Fat (g)	5.5
320.0	Cholesterol (mg)	80.0
2516.9	Sodium (mg)	629.2

1 tsp.＝5 mL   1 tbsp.＝15 mL   1 cup＝250 mL   1 oz.＝30 g

Lamb Specialties

Greek Broiled Lamb Chops

Makes 4 servings

4 lean loin lamb chops, 3/4-inch thick, trimmed of fat
2 tbsp. lemon juice
1 tbsp. dried mint leaves, crushed
1/8 tsp. cinnamon
1/8 tsp. ground nutmeg
1/8 tsp. garlic powder (optional)
Salt ● and pepper to taste (optional)
Fresh mint sprigs (optional)

● *HIGH SODIUM ALERT — Omit added salt.*

Sprinkle chops with lemon juice and seasonings; puncture repeatedly with a fork. Wrap in plastic; refrigerate several hours. Broil or grill chops, turning once, until brown and crisp outside but still pink in the middle or until done as desired. Garnish with fresh mint sprigs, if desired.

Total		Per Serving
1328.4	Calories	332.1
2.6	Carbohydrate (g)	0.7
126.2	Protein (g)	31.6
69.0	Total Fat (g)	17.3
39.0	Saturated Fat (g)	9.8
481.5	Cholesterol (mg)	120.4
465.2	Sodium (mg)	116.3

Chinese Lamb Chops ●

Makes 6 servings

6 lean loin lamb chops, 3/4-inch thick, trimmed of fat
1/3 cup soy sauce
1/4 cup dry sherry
2 tsp. dried marjoram
1 tsp. ground ginger
1 clove garlic, minced

● *HIGH SODIUM ALERT—Not recommended for low-sodium diets.*

Place chops in heavy plastic bag. Mix together remaining ingredients; pour over chops. Marinate in refrigerator 4 to 6 hours, turning occasionally. Broil chops 4 to 5 inches from heat 5 minutes; turn and broil 8 minutes, or until done as desired.

Total		Per Serving
2120.3	Calories	353.4
10.8	Carbohydrate (g)	1.8
194.5	Protein (g)	32.4
103.5	Total Fat (g)	17.3
58.5	Saturated Fat (g)	9.8
722.3	Cholesterol (mg)	120.4
6560.5	Sodium (mg)	1093.4

Crème de Menthe Lamb Chops ▲

Makes 4 servings

4 lean loin lamb chops, 3/4-inch thick, trimmed of fat
2 tbsp. white or green crème de menthe (mint liqueur)
Salt ● and coarsely ground pepper to taste (optional)
Fresh mint or parsley sprigs (optional)

● *HIGH SODIUM ALERT—Omit added salt.*

▲ *HIGH SUGAR ALERT—Not recommended for low-sugar diets.*

Sprinkle chops with crème de menthe, salt and pepper; puncture repeatedly with a fork. Wrap in plastic; refrigerate several hours. Broil or grill chops, turning once, until brown and crisp outside but still pink in the middle or until done as desired. Garnish with mint or parsley sprigs, if desired.

Total		Per Serving
1425.8	Calories	356.5
12.7	Carbohydrate (g)	3.2
126.0	Protein (g)	31.5
69.0	Total Fat (g)	17.3
39.0	Saturated Fat (g)	9.8
481.5	Cholesterol (mg)	120.8
465.0	Sodium (mg)	116.3

Polynesian Lamb Chops ●

Makes 8 servings

1 tbsp. safflower or corn oil
8 lean loin lamb chops, 3/4-inch thick, trimmed of fat
1 1/2 cups fat-skimmed chicken broth, canned or homemade
1/2 cup sliced onions
2 cups juice-packed pineapple chunks, drained, juice reserved
1 cup sliced celery
2 tbsp. cornstarch or arrowroot
3 tbsp. soy sauce
1 tbsp. vinegar
1/2 lb. fresh mushrooms, sliced

● *HIGH SODIUM ALERT—Not recommended for low-sodium diets.*

Heat oil in large nonstick skillet. Brown chops on both sides. Remove the chops; blot with paper towel. Pour off fat from skillet. Add broth, onions and the reserved juice from canned pineapple to skillet. Return chops to skillet. Simmer covered 30 minutes, or until chops are nearly tender. Stir in celery; simmer covered 10 minutes. Combine cornstarch with soy sauce and vinegar; mix well and stir into skillet. Stir in pineapple and mushrooms; simmer and stir until sauce thickens.

Total		Per Serving
3306.5	Calories	413.3
121.1	Carbohydrate (g)	15.1
324.9	Protein (g)	40.6
152.8	Total Fat (g)	19.1
79.0	Saturated Fat (g)	9.9
984.0	Cholesterol (mg)	123.0
5509.5	Sodium (mg)	688.7

Alert Symbols: ● Sodium ■ Cholesterol ▲ Sugar

63

Curried Lamb Chops and Apricots

Makes 6 servings

6 lean loin lamb chops, 3/4-inch thick, trimmed of fat
1 cup fat-skimmed chicken broth, canned or homemade ●
1/2 cup chopped onion
1/4 cup flour
1 tsp. salt ●
1 tsp. curry powder
1 tsp. ground turmeric
1/4 tsp. pepper
1 cup skim milk
16-oz. can juice-packed unpeeled apricot halves, drained

● *HIGH SODIUM ALERT — Use unsalted broth. Omit added salt.*

Spray large nonstick skillet with cooking spray; brown chops well on both sides. Remove chops from skillet. Pour off fat. Blot chops. Heat broth in same skillet. Add onion; cook and stir over low heat to get up any brown particles. Continue to cook over moderately low heat, stirring frequently. Combine flour, salt, curry powder, turmeric and pepper in small bowl; mix in milk gradually. Stir slowly into chicken broth. Cook, stirring constantly, until thickened; boil 1 minute. Place chops in a single layer in a baking dish. Add apricots; pour on sauce. Bake in a preheated 350° oven about 1 hour, or until chops are tender.

Total		Per Serving
2497.3	Calories	416.2
110.5	Carbohydrate (g)	18.4
210.4	Protein (g)	35.1
104.6	Total Fat (g)	17.4
58.5	Saturated Fat (g)	9.8
741.3	Cholesterol (mg)	123.6
3695.3	Sodium (mg)	615.9

Pineapple Lamburgers

Makes 4 servings

1 lb. lamb (from leg), trimmed of fat, ground
Salt ● and pepper to taste (optional)
1 cup undrained juice-packed crushed pineapple
Mint or parsley sprigs

● *HIGH SODIUM ALERT — Omit added salt.*

Combine meat with salt and pepper; shape meat into 4 patties. Spray nonstick skillet with cooking spray. Fry the patties over moderate heat in skillet, turning once, until cooked through. Remove patties to warm platter. Add pineapple to skillet; cook and stir over high heat until pineapple is hot and bubbling. Pour pineapple over lamburgers. Garnish with mint or parsley.

Total		Per Serving
991.4	Calories	247.9
39.0	Carbohydrate (g)	9.8
85.7	Protein (g)	21.4
45.4	Total Fat (g)	11.4
25.4	Saturated Fat (g)	6.4
320.0	Cholesterol (mg)	80.0
313.0	Sodium (mg)	78.3

Saucy Lamb Steaks

Makes 6 servings

3 leg-of-lamb steaks, trimmed of fat (about 1 3/4 lb.)
8-oz. can plain tomato sauce (check label for no added oil) ●
2 medium onions, sliced
1/4 cup dry white wine
1 tbsp. Worcestershire sauce ●
1 tsp. dried basil or oregano
Salt ● and pepper to taste (optional)

● *HIGH SODIUM ALERT—Use unsalted tomato sauce. Omit Worcestershire and added salt.*

Spray large nonstick skillet with cooking spray. Brown steaks in skillet. Pour off fat. Stir in remaining ingredients. Simmer tightly covered 45 minutes, or until steaks are done as desired.

Total		Per Serving
1677.9	Calories	279.7
42.3	Carbohydrate (g)	7.1
155.4	Protein (g)	25.9
79.9	Total Fat (g)	13.3
44.5	Saturated Fat (g)	7.4
560.0	Cholesterol (mg)	93.3
2263.3	Sodium (mg)	377.2

Souvlaki-Style Lamburger

Makes 4 servings

1 lb. lamb (from leg), trimmed of fat, ground
1 clove garlic, minced, or 1/8 tsp. garlic powder
1 tsp. dried oregano
1 tsp. dried mint leaves
1/4 tsp. ground nutmeg
1/4 tsp. cinnamon
Salt ● and pepper to taste (optional)
16-oz. can tomatoes, well broken-up ●
1 onion, chopped
1 small or 1/2 medium cucumber, pared, diced
1 1/3 cups cooked rice ● (optional)
1/4 cup plain low-fat yogurt (optional)

● *HIGH SODIUM ALERT—Omit added salt. Use unsalted tomatoes. Cook rice without salt.*

Spray large nonstick skillet with cooking spray. Spread lamb in skillet; sprinkle with garlic, oregano, mint, nutmeg, cinnamon, salt and pepper. Cook over moderate heat until underside is browned. Break up with a fork into bite-size chunks. Continue to cook and stir until chunks are well browned. Pour off fat. Add tomatoes and onion. Simmer uncovered, stirring frequently, until nearly all the liquid has evaporated. Stir in cucumber and heat through. Serve hot from the skillet (over rice, if desired). For an authentic touch, top with chilled yogurt.

Total		Per Serving
1009.4	Calories	252.4
37.4	Carbohydrate (g)	9.4
90.3	Protein (g)	22.6
46.3	Total Fat (g)	11.6
25.4	Saturated Fat (g)	6.4
320.0	Cholesterol (mg)	80.0
924.0	Sodium (mg)	231.0

1 tsp. = 5 mL   1 tbsp. = 15 mL   1 cup = 250 mL   1 oz. = 30 g

The Lean Way With Pork

Cashew Ham and Chicken with Vegetables•

Makes 8 servings

- 1 lb. ham steak, trimmed of fat, cut into 1-inch cubes
- 1 lb. chicken fillets (boneless, skinless breasts), cut into 1-inch cubes
- 1 tsp. safflower or corn oil
- 1 cup fat-skimmed chicken broth, canned or homemade
- 10-oz. package frozen Italian green beans or whole beans
- 1½ cups diagonally sliced celery
- 8-oz. can water chestnuts, drained, sliced (optional)
- 2 bell peppers (1 red, 1 green), cut into 1-inch squares
- 4-oz. can sliced mushrooms, drained
- 1 onion, sliced
- 1 tbsp. cornstarch or arrowroot
- 3 tbsp. dry-roasted cashews, broken up

● *HIGH SODIUM ALERT — Not recommended for low-sodium diets.*

Spray large nonstick skillet with cooking spray. Combine ham, chicken and oil in skillet. Cook and stir until lightly browned. Remove from skillet; blot; reserve. Pour off oil from skillet. Combine ¾ cup of the broth with the vegetables in skillet. Simmer covered 5 minutes, stirring occasionally. Mix cornstarch with remaining broth; stir into skillet. Cook and stir until mixture simmers and thickens. Stir in reserved ham and chicken; cook until heated through. Sprinkle with cashews and serve.

Total		Per Serving
1734.6	Calories	216.8
62.4	Carbohydrate (g)	7.8
225.8	Protein (g)	28.2
76.8	Total Fat (g)	9.6
25.3	Saturated Fat (g)	3.2
691.7	Cholesterol (mg)	86.5
5813.8	Sodium (mg)	726.7

Sweet-and-Sour Pork•

Makes 6 servings

- 2 cups juice-packed pineapple chunks
- 1½ lb. lean pork, trimmed of fat, cut into cubes
- 1 tbsp. safflower or corn oil
- 1 cup fat-skimmed beef broth, canned or homemade, or 1 bouillon cube dissolved in 1 cup boiling water
- ½ cup sliced onions
- 1 cup chopped celery
- 2 tsp. cornstarch or arrowroot
- 3 tbsp. soy sauce
- 1 tbsp. cider vinegar or wine vinegar

● *HIGH SODIUM ALERT — Not recommended for low-sodium diets.*

Drain pineapple; reserve juice. Brown pork on all sides in oil in nonstick skillet; pour off fat. Stir in beef broth, onions and reserved pineapple juice; simmer covered 45 minutes or until pork is nearly tender. Stir in celery; cook covered 10 minutes. Mix together cornstarch, soy sauce and vinegar; stir into skillet. Stir pineapple into skillet; cook and stir until mixture simmers and thickens.

Total		Per Serving
1869.4	Calories	311.6
99.3	Carbohydrate (g)	16.5
153.8	Protein (g)	25.6
82.1	Total Fat (g)	13.7
25.5	Saturated Fat (g)	4.3
448.0	Cholesterol (mg)	74.7
4612.8	Sodium (mg)	768.8

Applesauce Porkburgers

Makes 4 servings

- 2 slices rye bread, cut into ½-inch cubes ●
- Water
- 1 lb. lean pork, trimmed of fat, ground
- 1 cup unsweetened applesauce
- 3 tbsp. finely chopped onion or 1 tbsp. instant minced onion
- 1 egg, lightly beaten ■
- Salt ● and pepper to taste (optional)
- 2 cups tomato juice ●

● *HIGH SODIUM ALERT — Omit added salt. Use low-sodium bread and unsalted tomato juice.*

■ *HIGH CHOLESTEROL ALERT — Use 2 egg whites or ¼ cup liquid egg substitute.*

Moisten bread with water, then squeeze out. Combine bread with pork, applesauce, onion, egg, salt and pepper. Mix lightly. Shape into 4 large, 8 medium or 16 small meatballs. Brown meatballs on all sides under broiler. Heat tomato juice in large saucepan. Add meatballs; simmer uncovered until sauce is thick. Skim any fat from sauce.

Total		Per Serving
1284.2	Calories	321.1
74.9	Carbohydrate (g)	18.7
110.8	Protein (g)	27.7
52.0	Total Fat (g)	13.0
18.3	Saturated Fat (g)	4.6
532.6	Cholesterol (mg)	133.2
1573.0	Sodium (mg)	393.3

Alert Symbols: ● Sodium   ■ Cholesterol   ▲ Sugar

Baked Pork Chops Oregano

Makes 6 servings

6 lean center-cut pork chops (about 2¼ lb.), trimmed of fat
Salt ● and pepper to taste (optional)
1 tbsp. water
1 lb. fresh mushrooms, sliced
2 cups chopped canned tomatoes ●
2 green peppers, chopped
2 onions, sliced
2 tsp. dried oregano
1 clove garlic, minced, or ⅛ tsp. garlic powder (optional)

● *HIGH SODIUM ALERT — Omit added salt. Use unsalted tomatoes.*

Spray large nonstick skillet with cooking spray. Sprinkle chops with salt and pepper. Combine chops and the water in skillet. Simmer uncovered until water has evaporated and chops begin to brown. Brown quickly on both sides; blot. Arrange chops in single layer in shallow baking pan. Combine remaining ingredients and arrange over chops. Cover pan with foil. Bake 1 hour in a preheated 325° oven. Remove foil and continue to bake 20 to 30 minutes, or until chops are very tender.

Total		Per Serving
1879.0	Calories	313.2
67.0	Carbohydrate (g)	11.2
186.6	Protein (g)	31.1
82.9	Total Fat (g)	13.8
28.5	Saturated Fat (g)	4.8
490.0	Cholesterol (mg)	81.7
1175.3	Sodium (mg)	195.9

Oriental Pork Loin Roast

Makes 16 servings

5 lb. lean boneless pork loin roast, trimmed of fat
6-oz. can frozen unsweetened orange juice concentrate, defrosted, undiluted
¼ cup soy sauce ● (optional)
½ tsp. ground ginger
¼ tsp. garlic powder (optional)

● *HIGH SODIUM ALERT — Omit soy sauce.*

Place pork on rack in open roasting pan. Insert meat thermometer in

thickest part. Roast uncovered in a preheated 325° oven until thermometer registers 170°, 2½ to 3 hours (allow 30 minutes per pound). To make glaze, combine remaining ingredients and mix well. Baste roast with glaze during the last 20 minutes of roasting.

Total		Per Serving
4760.0	Calories	297.5
87.0	Carbohydrate (g)	5.4
478.0	Protein (g)	29.9
227.0	Total Fat (g)	14.2
81.5	Saturated Fat (g)	5.1
1400.0	Cholesterol (mg)	87.5
1259.0	Sodium (mg)	78.7

Pineapple Pork Roast

Makes 16 servings

5 lb. fat-trimmed, rolled pork roast
2 cups canned unsweetened pineapple juice
8-oz. can crushed juice-packed pineapple, undrained
½ cup chopped onion
½ cup sliced celery
¼ cup golden raisins
¼ cup cider vinegar
¼ cup soy sauce ● (optional)
½ tsp. ground ginger
¼ cup cornstarch
Cold water

● *HIGH SODIUM ALERT — Omit soy sauce.*

Place pork in roasting pan. Mix together remaining ingredients except cornstarch and cold water. Spoon pineapple mixture over pork. Bake covered in a preheated 325°

oven about 3 hours, or until tender, basting frequently with pineapple mixture. Remove meat to heated platter; keep warm. Mix cornstarch with a little cold water to make a thin paste. Stir into pan juices. Cook over moderate heat, stirring constantly until gravy thickens. Pour over roast.

Total		Per Serving
5101.8	Calories	318.9
180.9	Carbohydrate (g)	11.3
478.3	Protein (g)	29.9
227.1	Total Fat (g)	14.2
81.5	Saturated Fat (g)	5.1
1400.0	Cholesterol (mg)	87.5
1360.1	Sodium (mg)	85.0

Pork Chops with Cabbage

Makes 8 servings

8 lean pork chops (about 3 lb.), trimmed of fat, or 2 fresh ham steaks (about 2½ lb.), cut into 8 pieces, trimmed of fat
½ cup apple cider
3 tbsp. flour
⅓ cup cider vinegar
1 small head cabbage, shredded
1 cup chopped onion
2 tbsp. raisins
1 tsp. caraway seeds
1 clove garlic, minced, or ⅛ tsp. garlic powder (optional)
Salt ● and pepper to taste (optional)

● *HIGH SODIUM ALERT — Omit added salt.*

Spray large nonstick skillet with cooking spray. Combine meat and 2 tbsp. of the apple cider in skillet. Cook until liquid has evaporated and meat begins to brown. Brown meat on both sides; pour off fat. Add remaining cider. Simmer covered 1 hour. Remove meat from skillet; skim any fat from pan juices. Mix flour with vinegar; stir into skillet. Cook until simmering. Stir in remaining ingredients; place meat on top. Simmer tightly covered 25 to 30 minutes. Uncover and continue to cook, stirring occasionally, until most of the liquid has evaporated.

Total		Per Serving
2319.0	Calories	289.9
81.3	Carbohydrate (g)	10.2
221.8	Protein (g)	27.7
103.2	Total Fat (g)	12.9
36.7	Saturated Fat (g)	4.6
630.0	Cholesterol (mg)	78.8
649.4	Sodium (mg)	81.2

1 tsp. = 5 mL   1 tbsp. = 15 mL   1 cup = 250 mL   1 oz. = 30 g

Speedy Pork Skillet

Makes 4 servings

- 2 cups 1-inch cubes of lean roasted pork
- 2 onions, cut into chunks
- ¼ cup soy sauce ●
- ¼ cup unsweetened pineapple juice or apple juice
- 10-oz. package frozen asparagus spears, defrosted, sliced
- 2-oz. can sliced mushrooms, undrained ●
- 1 tsp. cornstarch or arrowroot
- ¼ cup dry white wine or water
- 8 cherry tomatoes, cut into halves

● *HIGH SODIUM ALERT — Substitute unsweetened pineapple or apple juice for soy sauce. Use unsalted mushrooms.*

Spray large nonstick skillet with cooking spray. Combine pork, onions, and soy sauce in skillet. Cook covered over high heat 1 minute. Stir in juice, asparagus and mushrooms (including liquid). Cook covered 6 to 8 minutes. Mix cornstarch with wine; stir into skillet. Cook, stirring constantly, until liquid thickens and meat and vegetables are glazed with sauce. (Don't overcook.) Stir in tomatoes; serve immediately.

Total		Per Serving
1028.4	Calories	257.1
57.9	Carbohydrate (g)	14.5
100.8	Protein (g)	25.2
40.6	Total Fat (g)	10.1
12.0	Saturated Fat (g)	3.0
240.0	Cholesterol (mg)	60.0
4852.5	Sodium (mg)	1213.1

Szechuan Ham Steaks●

Makes 6 servings

- 2 fresh ham slices (about ¾ lb. each), trimmed of fat
- ¾ cup Bloody Mary-seasoned tomato juice
- ½ cup dry white wine
- 6 tbsp. soy sauce
- ¼ tsp. garlic powder
- 2 tsp. cornstarch or arrowroot

● *HIGH SODIUM ALERT — Not recommended for low-sodium diets.*

Place ham in baking dish or heavy plastic cooking bag. For marinade, combine tomato juice, wine, soy sauce and garlic powder; pour over ham. Refrigerate covered all day or overnight. Drain well; reserve marinade. Broil or grill the ham, turning once, until cooked through. Meanwhile, combine reserved marinade with cornstarch in saucepan. Cook and stir until sauce is thick and hot. To serve, pour sauce over steaks.

Total		Per Serving
1533.1	Calories	255.5
22.9	Carbohydrate (g)	3.8
149.4	Protein (g)	24.9
68.1	Total Fat (g)	11.4
24.5	Saturated Fat (g)	4.1
420.0	Cholesterol (mg)	70.0
7339.0	Sodium (mg)	1223.2

Spanish Garlic Sausage

Makes 8 servings

- 2 lb. lean pork, trimmed of fat, ground
- 2 tbsp. wine vinegar
- 1 tbsp. dried oregano
- 1 tsp. pepper
- 1 tsp. cumin seeds
- 4 cloves garlic, minced
- Pinch cayenne pepper

Combine all ingredients and mix lightly. Shape into 16 flat patties. Broil, turning once, or fry over moderate heat in nonstick skillet sprayed with cooking spray, turning once, until well done with no trace of pinkness remaining.

Note: Recipe can be doubled or tripled. Label uncooked patties and store in freezer, well wrapped in foil. Remove as needed. Frozen patties may be grilled or broiled without defrosting, but be sure pork is cooked through, until no pinkness remains.

Total		Per Serving
1778.0	Calories	222.3
4.7	Carbohydrate (g)	0.6
190.0	Protein (g)	23.8
90.8	Total Fat (g)	11.4
32.6	Saturated Fat (g)	4.1
560.0	Cholesterol (mg)	70.0
506.0	Sodium (mg)	63.3

Pork and Veal Loaf

Makes 6 servings

- ¾ lb. lean veal, trimmed of fat, ground
- ¾ lb. lean pork, trimmed of fat, ground
- 1 onion, chopped
- 1 red bell pepper, chopped
- 1 green pepper, chopped
- 1 egg, beaten ■
- 2 tbsp. lemon juice
- 2 tsp. paprika
- 1 clove garlic, minced
- Salt ● and pepper to taste (optional)

● *HIGH SODIUM ALERT — Omit added salt.*

■ *HIGH CHOLESTEROL ALERT — Use 2 egg whites or ¼ cup liquid egg substitute.*

Mix together all ingredients. Shape into a loaf and place on rack in shallow roasting pan. Bake in a preheated 350° oven 50 to 60 minutes. Serve hot or cold.

Total		Per Serving
1417.6	Calories	236.3
22.2	Carbohydrate (g)	3.7
147.2	Protein (g)	24.5
74.2	Total Fat (g)	12.4
30.6	Saturated Fat (g)	5.1
705.0	Cholesterol (mg)	117.5
502.1	Sodium (mg)	83.7

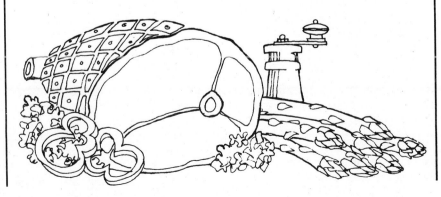

Alert Symbols: ● Sodium   ■ Cholesterol   ▲ Sugar

The Perfection
Of Poultry

Q. *Which should I choose—fryers, roasters, broilers, stewing hens, capons, breasts, legs, necks or thighs?*

A. Compared with most meats, all chicken is relatively low in fat and calories, but your best bet of all is young frying chickens. Don't let the word fryer mislead you. Frying is the one thing you don't want to do with it! You can use a frying chicken in place of any other chicken. The word fryer simply refers to age. Frying chickens are the only ones that are young and tender enough to quick-cook in high heat. That means they're also ideal for broiling or cooking on the grill. If you use fryers in place of the fatter, tougher, older chickens, be sure to cut the normal cooking time.

Q. *Which is the best part, calorically speaking?*

A. The breast is the chicken part that offers the most lean meat and protein, the least calories, fat and waste. But chicken is still so low in calories and fat that you can enjoy the other parts as well. Listed in order of fat content—from least fat to most fat—poultry parts rank as follows: (1) breast, (2) drumstick, (3) thigh, (4) wing, (5) neck and (6) back.

Q. *What are chicken fillets? How can I do it myself?*

A. Chicken fillets are boneless, skinless fillets of white meat cut from chicken breasts. They're premium priced (for chicken) but a bargain in terms of calories, cholesterol, fat and protein. You can save money by buying whole breasts and filleting them yourself with a small, sharp, pointed knife—a boning knife works best. Simply strip off the skin, then slice the meat away from the bones in a single piece. (You may use the skin and bones to make chicken broth. Simmer them in water, then fat-skim and refrigerate or freeze the broth for later use.)

Q. *What's my best buy in turkey?*

A. Younger turkeys have proportionally less fat and fewer calories per pound of meat than older birds. Contrary to popular opinion, young birds have the same proportion of meat-to-bone as older birds. In other words, you're *not* getting more meat and less bone with older birds; what you *are* getting is more fat! Unfortunately, younger birds cost more per pound than older ones.

Q. *Is there any difference between hens and toms?*

A. Well, yes, but the difference only matters to turkeys. In terms of tenderness, leanness and waste, there's no real difference.

LEAN CUISINE POULTRY GUIDE*

	Calories	Fat (g)	Protein (g)
Chicken			
Fryer/Broiler	382	15.1	57.4
Roaster	791	59.3	60.3
Capon	937	70.2	70.9
Turkey			
Young (24 weeks and under)	480	19.9	70.9
Medium (26-32 weeks)	752	52.3	65.9
Mature (over 32 weeks)	1136	97.0	60.9
Duck (domestic)	1213	106.4	59.5
Goose (domestic)	1172	104.3	54.3

Source: U.S. Department of Agriculture, Agricultural Research Service, *Composition of Foods* (Agriculture Handbook No. 8), 1963, 1975.

Figures reflect the average content of the edible portion of 1 pound of a ready-to-cook whole bird.

Q. *What about so-called self-basting turkeys?*

A. Here's where you can save cash as well as calories and cholesterol. Don't, repeat *do not,* waste money and calories on self-basting turkeys which have been artificially pumped full of oil and additives. Despite the implications of butter on self-basters' labels, the fat generally is not butter. In addition to adding fat and calories, the basting oil and additives add an artificial taste. Those who have been cautioned to watch salt intake should also be wary of basted birds since the baste usually contains high-sodium ingredients.

Q. *Are there any self-basting birds without added fat?*

A. Yes, in some areas, birds are available with an added broth baste. These are acceptable for fat-fighters but not a wise choice for low-sodium dieters. They also cost more than plain birds.

Q. *Are fresh-killed birds better than frozen?*

A. They cost more, and many cooks claim that they are juicier and moister than a bird that has been frozen and defrosted. Since juiciness is an important factor to fat-fighting cooks, the price difference may be worth it. One way to minimize moisture loss in frozen poultry is to follow proper defrosting techniques.

Q. *Turkey seems so calorie-wise, but so big for our small family. Can you give me any practical ways to enjoy it more often?*

A. Try the following tips: Turkeys come as small as six pounds. Roast a small turkey for a weekend family dinner. Cut the remaining meat off the bones and divide into one-pound or meal-size packages. Simmer the bones in water to make a fat-skimmed broth. Store both in your freezer and defrost for interesting, quick-and-easy meals.

Buy a larger frozen turkey on sale and ask the supermarket to cut it in quarters. Yes they can! They simply power-saw right through it. At home, rewrap each frozen quarter and store in the freezer. Thaw and roast a quarter at a time. Freeze the cooked leftovers as suggested above.

Buy a whole or half turkey breast. This is the leanest, least fattening part.

Buy other turkey parts. A turkey thigh has enough meat to make four servings. You can trim the meat from the bone, dice it in cubes, and use it any way you might use beef stew meat.

Q. *What about rock cornish hens? Are they fattening?*

A. Cornish hens are elegant little birds with the same general low calorie count as young frying chickens. They're ideal for small families and for rotisserie cooking, and great for company meals, too.

Q. *How about ducks and geese?*

A. Domesticated waterfowl grow their own wetsuit of blubber to keep them warm and are not a good buy for fat-fighters. Wild gamebirds have a lower fat and calorie count (as does all game). Dressed wild duck is 613 calories per pound; domestic duck is 961 and a pound offers only two servings. The calorie count for geese is similar. It's best to puncture or slit the skin in several places and roast in a very hot oven (about 425°), to render as much fat as possible. Naturally, eat only the meat, not the skin or fat. (A roast thigh of turkey basted with orange juice or served with cherry sauce makes a tasty calorie-wise stand-in for duck.)

Roast Turkey—Easy as 1-2-3

Be sure to buy a plain turkey and *not* a self-basting bird, which has added fat. It's less expensive and less fattening.

1. How to Thaw a Turkey. Leave wrapped in original plastic bag and thaw in the refrigerator on a tray for three or four days, or at room temperature, allowing one hour per pound. You may also cover frozen plastic-wrapped turkey with cold water, allowing 30 minutes per pound to defrost. (Change water frequently.) Refrigerate or cook turkey as soon as it is thawed.

2. How to Prepare a Turkey. Remove turkey from its plastic bag; remove neck and giblets from cavities; rinse turkey and wipe dry inside and out. (Cook neck and giblets in water to cover for broth to flavor dressing or for giblet gravy.) If dressing is used, stuff it loosely into neck cavity, then skewer neck skin to back. Stuff body cavity loosely. Fasten down legs either by tying or tucking under skin band. Twist wings so that wing tips are under turkey, and the weight of the bird holds them in that position.

3. How to Roast a Turkey. Place turkey, breast up, on rack in shallow roasting pan. Brush with wine or lemon juice, if desired. If a roast-meat thermometer is used, insert into thick part of thigh. Bulb should not touch bone. Roast at 325°. Consult the Time Chart for Roasting Turkey for cooking times. A tent of foil placed loosely over turkey keeps it from browning too fast, and it may be removed when necessary to baste turkey. Remove foil for last half hour of final browning. Turkey is done when roast-meat thermometer registers 180° to 185°. Other tests for doneness are: thick part of drumstick feels soft when pressed with thumb and forefinger, or drumstick and thigh move easily.

Do's and Don'ts for a Better Stuffed Bird

Use bread that is stale, dry or toasted. Include the crust. (Use additional liquid if too dry.)

Stuffings can be prepared ahead except for adding liquid, but *do* keep in refrigerator until ready to use. Just before roasting, add liquid and stuff the bird. *Do not* stuff turkey the night before.

Allow about ½ to ¾ cup of stuffing for each pound of ready-to-cook poultry.

Fill the bird loosely; stuffing swells during roasting and will be soggy if packed too tightly.

Pack extra stuffing in a covered casserole. Bake about 1 hour in same oven as the bird.

Remove any leftover stuffing from the bird and refrigerate separately in a covered container. Use both meat and stuffing within 5 days, unless you plan to freeze it.

Barbecued Turkey

For rotisserie roasting, an 8- to 12-pound bird is a good size; it will cook in 3 to 4 hours.

If you buy a frozen turkey, thaw according to directions given above.

TIME CHART FOR ROASTING TURKEY*

Ready-to-Cook Weight	Approximate Cooking Time
6 to 8 pounds	3 to 3½ hours
8 to 12 pounds	3½ to 4½ hours
12 to 16 pounds	4½ to 5½ hours
16 to 20 pounds	5½ to 6½ hours
20 to 24 pounds	6½ to 7 hours

*Roast in a preheated 350° oven until roast-meat thermometer registers a temperature of 180° to 185°.

Once the turkey is thawed, remove the plastic bag, take out the packet of giblets from its interior, then wipe dry inside and out with paper toweling.

Rinse inside with a tablespoon of wine or lemon juice, and sprinkle generously with seasoned salt (if not on a sodium-restricted diet), poultry seasoning or herbs and pepper. Do not stuff a turkey for rotisserie roasting, but do put in a few sprigs of fresh parsley. Try to time it so that you are ready to cook the bird as soon as it is thawed. If this isn't possible, refrigerate the thawed turkey until cooking time.

Skewer flap of neck skin to back. Skewer wings flat to sides, or tie them in place with white cord around the body. Tie legs together. Adjust rotisserie rod and forks, and do a test run to see that weight is balanced properly. Brush bird with wine or lemon juice and turn on the current. If you are using a charcoal grill, wait until the charcoal has burned down to gray-red coals.

During the final half hour, brush the turkey with a little soy sauce or Worcestershire sauce, or with your favorite barbecue sauce thinned a bit with wine, water or giblet broth. (If you are on a low-sugar diet, use sugarless barbecue sauce. If you are on a sodium-restricted diet, use low-sodium barbecue sauce thinned with wine, water or unsalted broth; do not use soy sauce or Worcestershire sauce.)

How to Roast Turkey Breast

Thaw turkey in its plastic wrap (in the refrigerator several hours, or in a pan of cold water 3 to 4 hours). Wipe with damp paper toweling and sprinkle with salt or herbs. (Do not use salt if on a low-sodium diet.) Place skin-side up in an open baking pan. Brush lightly with lemon juice or white wine. Place a loose tent of foil over turkey, and roast at 325° about 1½ hours. From then on baste with pan drippings every half hour or so, until meat is nicely browned and thoroughly tender. Total oven time for either whole or half breast probably will be 3 to 3½ hours, or until roast-meat thermometer registers 180° to 185°. When done, pour off pan drippings. Skim fat from drippings and use to make gravy.

Oriental Chicken with Pineapple and Peppers

Makes 8 servings

2 frying chickens (about 1½ lb. each), cut up, trimmed of fat
1-lb. can juice-packed pineapple chunks, drained, juice reserved
3 tbsp. wine vinegar
2 tbsp. soy sauce ● (optional)
1 tsp. prepared mustard ●
1 red bell pepper, cut into strips
1 green pepper, cut into strips
2 tsp. cornstarch or arrowroot
¼ cup water

● *HIGH SODIUM ALERT—Omit soy sauce. Substitute dry mustard to taste for prepared mustard.*

Broil chicken pieces skin-side up 10 to 15 minutes, or until skin is crisp. Pour off fat. Blot chicken. Place chicken skin-side up in shallow baking dish; surround with pineapple chunks. Mix reserved juice with vinegar, soy sauce and mustard; pour over chicken. Bake uncovered in a preheated 325° oven, basting occasionally, 40 minutes. Add pepper strips. Stir cornstarch into water; blend well. Stir into liquid in baking dish. Bake 15 minutes, or until thick and bubbling.

Total		Per Serving
1642.8	Calories	205.4
86.7	Carbohydrate (g)	10.8
199.9	Protein (g)	25.0
54.1	Total Fat (g)	6.8
20.6	Saturated Fat (g)	2.6
834.3	Cholesterol (mg)	104.3
675.1	Sodium (mg)	84.4

Chicken Cacciatore

Makes 6 servings

3 whole chicken breasts (about 2 lb.), split, trimmed of fat
16-oz. can tomatoes, undrained, broken up ●
1 green pepper, sliced
½ cup dry white wine
1 to 2 tsp. dried oregano
   Salt ● and pepper to taste (optional)
2 tbsp. grated extra-sharp Romano cheese ● ■

● *HIGH SODIUM ALERT—Use unsalted tomatoes. Use low-sodium cheese, or omit. Omit added salt.*

■ *HIGH CHOLESTEROL ALERT—Use low-fat cheese, or omit.*

Broil chicken skin-side up 10 to 15 minutes, or until skin is crisp. Pour off fat. Blot chicken. Mix together remaining ingredients, except cheese, in skillet or baking dish. Add chicken. Simmer covered over moderate heat or bake covered in a preheated 325° oven 45 to 50 minutes, or until chicken is tender. Uncover; cook until pan juices are reduced to sauce consistency. Sprinkle with cheese before serving.

Total		Per Serving
1098.3	Calories	183.1
28.2	Carbohydrate (g)	4.7
169.4	Protein (g)	28.2
24.3	Total Fat (g)	4.1
12.5	Saturated Fat (g)	2.1
522.7	Cholesterol (mg)	87.1
1131.3	Sodium (mg)	188.6

1 tsp. = 5 mL   1 tbsp. = 15 mL   1 cup = 250 mL   1 oz. = 30 g

No-Fat-Added "Southern Fried" Chicken

Makes 8 servings

2 frying chickens (about 2 lb. each),
  cut up, trimmed of fat
  Water
½ cup plain bread crumbs ●
½ tsp. paprika
¼ tsp. salt ●
¼ tsp. monosodium glutamate ●
  (optional)
¼ tsp. celery salt ●
¼ tsp. celery seed ●
  Pinch pepper

● *HIGH SODIUM ALERT—Use low-sodium bread crumbs. Substitute marjoram, thyme and poultry seasoning for salt, monosodium glutamate and celery seasonings.*

Brush chicken pieces with water to moisten. Combine remaining ingredients in heavy paper bag. Place chicken pieces, a few at a time, in paper bag; shake to coat chicken. Arrange, skin-side up in nonstick pan or baking sheet. Bake uncovered in a preheated 375° oven about 50 minutes, or until crisp.

Total		Per Serving
1921.2	Calories	240.2
36.5	Carbohydrate (g)	4.6
266.8	Protein (g)	33.4
71.0	Total Fat (g)	8.9
27.9	Saturated Fat (g)	3.5
1112.2	Cholesterol (mg)	139.0
2201.8	Sodium (mg)	275.2

Coq au Vin Rouge

Makes 4 servings

1 frying chicken (about 2 lb.), cut up,
  trimmed of fat
1 cup fresh, frozen or drained canned
  small onions ●
¾ cup dry red wine
¼ cup tomato juice ●
1 small bay leaf
⅛ tsp. thyme
⅛ tsp. sage
  Salt ● and pepper to taste
  (optional)

● *HIGH SODIUM ALERT—Use fresh, frozen or unsalted canned onions. Use unsalted tomato juice. Omit added salt.*

Broil chicken pieces skin-side up 10 to 15 minutes, or until skin is crisp. Pour off fat. Blot chicken; combine with remaining ingredients in heavy Dutch oven. Simmer covered over moderate heat or bake in a preheated 350° oven 45 to 50 minutes, or until chicken is tender. Uncover and continue to cook until liquid is reduced to a thick sauce.

Total		Per Serving
1069.2	Calories	267.3
19.7	Carbohydrate (g)	4.9
132.5	Protein (g)	33.1
34.3	Total Fat (g)	8.6
13.7	Saturated Fat (g)	3.4
555.4	Cholesterol (mg)	138.9
537.2	Sodium (mg)	134.3

Turkey-Cheese Roll

Makes 4 servings

1¼ lb. package frozen turkey thigh,
  defrosted, boned
  Garlic salt ● and pepper to taste
  (optional)
3 tbsp. minced onion
2 oz. (4 thin slices) sharp Cheddar
  cheese ● ■
3 tbsp. chopped fresh parsley
1 cup tomato juice ●
2 tsp. Worcestershire sauce ●
  Dash red pepper sauce (optional)

● *HIGH SODIUM ALERT—Substitute garlic powder to taste for garlic salt. Use low-sodium cheese and unsalted tomato juice. Omit Worcestershire.*

■ *HIGH CHOLESTEROL ALERT—Use low-fat cheese.*

Lay the turkey meat flat, skin-side down. Sprinkle with garlic salt, pepper and onion. Arrange cheese slices over meat; sprinkle with parsley. Roll up tightly. Place roll in baking dish just large enough to hold it (so that it will not unroll). Mix together the tomato juice, Worcestershire and pepper sauce; pour over turkey roll. Bake covered in a preheated 350° oven, basting occasionally, 2½ to 3 hours, or until tender. Uncover during the last hour of baking. Slice to serve.

Total		Per Serving
917.8	Calories	229.5
17.9	Carbohydrate (g)	4.5
108.8	Protein (g)	27.2
43.4	Total Fat (g)	10.9
17.4	Saturated Fat (g)	4.4
365.1	Cholesterol (mg)	91.3
1302.7	Sodium (mg)	325.7

Thousand Island Chicken Thighs

Makes 6 servings

2 lb. chicken thighs, trimmed of fat
⅓ cup low-calorie low-fat Thousand
  Island salad dressing ●
¼ cup unsweetened pineapple juice
¼ cup dry white wine

● *HIGH SODIUM ALERT—Use unsalted salad dressing.*

Place chicken in plastic bag or large bowl. Mix together remaining ingredients; pour over chicken. Marinate 30 minutes at room temperature or several hours in refrigerator, turning frequently. Place chicken skin-side up in shallow baking dish; pour marinade over chicken. Bake uncovered in a preheated 350° oven, basting occasionally, 35 to 45 minutes, or until tender.

Total		Per Serving
1113.7	Calories	185.6
21.6	Carbohydrate (g)	3.6
123.4	Protein (g)	20.6
48.9	Total Fat (g)	8.2
14.6	Saturated Fat (g)	2.4
572.0	Cholesterol (mg)	95.3
1188.5	Sodium (mg)	198.1

Alert Symbols: ● Sodium   ■ Cholesterol   ▲ Sugar

Spanish Chicken in Orange-Wine Sauce

Makes 6 servings

3 whole chicken breasts (about 2 lb.), split, trimmed of fat
1 onion, sliced
1 green pepper, chopped
1 cup sliced fresh or drained canned mushrooms ●
Paprika
1 cup unsweetened orange juice
1/4 cup dry red wine
1 tsp. grated orange rind
Salt ● and pepper to taste (optional)
2 tbsp. chopped fresh parsley
6 thin orange slices (optional)

● *HIGH SODIUM ALERT—Use fresh or unsalted canned mushrooms. Omit added salt.*

Broil chicken skin-side up 10 to 15 minutes, or until skin is crisp. Pour off fat. Blot chicken. Combine onion, green pepper and mushrooms in shallow baking dish. Arrange chicken over vegetables; sprinkle with paprika. Mix together remaining ingredients except parsley; pour over chicken. Bake uncovered in a preheated 375° oven, basting occasionally, 40 to 50 minutes, or until tender. Sprinkle with parsley. Garnish with fresh orange slices, if desired.

Total		Per Serving
1928.0	Calories	321.3
192.9	Carbohydrate (g)	32.2
167.3	Protein (g)	27.9
48.4	Total Fat (g)	8.1
18.0	Saturated Fat (g)	3.0
752.5	Cholesterol (mg)	125.4
3627.9	Sodium (mg)	604.7

Chicken Noodle Stroganoff

Makes 6 servings

2 lb. chicken thighs, trimmed of fat
3/4 cup tomato juice ●
1 onion, chopped
4-oz. can sliced mushrooms, undrained ●
1/4 tsp. dry mustard
1/2 cup skim milk
1/2 cup plain low-fat yogurt
2 tbsp. flour
Salt ● and pepper to taste (optional)
4 cups tender-cooked wide noodles ● ■

● *HIGH SODIUM ALERT—Use unsalted tomato juice and mushrooms. Omit added salt. Cook noodles without salt.*

■ *HIGH CHOLESTEROL ALERT—Use noodles made without egg yolks.*

Broil chicken skin-side up 10 to 15 minutes, or until skin is crisp. Pour off fat. Blot chicken. Combine tomato juice, onion, mushrooms and mustard in large saucepan; add chicken. Simmer covered over very low heat about 50 minutes, or until chicken is tender, adding water if needed. Skim off fat.

Mix together milk, yogurt and flour and stir into saucepan. Cook and stir until sauce simmers and thickens. Sprinkle with salt and pepper. Serve over hot noodles.

Total		Per Serving
1081.8	Calories	180.3
46.0	Carbohydrate (g)	7.7
167.0	Protein (g)	27.8
21.3	Total Fat (g)	3.6
10.0	Saturated Fat (g)	1.7
510.0	Cholesterol (mg)	85.0
420.1	Sodium (mg)	70.0

Greek-Seasoned Oven-Fried Chicken

Makes 8 servings

2 frying chickens (about 2 lb. each), cut up, trimmed of fat
2/3 cup water
1/3 cup lemon juice
2 tsp. dried mint leaves
1/2 cup Italian-seasoned bread crumbs ●
1 tsp. ground nutmeg
1 tsp. cinnamon
1 tsp. paprika
1 tsp. onion or garlic salt ●

● *HIGH SODIUM ALERT—Use plain low-sodium bread crumbs. Substitute onion or garlic powder to taste for onion or garlic salt.*

Place chicken pieces in plastic bag or large bowl. Mix together water, lemon juice and mint; pour over chicken. Marinate 30 minutes at room temperature or several hours in refrigerator, turning frequently. Drain chicken. Combine remaining ingredients in heavy paper bag. Place chicken pieces, a few at a time, in paper bag; shake to coat chicken. Arrange chicken pieces skin-side up in nonstick pan or baking sheet. Bake uncovered in a preheated 375° oven 1 hour, or until crisp.

Total		Per Serving
1951.7	Calories	244.0
46.7	Carbohydrate (g)	5.8
268.6	Protein (g)	33.6
70.0	Total Fat (g)	8.8
27.4	Saturated Fat (g)	3.4
1109.7	Cholesterol (mg)	138.7
4457.8	Sodium (mg)	557.2

1 tsp. = 5 mL   1 tbsp. = 15 mL   1 cup = 250 mL   1 oz. = 30 g

Color-Me-Slim Photo Gallery 3

Savor the dieter's forbidden treats, and stay slim too!
Noodle Lasagne, Quick Spanish Rice, Hot German Potato Salad,
Banana-Raspberry Layer Cake, Slim and Speedy Chocolate Cream Pie—they
all can be yours the *Lean Cuisine* way.
Feast your eyes on the colorful dishes that have been miraculously
transformed into a dieter's delights.

Banana-Raspberry Layer Cake, page 111

◁Hot German Potato Salad,
page 104

Blushing Pears, ▷
page 117

Raisin Chip Chewies,
page 115

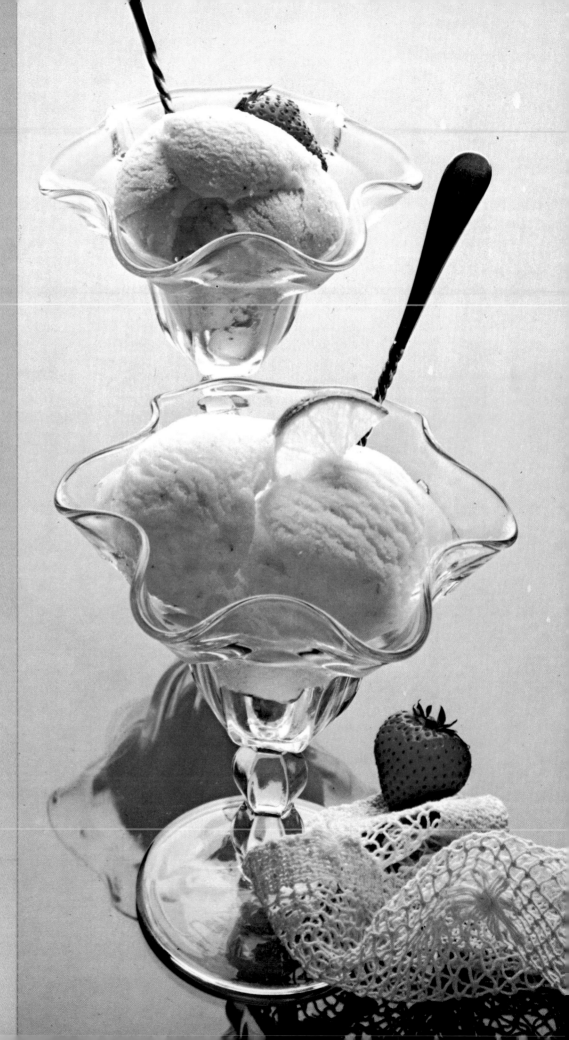

△
**Chilled
Orange Souffle,**
page 108

Hungarian Turkey Skillet

Makes 4 servings

1¼ lb. package frozen turkey thigh, defrosted, skinned, boned, cut into ¼-inch cubes
2 cups onions, cut into strips
2 green peppers, cut into strips
1 red bell pepper, cut into strips
2 tomatoes, peeled, seeded, diced
1 cup water
    Salt ● and pepper to taste (optional)
    Pinch cayenne pepper (or to taste)

● *HIGH SODIUM ALERT—Omit added salt.*

Combine all ingredients in heavy skillet. Simmer covered 35 minutes, or until meat is tender. Uncover and continue to simmer until sauce is thick.

Total		Per Serving
844.3	Calories	211.1
50.2	Carbohydrate (g)	12.5
102.0	Protein (g)	25.5
25.8	Total Fat (g)	6.5
7.4	Saturated Fat (g)	1.9
309.1	Cholesterol (mg)	77.3
358.9	Sodium (mg)	89.7

Chicken Paprika

Makes 4 servings

1 lb. frying chicken (about 2¼ lb.), cut up, trimmed of fat
1 cup water
¼ lb. fresh mushrooms, sliced
1 onion, sliced
1 clove garlic, chopped (optional)
    Salt ● and pepper to taste (optional)
½ cup plain low-fat yogurt
1 tbsp. instant-blend flour
1 tbsp. paprika

● *HIGH SODIUM ALERT—Omit added salt.*

Place chicken pieces skin-side down in cold large nonstick skillet. Add 2 tablespoons of the water. Cook covered over moderate heat until water has evaporated and chicken begins to brown in its own fat. Continue to cook; turn pieces to brown evenly. Remove chicken; pour off fat from skillet. Blot chicken and return to skillet skin-side up. Add remaining water, the mushrooms, onion, garlic, salt and pepper. Simmer covered 35 to 40 minutes, or until chicken is tender. Remove chicken to serving dish.

Skim fat from pan juices and discard. Mix together yogurt, flour and paprika; stir into skillet. Cook and stir over low heat until sauce is thick. Pour sauce over chicken and serve immediately.

Total		Per Serving
1104.4	Calories	276.1
27.6	Carbohydrate (g)	6.9
189.0	Protein (g)	47.3
24.8	Total Fat (g)	6.2
12.2	Saturated Fat (g)	3.1
581.2	Cholesterol (mg)	145.3
516.3	Sodium (mg)	129.1

Italian-Seasoned Oven-Fried Chicken I

Makes 8 servings

2 frying chickens (about 2 lb. each), cut up, trimmed of fat
1 cup tomato juice ●
½ cup Italian-seasoned bread crumbs ●
1 tsp. garlic salt ●
1 tsp. onion powder
1 tsp. paprika
¼ cup grated extra-sharp Romano cheese ● ■

● *HIGH SODIUM ALERT—Use unsalted tomato juice and plain low-sodium bread crumbs. Substitute garlic powder to taste for garlic salt. Use low-sodium cheese, or omit.*

■ *HIGH CHOLESTEROL ALERT—Use low-fat cheese, or omit.*

Combine chicken pieces with tomato juice in plastic bag or large bowl. Marinate 30 minutes at room temperature or several hours in refrigerator, turning frequently. Drain chicken. Combine remaining ingredients in heavy paper bag. Place chicken pieces, a few at a time, in paper bag; shake to coat chicken.

Total		Per Serving
2072.3	Calories	259.1
51.1	Carbohydrate (g)	6.4
278.5	Protein (g)	34.8
72.9	Total Fat (g)	9.1
32.5	Saturated Fat (g)	4.1
1135.2	Cholesterol (mg)	141.9
5130.6	Sodium (mg)	641.3

Chicken Teriyaki●

Makes 6 servings

3 whole chicken breasts (about 2 lb.), split, trimmed of fat
½ cup dry white wine
¼ cup water
3 tbsp. soy sauce
¼ tsp. ground ginger
⅛ tsp. garlic powder

● *HIGH SODIUM ALERT—Not recommended for low-sodium diets.*

Place chicken in glass or ceramic bowl. Mix together remaining ingredients; pour over chicken. Marinate covered several hours or overnight in refrigerator. Drain and reserve marinade. Grill or broil chicken, turning once, about 10 inches from heat, about 30 minutes, or until tender. Baste frequently with reserved marinade.

Total		Per Serving
970.0	Calories	161.7
7.8	Carbohydrate (g)	1.3
163.0	Protein (g)	27.2
20.0	Total Fat (g)	3.3
10.0	Saturated Fat (g)	1.7
510.0	Cholesterol (mg)	85.0
3681.0	Sodium (mg)	613.5

Alert Symbols: ● Sodium ■ Cholesterol ▲ Sugar

Temple Chicken Breasts

Makes 4 servings

2 whole chicken breasts (about 1¼ lb.), split, trimmed of fat
¼ tsp. pepper
⅛ tsp. garlic powder (optional)
¼ cup unsweetened orange juice
2 tbsp. soy sauce ● (optional)
2 tbsp. dry white wine
1 large Temple orange, peeled, segmented

● *HIGH SODIUM ALERT—Omit soy sauce.*

Sprinkle chicken with pepper and garlic; broil skin-side up 10 to 15 minutes, or until skin is crisp. Pour off fat. Blot chicken; place skin-side up in shallow baking dish. Mix orange juice with soy sauce and wine; pour over chicken. Bake uncovered in a preheated 350° oven, basting frequently, 45 to 50 minutes. Add orange sections and bake 5 minutes, or until just heated through. Serve chicken with sauce.

Total		Per Serving
656.2	Calories	164.1
27.7	Carbohydrate (g)	6.9
101.2	Protein (g)	25.3
12.6	Total Fat (g)	3.2
6.2	Saturated Fat (g)	1.6
317.2	Cholesterol (mg)	79.3
240.4	Sodium (mg)	60.1

Italian-Seasoned Oven-Fried Chicken II

Makes 8 servings

2 frying chickens (about 2 lb. each), cut up, trimmed of fat
½ cup low-calorie low-fat Italian salad dressing ●
½ cup water
½ cup plain bread crumbs ●

● *HIGH SODIUM ALERT—Use unsalted dressing and low-sodium bread crumbs.*

Place chicken pieces in plastic bag or large bowl. Mix together dressing and water; pour over chicken. Marinate 30 minutes at room temperature or several hours in refrigerator, turning frequently. Drain chicken. Shake chicken pieces, a few at a time, with bread crumbs in heavy paper bag. Arrange chicken pieces skin-side up in nonstick pan or baking sheet. Bake uncovered in a preheated 375° oven 1 hour, or until crisp.

Total		Per Serving
1985.2	Calories	248.2
39.6	Carbohydrate (g)	5.0
266.8	Protein (g)	33.4
79.0	Total Fat (g)	9.9
27.9	Saturated Fat (g)	3.5
1112.2	Cholesterol (mg)	139.0
2170.6	Sodium (mg)	271.3

Turkey Steaks with Mushrooms

Makes 4 servings

1 lb. turkey breast steaks
1 tbsp. diet margarine ● ■
2 cups sliced fresh mushrooms
½ cup sherry
Salt ● and pepper to taste (optional)

● *HIGH SODIUM ALERT—Use unsalted margarine. Omit added salt.*

■ *HIGH CHOLESTEROL ALERT—Use polyunsaturated margarine.*

Sauté steaks in margarine in nonstick skillet until done. Remove to serving platter. Sauté mushrooms; stir in sherry, salt and pepper. Cook 2 to 3 minutes. Top steaks with mushroom mixture.

Total		Per Serving
969.0	Calories	242.2
10.7	Carbohydrate (g)	2.7
153.1	Protein (g)	38.3
24.1	Total Fat (g)	6.0
6.1	Saturated Fat (g)	1.5
406.8	Cholesterol (mg)	101.7
506.0	Sodium (mg)	126.5

Tarragon Chicken

Makes 4 servings

1 frying chicken (about 2 lb.), cut up, trimmed of fat
¼ cup dry sherry
¼ cup water
2 tbsp. lemon juice
½ tsp. dried tarragon
2 onions, quartered
Salt ● and pepper to taste (optional)
Pinch garlic powder (optional)
2 tbsp. chopped fresh parsley
4 or 5 thin lemon slices

● *HIGH SODIUM ALERT—Omit added salt.*

Place chicken pieces in plastic bag or large bowl. Mix together wine, water, lemon juice and tarragon; pour over chicken. Marinate, 30 minutes at room temperature or several hours in refrigerator. Drain and reserve marinade. Broil chicken skin-side up 10 to 15 minutes or until skin is crisp. Pour off fat. Blot chicken.

1 tsp. = 5 mL   1 tbsp. = 15 mL   1 cup = 250 mL   1 oz. = 30 g

Place onion quarters in shallow baking dish. Arrange chicken over onions. Sprinkle with salt, pepper and garlic powder. Pour reserved marinade over chicken. Bake uncovered in a preheated 375° oven, basting occasionally, about 1 hour, or until chicken is tender. Spoon pan juices over chicken. Garnish with parsley and lemon slices.

Total		Per Serving
1005.6	Calories	251.4
25.6	Carbohydrate (g)	6.4
134.7	Protein (g)	33.7
34.3	Total Fat (g)	8.6
13.7	Saturated Fat (g)	3.4
555.4	Cholesterol (mg)	138.9
425.9	Sodium (mg)	106.5

Chicken-Stuffed Acorn Squash

Makes 4 servings
2 small acorn squashes (3/4 lb. each), halved, seeded
1/2 cup fat-skimmed chicken broth, canned or homemade ●
1/2 cup skim milk
2 tbsp. flour
1 tbsp. instant minced onion
1 tsp. parsley flakes
2 cups cooked white-meat chicken, diced
Salt ● and pepper to taste (optional)
Poultry seasoning to taste (optional)

● HIGH SODIUM ALERT—Use unsalted broth. Omit added salt.

Place squash halves cut-sides down on baking sheet. Bake in a preheated 400° oven about 30 minutes, or until tender. Meanwhile, combine broth, milk, flour, onion and parsley in saucepan. Cook and stir until sauce simmers and thickens. Stir in chicken and heat through. Sprinkle with salt, pepper and poultry seasoning. Spoon into squash halves and serve.

Total		Per Serving
858.2	Calories	214.5
90.0	Carbohydrate (g)	22.5
105.4	Protein (g)	26.3
10.4	Total Fat (g)	2.6
3.0	Saturated Fat (g)	0.7
230.2	Cholesterol (mg)	57.6
614.3	Sodium (mg)	153.6

Chicken with Linguine and Eggplant Sauce

Makes 6 servings
2 lb. chicken thighs, trimmed of fat
2 tbsp. water
1 1/4 cups fat-skimmed chicken broth, canned or homemade ●
6-oz. can tomato paste
1/2 medium eggplant, pared, cut into 1/4-inch cubes
1 onion, finely chopped
2 tsp. dried oregano
1 tsp. dried basil
1 tsp. garlic salt ● (optional)
4 cups tender-cooked protein-enriched linguine or spaghetti ●

● HIGH SODIUM ALERT—Use unsalted broth. Substitute garlic powder to taste for garlic salt. Cook pasta without salt.

Place chicken skin-side down in cold large nonstick skillet. Add the water. Cook covered over moderate heat until water has evaporated and chicken begins to brown in its own fat. Continue to cook; turn pieces to brown evenly. Remove chicken; pour off fat from skillet. Blot chicken and return to skillet skin-side up. Combine remaining ingredients except linguine; pour over chicken. Simmer covered 1 hour. Uncover and continue to cook until sauce is the consistency of gravy. Serve over linguine.

Total		Per Serving
1741.1	Calories	290.2
182.4	Carbohydrate (g)	30.4
156.2	Protein (g)	26.0
41.0	Total Fat (g)	6.8
13.0	Saturated Fat (g)	2.2
557.5	Cholesterol (mg)	92.9
3327.1	Sodium (mg)	554.5

Cornish Hens with Cherries

Makes 8 servings
4 Rock Cornish hens, (about 4 lb. total) cut into halves lengthwise
16-oz. can juice-packed dark cherries, drained, juice reserved
1/4 tsp. poultry seasoning
Salt ● and pepper to taste (optional)
1/2 cup undiluted bottled unsweetened red grape juice
Water
2 tsp. cornstarch or arrowroot

● HIGH SODIUM ALERT—Omit added salt.

Broil hen halves skin-side up 10 to 15 minutes, or until skin is crisp. Pour off fat. Blot hen halves; place skin-side up in shallow baking dish. Pour 1/2 cup of the reserved juice from the cherries over the hen halves. Sprinkle with poultry seasoning, salt and pepper. Bake uncovered in a preheated 350° oven, basting frequently, about 1 hour, or until hen halves are tender. Meanwhile, pour remaining cherry juice into a 2-cup measure; add grape juice and enough water to measure 1 3/4 cups liquid; combine liquid and cornstarch in saucepan. Cook and stir over low heat until mixture thickens and clears. Stir in cherries and heat through. Pour sauce over hens and serve.

Total		Per Serving
1964.0	Calories	245.5
100.2	Carbohydrate (g)	12.5
240.3	Protein (g)	30.0
63.0	Total Fat (g)	7.9
24.9	Saturated Fat (g)	3.1
1004.4	Cholesterol (mg)	125.6
727.4	Sodium (mg)	90.9

Alert Symbols:　● Sodium　■ Cholesterol　▲ Sugar

Chicken Cordon Bleu

Makes 8 servings

8 chicken fillets (about 2 lb.) (4 whole breasts, split, skinned and boned)
8 tsp. chopped parsley
8 thin slices (4 oz.) part-skim mozzarella cheese ●
4 thin slices (4 oz.) boiled ham, cut into halves ●
1 tbsp. low-calorie low-fat mayonnaise ●
1 tbsp. warm water
¼ cup seasoned bread crumbs ●
White Wine Sauce (optional) (recipe in this chapter)

● *HIGH SODIUM ALERT—Use low-sodium cheese and bread crumbs. Omit ham. Use unsalted mayonnaise.*

Pound fillets until they are thin. Lay out flat and sprinkle with parsley. Top each fillet with a slice of cheese, then a half-slice of ham. Roll up tightly. Stir together mayonnaise and water in shallow dish. Roll each chicken fillet in the mayonnaise mixture, then in the bread crumbs. Spray a baking sheet with cooking spray. Arrange the chicken rolls, seamside down, in a single layer on baking sheet. Bake in a preheated 425° oven 15 to 20 minutes, or until browned, cooked through and cheese is melted. Top with White Wine Sauce, if desired.

Total		Per Serving
1725.8	Calories	215.7
23.2	Carbohydrate (g)	2.9
252.1	Protein (g)	31.5
66.1	Total Fat (g)	8.3
31.8	Saturated Fat (g)	4.0
809.6	Cholesterol (mg)	101.2
3196.3	Sodium (mg)	399.5

Cantonese Chicken and Vegetables

Makes 6 servings

2 tsp. safflower or corn oil
6 chicken fillets (about 1½ lb.) (3 whole breasts, split, skinned and boned), cut into 1-inch cubes
¼ cup thinly sliced green onions
1 clove garlic, minced
1¼ cups fat-skimmed chicken broth, canned or homemade ●
10-oz. package frozen cut green beans, defrosted
10-oz. package frozen cut broccoli, defrosted
4-oz. can sliced mushrooms, drained ●
½ tsp. ground ginger
1 tbsp. cornstarch or arrowroot
¼ cup soy sauce ●

● *HIGH SODIUM ALERT—Use unsalted broth and mushrooms. Substitute ¼ cup cold water for soy sauce.*

Heat oil over high heat in large nonstick skillet. Add chicken, onions and garlic to skillet. Stir-fry 2 minutes. Reduce heat. Stir in broth, green beans, broccoli, mushrooms and ginger. Simmer covered, 6 to 8 minutes, until vegetables are crisp-tender. Mix together cornstarch and soy sauce; stir into skillet. Cook and stir until sauce simmers and clears.

Total		Per Serving
1246.0	Calories	207.7
54.3	Carbohydrate (g)	9.0
155.5	Protein (g)	25.9
44.8	Total Fat (g)	7.5
14.4	Saturated Fat (g)	2.4
572.9	Cholesterol (mg)	95.5
6242.2	Sodium (mg)	1040.4

Turkey Spaghetti Sauce

Makes 8 servings

3 frozen turkey legs (about 3 lb. total)
4 cups canned tomatoes, undrained, well broken up ●
3 cups water
2 cans (6 oz. each) tomato paste
1 cup dry red wine
1 onion, minced
2 tsp. dried oregano or mixed Italian seasoning
1 tsp. garlic salt ● (optional)

● *HIGH SODIUM ALERT—Use unsalted tomatoes. Substitute garlic powder to taste for garlic salt.*

Combine all ingredients in large stockpot. Heat to boiling. Simmer covered over very low heat 1½ to 2 hours, or until turkey is tender. Cool. Remove and discard turkey skin, bones and tendons. Cut meat into small pieces; return meat to sauce. Refrigerate covered several hours.

Remove and discard hardened fat from surface of sauce. Heat sauce to boiling. Reduce heat; simmer uncovered until sauce is the consistency of thick gravy.

Total		Per Serving
2213.1	Calories	276.6
124.7	Carbohydrate (g)	15.6
240.7	Protein (g)	30.1
64.9	Total Fat (g)	8.1
17.6	Saturated Fat (g)	2.2
742.4	Cholesterol (mg)	92.8
2128.7	Sodium (mg)	266.1

South Seas Chilled Chicken●

Makes 6 servings

2 lb. chicken thighs or drumsticks, trimmed of fat
⅓ cup soy sauce
¼ cup rice wine vinegar or white vinegar
2 cloves garlic, finely minced, or ¼ tsp. garlic powder

● *HIGH SODIUM ALERT—Not recommended for low-sodium diets.*

Broil chicken skin-side up 10 to 15 minutes, or until skin is crisp. Pour off fat. Blot chicken; place skin-side

1 tsp. = 5 mL   1 tbsp. = 15 mL   1 cup = 250 mL   1 oz. = 30 g

up in shallow baking dish. Mix together remaining ingredients; pour over chicken. Bake covered in a preheated 325° oven 40 to 50 minutes, or until tender. Uncover and continue to bake until sauce is somewhat reduced. Cool to room temperature. Chill in sauce; serve cold.

Total		Per Serving
935.3	Calories	155.9
11.1	Carbohydrate (g)	1.9
128.9	Protein (g)	21.5
38.2	Total Fat (g)	6.4
13.0	Saturated Fat (g)	2.2
540.0	Cholesterol (mg)	90.0
6249.0	Sodium (mg)	1041.5

Arroz con Pollo

Makes 8 servings

2 frying chickens (about 2 lb. each), cut up, trimmed of fat
4 tbsp. sherry
16-oz. can tomatoes, undrained, well broken up ●
1 cup uncooked brown rice
1 cup water
2 onions, chopped
2 cloves garlic, minced, or ¼ tsp. garlic powder
1 bay leaf
½ tsp. ground turmeric
½ tsp. pepper
1 green pepper, diced
8 stuffed green (Spanish) olives, thinly sliced ●

● *HIGH SODIUM ALERT—Use unsalted tomatoes. Omit olives.*

Place chicken pieces skin-side down in cold large nonstick skillet. Add 2 tablespoons of the wine. Cook uncovered over moderate heat until wine has evaporated and chicken begins to brown in its own fat. Continue to cook; turn pieces to brown evenly. Remove chicken; pour off fat from skillet. Blot chicken and return to skillet skin-side up. Add tomatoes, rice, water, onions, garlic, bay leaf, turmeric and ½ teaspoon pepper. Simmer covered 30 minutes. Stir in green pepper, olives and remaining wine. Simmer covered 30 minutes, adding more water if necessary.

Total		Per Serving
2648.6	Calories	331.1
192.1	Carbohydrate (g)	24.0
342.1	Protein (g)	42.8
48.3	Total Fat (g)	6.1
19.9	Saturated Fat (g)	2.5
1014.9	Cholesterol (mg)	126.9
2167.2	Sodium (mg)	270.9

Moo Goo Gai Pan

Makes 4 servings

1 tsp. safflower or corn oil
4 chicken fillets (about 1 lb.) (2 whole breasts, split, skinned and boned), cut into 1-inch cubes
1 lb. Chinese or savoy cabbage
9-oz. package frozen snow peas, defrosted
8-oz. can sliced mushrooms, drained ●
1 cup drained canned Chinese vegetables ●
¾ cup fat-skimmed chicken broth, canned or homemade ●
¼ tsp. ground ginger
1 tsp. cornstarch or arrowroot

● *HIGH SODIUM ALERT—Use unsalted mushrooms, Chinese vegetables and broth.*

Heat oil over high heat in large nonstick skillet. Add chicken to skillet; stir-fry until chicken turns white. Stir in cabbage, snow peas, mushrooms, Chinese vegetables, ½ cup of the chicken broth, and the ginger. Cook covered 2 minutes. Reduce heat. Mix together cornstarch and remaining ¼ cup broth; stir into skillet. Cook and stir 1 to 2 minutes, until mixture thickens.

Total		Per Serving
805.1	Calories	201.3
45.8	Carbohydrate (g)	11.5
121.2	Protein (g)	30.3
18.5	Total Fat (g)	4.6
6.5	Saturated Fat (g)	1.6
326.7	Cholesterol (mg)	81.7
3101.1	Sodium (mg)	775.3

Chicken Portuguaise

Makes 4 servings

1 frying chicken (about 2 lb.), cut up, trimmed of fat
1 onion, thinly sliced
1 large or 2 small bell peppers, thinly sliced
¼ pound fresh mushrooms, thinly sliced
1 stalk celery, chopped ●
16-oz. can tomatoes, undrained, well broken up ●
¼ cup rosé or white wine
4 cloves garlic, minced, or ½ tsp. garlic powder
Salt ● and pepper to taste (optional)

● *HIGH SODIUM ALERT—Omit celery and added salt. Use unsalted tomatoes.*

Broil chicken pieces skin-side up 10 to 15 minutes, or until skin is crisp. Pour off fat. Blot chicken. Place the onion, bell pepper, mushrooms and celery in shallow baking dish. Arrange chicken over vegetables. Mix together tomatoes, wine, garlic, salt and pepper; pour over chicken. Bake uncovered in a preheated 400° oven, basting frequently, 50 to 60 minutes, or until chicken is tender and sauce is thick.

Total		Per Serving
1139.7	Calories	284.9
39.1	Carbohydrate (g)	9.8
143.0	Protein (g)	35.8
35.8	Total Fat (g)	9.0
13.7	Saturated Fat (g)	3.4
555.4	Cholesterol (mg)	138.9
1092.7	Sodium (mg)	273.7

Alert Symbols: ● Sodium ■ Cholesterol ▲ Sugar

Mexican Oven-Fried Chicken

Makes 8 servings

2 frying chickens (about 2 lb. each), cut-up, trimmed of fat
1 cup plain or Bloody-Mary seasoned tomato juice ●
1 cup cornflakes, crushed into crumbs ●
1 tsp. onion or garlic salt ●
1 tsp. paprika
1 tsp. chili powder (optional)
1 tsp. ground cumin
1 tsp. dried oregano

● *HIGH SODIUM ALERT—Use unsalted tomato juice. Substitute onion or garlic powder to taste for onion or garlic salt. Substitute soda-free cracker crumbs or low-sodium cornflakes for regular cornflakes.*

Combine chicken pieces with tomato juice in plastic bag or large bowl. Marinate 30 minutes at room temperature or several hours in refrigerator, turning frequently. Drain chicken. Combine remaining ingredients in heavy paper bag. Place chicken pieces, a few at a time, in paper bag; shake to coat chicken. Arrange chicken pieces skin-side up in nonstick pan or baking sheet. Bake uncovered in a preheated 375° oven 1 hour, or until crisp.

Total		Per Serving
1872.2	Calories	234.0
31.4	Carbohydrate (g)	3.9
264.5	Protein (g)	33.1
68.7	Total Fat (g)	8.6
27.4	Saturated Fat (g)	3.4
1109.7	Cholesterol (mg)	138.7
3663.6	Sodium (mg)	457.9

Curried Pineapple Glaze

Makes 1 cup

8-oz. can juice-packed crushed pineapple, undrained
2 tbsp. cold water
2 tsp. cornstarch
1 tsp. curry powder
1/4 tsp. onion powder
1/8 tsp. garlic salt ● or garlic powder

● *HIGH-SODIUM ALERT—Use garlic powder, not garlic salt.*

Combine all ingredients in saucepan. Cook and stir over low heat until smooth and clear. Spread over a turkey breast after it is tender and nicely browned, and return to oven for 10 or 15 minutes. (Makes enough to glaze a medium-size turkey breast. Double recipe if you wish to serve more sauce at table.)

Total		Per Tablespoon
170.0	Calories	10.6
43.7	Carbohydrate (g)	2.7
1.0	Protein (g)	0.1
0.0	Total Fat (g)	0.0
0.0	Saturated Fat (g)	0.0
0.0	Cholesterol (mg)	0.0
256.1	Sodium (mg)	16.0

White Wine Sauce

Makes about 2 cups

1 cup fat-skimmed chicken or turkey broth, canned or homemade ●
3 tbsp. dry white wine
3 tbsp. instant-blend flour
2/3 cup skim milk
Onion salt ● and pepper to taste (optional)
Pinch nutmeg (optional)
1 tbsp. minced fresh parsley

● *HIGH SODIUM ALERT—Use unsalted broth. Substitute onion powder to taste for onion salt.*

Combine broth and wine in nonstick saucepan. Heat to boiling; reduce heat. Mix together flour and milk; stir into simmering broth. Cook and stir until mixture is thick and bubbling. Sprinkle with onion salt, pepper and nutmeg. (Thin with a little water, if necessary.) Sprinkle with parsley.

Total		Per 1/4 cup
209.7	Calories	26.2
30.4	Carbohydrage (g)	3.8
11.5	Protein (g)	1.4
0.0	Total Fat (g)	0.0
0.0	Saturated Fat (g)	0.0
17.3	Cholesterol (mg)	2.2
810.8	Sodium (mg)	101.4

High-Fiber Fruit Stuffing

Makes 4 servings

4 slices stale high-fiber bread, crumbled ●
1 1/2 cups finely diced unpared apple
1 medium onion, chopped
5 tbsp. raisins
3/4 tsp. salt ● (optional)
1/2 tsp. pepper
1/4 tsp. dried sage
1/4 tsp. dried rosemary

● *HIGH SODIUM ALERT—Use low-sodium bread. Omit added salt.*

Toss all ingredients together. Use to stuff chicken or Cornish hens.

Total		Per Serving
469.3	Calories	117.3
108.7	Carbohydrate (g)	27.2
12.3	Protein (g)	3.1
3.0	Total Fat (g)	0.7
0.0	Saturated Fat (g)	0.0
0.0	Cholesterol (mg)	0.0
655.8	Sodium (mg)	163.9

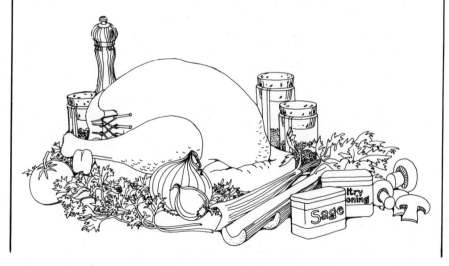

1 tsp. = 5 mL   1 tbsp. = 15 mL   1 cup = 250 mL   1 oz. = 30 g

Superior Seafood

Compared with most meats, virtually all seafood is low in fat and calories. Even the supposedly fatty fish such as salmon, bluefish and mackerel seem like diet fare compared with most meats. Mackerel, for example, is only 12 percent fat. The fat content of cod is so low that it's measured in fractions of a percent. So a fat-fighter can enjoy any seafood that's available, as long as the cooking method doesn't inflate the calorie count excessively.

(For those on cholesterol- or sodium-restricted diets, however, there are some special considerations. As we mentioned at the beginning of this book, shrimp is moderately high in cholesterol; its use should be limited if you are on a low-cholesterol diet. All shellfish is relatively high in sodium and is, therefore, usually not recommended for low-sodium diets. Also, when any fish is frozen, it may be dipped in a brine solution, thus raising the sodium content to an unacceptably high level for low-sodium diets. It is suggested that you always use fresh fish if you must restrict your sodium intake.)

Questions and Answers on Seafood Shopping

Q. *How can you tell fish is fresh?*

A. Look it in the eye. Fresh fish is bright-eyed, the eyes are clear and transparent, almost protruding. Sunken, cloudy, pinkish eyes indicate the fish has been out of the water for a considerable time, too long for a just-caught flavor. Seafood should have a fresh, clean smell. The longer the seafood is out of water, the stronger the fishy odor. Fresh fish also has a shiny, irridescent appearance with bright red gills. Faded color and pinkish gills indicate a lack of freshness.

Q. *How can you judge freshness when the fish is already cut into steaks or fillets?*

A. The absence of any fishy odor is the first clue. The flesh should have a firm, moist, fresh-cut appearance with no signs of drying or browning at the edges. Steaks should not be shrinking away from the bone, a sign of moisture loss.

Q. *How can you judge quality when the seafood is frozen, and wrapped in a box or plastic bag?*

A. Properly handled frozen fish can be as fresh as fresh fish, maybe even fresher, if flash-frozen shortly after the catch and carefully handled up until you thaw it for cooking. Unfortunately, there are many opportunities for mishandling. Accidental defrosting and refreezing can impair quality and flavor. In choosing boxes of fish fillets from the frozen-food cabinet, look for containers that have kept their shape. A misshapen box indicates that the fish may have thawed and become soft enough for the box to become pushed in or wrinkled—so pass it by. With seafood in plastic bags, look for, and then avoid, large amounts of frost inside the bag, an indication that improper handling caused the seafood to lose its natural moisture. When frozen fish is defrosted, it should be as firm, shiny and odor-free as fresh fish, not soft, pungent or dried out. If you discover after thawing that frozen seafood has been mishandled, refrigerate it until you can take it back to the store for a refund. Fish that's been mishandled probably won't harm you, but it won't be pleasant to eat.

Q. *How can I tell if so-called fresh fish is actually frozen fish that has been defrosted?*

A. Ask! Non-local or out-of-season seafood specialties are

LEAN CUISINE GUIDE TO SEAFOOD*

	Calories	Protein (g)	Fat (g)		Calories	Protein (g)	Fat (g)
Bass, striped	476	85.7	12.2	Pike, northern	399	83.0	5.0
Bass, sea, black	422	87.1	5.4	Pike, walleye	422	87.5	5.4
Bluefish	530	93.0	15.0	Pollack	431	92.5	4.1
Bonito	762	108.9	33.1	Pompano	753	85.3	43.1
Buffalofish	513	79.4	19.1	Porgy	508	86.2	15.4
Butterfish, Gulf	431	73.5	13.2	Red snapper	422	89.8	4.1
Carp	522	81.6	19.1	Rockfish	440	85.7	8.2
Catfish	467	79.8	14.1	Salmon, Atlantic	984	102.1	60.8
Clams, soft	372	63.5	8.6	Salmon, Chinook	1007	86.6	70.8
Clams, hard or round	363	50.3	4.1	Sole	358	75.8	3.6
Cod	354	79.8	1.4	Sardines, canned in oil, drained	755	89.3	41.3
Crab	422	78.5	8.6	Sauger	381	81.2	3.6
Flounder	358	75.8	3.6	Scallops	367	69.4	0.9
Grouper	395	87.5	2.3	Shrimp	412	82.1	3.6
Haddock	358	83.0	0.5	Smelt	445	84.4	9.5
Halibut	453	94.8	5.4	Sole	358	75.8	3.6
Kingfish	476	83.0	13.6	Sturgeon	426	82.1	8.6
Lobster	413	76.7	8.6	Swordfish	535	87.1	18.1
Mackerel	866	86.2	55.3	Trout, brook	458	87.1	9.5
Mullet, striped	662	88.9	31.3	Trout, lake	762	83.0	45.4
Mussels	431	65.3	10.0	Trout, rainbow	885	97.5	51.7
Oysters	299	38.1	8.2	Tuna, canned in oil, drained	894	130.6	37.2
Perch, ocean	430	86.2	6.8	Tuna, canned in water	576	127.0	3.6
Perch, yellow	413	88.5	4.1	Whitefish, lake	703	85.7	37.2
Pike, blue	408	86.6	4.1				

Source: U.S. Department of Agriculture, Agricultural Research Service, *Composition of Foods* (Agriculture Handbook No. 8), 1963, 1975.
Figures reflect content of 1 pound of ready-to-cook (or, for canned items, cooked) flesh only.

likely to be defrosted. Don't buy defrosted fish unless you plan to use it immediately. Ask the counter-person for the still-frozen fish. Thaw frozen fish overnight in your refrigerator or for one or two hours in cold (never hot) water. Always defrost fish for use in any recipe unless directions say otherwise. Never refreeze defrosted raw fish.

Q. *How much fish should you buy?*

A. Whole (fish as it comes from the water): Before cooking, the fish must be scaled and gutted. The head, tail and fins can be removed, if desired. The fish may then be cooked, filleted or cut into steaks or chunks. Allow 2/3 to 3/4 pound per serving.

Dressed (fish with scales and entrails removed): The head,

TIMETABLE FOR COOKING FISH

Method of Cooking	Market Form	Cooking Temperature	Approximate Cooking Time
Baking	Dressed	350°	45 to 60 min.
	Pan-dressed	350°	25 to 30 min.
	Fillets or steaks	350°	20 to 25 min.
Broiling	Pan-dressed	3 to 4 inches from heat	10 to 16 min. turning once
	Fillets or steaks		10 to 15 min.
	Frozen fried fish		10 to 15 min.
	Frozen fried fish sticks		10 to 15 min.
Charcoal Broiling	Pan-dressed	Moderate	10 to 16 min. turning once
	Fillets or steaks	Moderate	10 to 16 min.
Oven-Frying	Pan-dressed	500°	15 to 20 min.
	Fillets or steaks	500°	10 to 12 min.
Pan-Frying	Pan-dressed	Moderate	8 to 10 min. turning once
	Fillets or steaks	Moderate	8 to 10 min.
Poaching	Whole Fish	Simmer	30 to 60 min.
	Fillets or steaks	Simmer	5 to 10 min.
Steaming	Fillets or steaks	Boil	5 to 10 min.

tail and fins can also be removed, if you wish. The fish may then be cooked, filleted or cut into steaks or chunks. (The smaller size fish are called pan-dressed and are ready to cook as purchased.) About ⅓ to ½ pound equals one serving.

Fillets (the boneless, usually skinless sides of the fish cut lengthwise away from the backbone): They are ready to cook as purchased. Allow about ¼ to ½ pound per serving.

Steaks (cross-section slices from large dressed fish, cut ½- to 1-inch thick): A cross section of the backbone is the only bone in a steak. Steaks are ready to cook as purchased. Allow ¼ to ⅓ pound per serving.

Chunks (cross-sections of large dressed fish): A cross section of the backbone is the only bone in a chunk. They are ready to cook as purchased. Allow ¼ to ⅓ pound per serving.

Q. *Is there any fish dieters should avoid?*

A. There are some types of frozen fish that dieters should stay away from. Fish is often frozen already breaded as a convenience to busy homemakers. You pay as much for the breading as you do for the fish, and you get a lot of extra calories.

Raw breaded fish portions: These are portions cut from frozen fish blocks, coated with a batter, breaded, packaged and frozen. Raw breaded fish portions generally contain only 75 percent fish.

Fried fish sticks: These are cut from frozen fish blocks. They are coated with a batter, then fried in fat and frozen. Fried fish sticks are only 60 percent fish.

Italian Fish Stew

Makes 4 servings

1 tsp. safflower or corn oil
2 tbsp. water
1 cup chopped onion
1 clove garlic, minced (optional)
16-oz. can tomatoes, undrained, well broken up ●
1 green pepper, diced
2 stalks celery, diced ●
3 tbsp. chopped Italian parsley
3 tbsp. dry white wine
1 small bay leaf
Salt ● and pepper to taste (optional)
1 tsp. dried oregano
1 tsp. fennel seeds
1 lb. frozen cod fillets, slightly defrosted ●

● *HIGH SODIUM ALERT—Use fresh fish fillets; freeze until firm. Use unsalted tomatoes. Omit celery and added salt.*

Spray a large nonstick skillet with cooking spray. Add oil, water, onions and garlic. Cook, stirring frequently, until water evaporates and onions are lightly browned. Add remaining ingredients except fish. Cover and simmer 25 to 30 minutes. With a sharp knife, cut fillets into 1½-inch chunks. Add to the skillet. Cover and simmer 12 to 15 minutes, only until fish flakes easily with a fork. Remove bay leaf before serving.

Total		Per Serving
629.2	Calories	157.3
43.7	Carbohydrate (g)	10.9
88.9	Protein (g)	22.2
7.3	Total Fat (g)	1.8
0.8	Saturated Fat (g)	0.2
227.0	Cholesterol (mg)	56.8
1042.5	Sodium (mg)	260.6

Quick Seafood Newburg

Makes 4 servings

1 cup skim milk
2 tbsp. instant-blend flour
¼ cup sherry
Salt ● and black pepper to taste (optional)
Pinch nutmeg
Pinch cayenne pepper
2 cups cold cooked shelled lobster or shrimp, or 2 cans (7 oz. each) water-packed tuna ● ■
4 slices toasted high-fiber bread, cut into halves diagonally ●
2 tbsp. minced parsley
Paprika
Lemon wedges (optional)

● *HIGH SODIUM ALERT—Use unsalted tuna (do not use lobster or shrimp) and low sodium bread. Omit added salt.*

■ *HIGH CHOLESTEROL ALERT—Use lobster or tuna (do not use shrimp).*

Stir milk and flour together in saucepan; cook and stir over low heat, until sauce simmers and thickens. Stir in sherry, salt, black pepper, nutmeg and cayenne pepper. Stir in seafood until heated through. Spoon over toast triangles and sprinkle with parsley and paprika. Garnish with lemon wedges, if desired.

Total		Per Serving
710.7	Calories	177.7
68.3	Carbohydrate (g)	17.1
75.1	Protein (g)	18.8
6.6	Total Fat (g)	1.6
0.0	Saturated Fat (g)	0.0
245.3	Cholesterol (mg)	61.3
1373.4	Sodium (mg)	343.3

Flounder Fillets in Mock Sour Cream Sauce

Makes 4 servings

1 lb. flounder or sole fillets, fresh or frozen, defrosted ●
½ cup dry white wine
½ cup water
½ tsp. dried dillweed
Salt ● and pepper to taste (optional)
1 cup plain low-fat yogurt
2 tbsp. chopped parsley

● *HIGH SODIUM ALERT—Use fresh fish. Omit added salt.*

Cut fillets into serving-size pieces; place in a shallow baking dish. Add wine and water. Sprinkle with dillweed, salt and pepper. Bake in preheated 350° oven 20 to 25 minutes, or until fish flakes easily with a fork. Baste several times with liquid while baking. Drain liquid from baking dish into a saucepan. Cook liquid over high heat until reduced to about ⅓ cup. Reduce heat, stir in yogurt; heat, do not boil, just until sauce is heated through. Place fish on serving platter; pour sauce over fish. Top with parsley.

Total		Per Serving
587.0	Calories	146.8
18.4	Carbohydrate (g)	4.6
84.0	Protein (g)	21.0
7.6	Total Fat (g)	1.9
3.2	Saturated Fat (g)	0.8
247.0	Cholesterol (mg)	61.8
487.0	Sodium (mg)	121.8

Alert Symbols: ● Sodium   ■ Cholesterol   ▲ Sugar

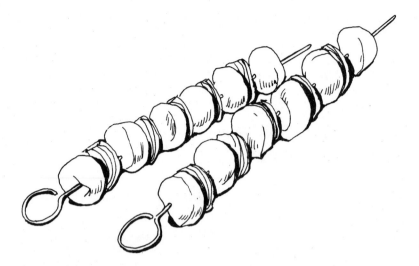

Cod Creole

Makes 4 servings
- 1 tbsp. diet margarine ● ■
- 1/2 cup chopped onion
- 1/2 cup chopped green pepper
- 1/4 lb. fresh mushrooms, sliced
- 16-oz. can tomatoes, undrained, chopped ●
- 1 tbsp. lemon juice
- 1/8 tsp. dry mustard
- 1 bay leaf
- 1/4 tsp. liquid red pepper seasoning ● (optional)
- Salt ● and pepper to taste (optional)
- 1 lb. fresh or frozen, defrosted, cod fillets ●

● *HIGH SODIUM ALERT—Use unsalted margarine and tomatoes. Omit red pepper seasoning and added salt. Use fresh fish.*

■ *HIGH CHOLESTEROL ALERT—Use polyunsaturated margarine.*

Melt margarine in large nonstick skillet. Add onion and green pepper; sauté until tender. Add mushrooms; cook 3 minutes. Add tomatoes, lemon juice, mustard, bay leaf, red pepper seasoning, salt and pepper. Cover; simmer 15 minutes. Cut cod fillets into serving-size pieces; add to skillet. Cover; simmer 8 to 10 minutes, or until fish flakes easily with a fork.

Total		Per Serving
583.5	Calories	145.9
36.8	Carbohydrate (g)	9.2
89.6	Protein (g)	22.4
8.8	Total Fat (g)	2.2
1.5	Saturated Fat (g)	0.4
227.0	Cholesterol (mg)	56.8
1053.6	Sodium (mg)	263.4

Skewered Scallops Hawaiian

Makes 4 servings
- 1 lb. sea scallops, fresh or frozen, defrosted ●
- 8-oz. can juice-packed pineapple chunks, undrained
- 4-oz. can whole mushrooms, undrained ●
- 2 small bell peppers (1 green and 1 red), cut into 1-inch squares
- 1/4 cup lemon juice
- 1/4 cup soy sauce ●
- 2 tsp. safflower oil

● *HIGH SODIUM ALERT—Substitute 1 lb. fresh fish fillets, cut into bite-size chunks, for scallops. Use unsalted mushrooms. Omit soy sauce.*

Combine all ingredients, except safflower oil. Refrigerate, covered, 1 hour, stirring occasionally. Drain scallops, pineapple and vegetables, reserving marinade. Thread scallops on long skewers alternately with pineapple, mushrooms and pepper squares. Brush with marinade, then with oil. Broil, turning once, 10 minutes, or until scallops are opaque. Brush with remaining marinade as they broil.

Total		Per Serving
704.3	Calories	176.1
70.7	Carbohydrate (g)	17.7
79.0	Protein (g)	19.8
11.5	Total Fat (g)	2.9
0.6	Saturated Fat (g)	0.2
159.0	Cholesterol (mg)	39.8
6097.5	Sodium (mg)	1524.4

Tuna Napoleon

Makes 4 servings
- 1 tsp. safflower or corn oil
- 1 tbsp. water
- 1 onion, chopped
- 1 clove garlic, minced, or 1/8 tsp. garlic powder
- 2 cans (7 oz. each) water-packed tuna, drained, flaked ●
- Salt ● and pepper to taste (optional)
- 1/4 tsp. dried basil or marjoram
- 1/4 cup dry sherry
- 4-oz. can mushroom stems and pieces, undrained ●
- 16-oz. can stewed tomatoes, undrained, broken-up ●
- 1 tbsp. chopped parsley

● *HIGH SODIUM ALERT—Use unsalted tuna, mushrooms and tomatoes. Omit added salt.*

Combine oil and water in a large nonstick skillet. Add onion and garlic; sauté until tender. Add remaining ingredients. Cover; heat to boiling. Reduce heat; simmer covered 15 minutes, stirring occasionally.

Total		Per Serving
791.7	Calories	197.9
38.3	Carbohydrate (g)	9.6
121.3	Protein (g)	30.3
14.2	Total Fat (g)	3.5
0.3	Saturated Fat (g)	0.1
252.0	Cholesterol (mg)	63.0
4560.0	Sodium (mg)	1140.0

Spicy Snapper

Makes 8 servings
- 2 lb. snapper fillets or other fish fillets, fresh or frozen, defrosted ●
- 2/3 cup tomato juice ●
- 3 tbsp. vinegar
- 1 envelope (3/8 oz.) old-fashioned French dressing mix ●

● *HIGH SODIUM ALERT—Use fresh fish and unsalted tomato juice. Substitute 1 tsp. paprika and dash pepper for dressing mix.*

Cut fillets into serving-size pieces. Place fish in a single layer in a shallow baking dish. Combine remaining ingredients; mix thoroughly. Pour sauce over fish and refrigerate covered for 30 minutes, turning once. Drain fish, reserving marinade for basting. Place fish on a broiler pan sprayed with cooking

1 tsp. = 5 mL   1 tbsp. = 15 mL   1 cup = 250 mL   1 oz. = 30 g

spray. Broil about 4 inches from heat for 4 to 5 minutes. Turn carefully and brush with marinade. Broil 4 to 5 minutes longer, or until fish flakes easily with a fork.

Total		Per Serving
910.8	Calories	113.9
15.1	Carbohydrate (g)	1.9
182.7	Protein (g)	22.8
8.8	Total Fat (g)	1.1
2.7	Saturated Fat (g)	0.3
544.0	Cholesterol (mg)	68.0
2480.0	Sodium (mg)	310.0

Seafood Chow Mein

Makes 4 servings

1 large Bermuda onion, thinly sliced
1 red or green bell pepper, cut into squares
2 stalks celery, diagonally sliced ●
2-oz. can mushroom stems and pieces, undrained ●
1/4 cup soy sauce ●
1/2 cup fat-skimmed canned chicken broth, undiluted ●
2 cups fresh or canned drained bean sprouts ●
5-oz. can water chestnuts, drained and sliced ● (optional)
1 lb. cooked cleaned small shrimp, or 2 cans (7 oz. each) water-packed tuna ● ■
1/4 cup cold water
1 tbsp. cornstarch or arrowroot

● HIGH SODIUM ALERT—Use unsalted broth, mushrooms and tuna. Omit celery and soy sauce. Use fresh bean sprouts. Substitute 1/4 cup sliced fresh white radishes for water chestnuts.

■ HIGH CHOLESTEROL ALERT—Use tuna (do not use shrimp).

Combine onion, pepper, celery, mushrooms, soy sauce and broth in a large nonstick skillet. Cover and simmer 5 minutes, just until vegetables are crisp-tender. Uncover and stir in bean sprouts, water chestnuts and shrimp. Cook and stir over moderate heat until mixture is bubbling. Stir water and cornstarch together. Add to skillet. Cook and stir until mixture thickens and clears.

Total		Per Serving
814.0	Calories	203.5
50.9	Carbohydrate (g)	12.7
143.1	Protein (g)	35.8
12.4	Total Fat (g)	3.1
4.0	Saturated Fat (g)	1.0
1027.0	Cholesterol (mg)	256.8
5759.4	Sodium (mg)	1439.9

Saucy Seafood

Makes 8 servings

2 lb. sole fillets or other fish fillets, fresh or frozen, defrosted ●
1/4 cup tomato juice ●
1/4 cup steak sauce ●
2 tbsp. low-calorie Italian salad dressing ●
Pinch curry powder
Dash red pepper sauce (optional)

● HIGH SODIUM ALERT—Use fresh fish, unsalted tomato juice and salad dressing. Omit steak sauce.

Cut fillets into serving-size pieces; place in nonstick broiler pan sprayed with cooking spray. Combine remaining ingredients; spread half of mixture on fish. Broil 4 to 5 minutes. Turn fillets carefully; spread with remaining basting sauce. Broil an additional 4 to 5 minutes until fish flakes easily with a fork.

Total		Per Serving
791.2	Calories	98.9
19.3	Carbohydrate (g)	2.4
152.1	Protein (g)	19.0
9.2	Total Fat (g)	1.2
2.4	Saturated Fat (g)	0.3
454.0	Cholesterol (mg)	56.8
2181.5	Sodium (mg)	272.7

Teriyaki Cod

Makes 4 servings

1 lb. fresh or frozen, defrosted, cod steaks ●
1/2 cup dry white wine
3 tbsp. soy sauce ●
1/2 tsp. dry mustard
1/2 tsp. ground ginger
1/4 tsp. garlic powder (optional)
Few drops liquid smoke seasoning (optional)
2 tsp. safflower or corn oil

● HIGH SODIUM ALERT—Use fresh fish. Omit soy sauce.

Cut cod steaks into serving-size pieces; place in a plastic bag or shallow dish. Combine remaining ingredients except oil; pour mixture over fish. Allow fish to marinate, covered, about 2 hours in the refrigerator. Drain fish; reserve marinade. Brush steaks with oil. Broil or grill, turning once, 10 to 12 minutes, or until fish flakes easily. While fish is broiling, brush occasionally with reserved marinade.

Total		Per Serving
567.3	Calories	141.8
7.8	Carbohydrate (g)	2.0
82.3	Protein (g)	20.6
10.7	Total Fat (g)	2.7
1.2	Saturated Fat (g)	0.3
227.0	Cholesterol (mg)	56.8
3619.0	Sodium (mg)	904.8

Alert Symbols: ● Sodium   ■ Cholesterol   ▲ Sugar

Striped Bass with Low-Cal Stuffing

Makes 6 servings

3 lb. dressed striped bass or other dressed fish, fresh or frozen, defrosted ●
1½ tsp. salt ● (optional)
    Low-Cal Stuffing (recipe in this chapter)
1 tbsp. safflower or corn oil
    Lemon wedges (optional)

● *HIGH SODIUM ALERT—Use fresh fish. Omit added salt.*

Clean, wash, and dry fish. Sprinkle inside and out with salt. Prepare Low-Cal Stuffing; stuff fish loosely with stuffing. Close opening with small skewers or wooden picks. Place fish in nonstick baking dish sprayed with cooking spray; brush fish with oil. Bake in preheated 350° oven for 40 to 60 minutes or until fish flakes easily when tested with a fork. Remove skewers. Serve with lemon wedges; if desired.

NOTE: If not all of the stuffing will fit into the cavity of the fish, place remainder of stuffing in covered casserole and bake separately.

Total		Per Serving
1160.0	Calories	193.3
56.5	Carbohydrate (g)	9.4
127.2	Protein (g)	21.2
32.7	Total Fat (g)	5.5
6.8	Saturated Fat (g)	1.1
391.8	Cholesterol (mg)	65.3
517.9	Sodium (mg)	86.3

Hearty Halibut

Makes 8 servings

2 lb. halibut steaks or other fish steaks, fresh or frozen, defrosted ●
⅔ cup thinly sliced onion
1½ cups chopped fresh mushrooms
⅓ cup chopped tomato
¼ cup chopped green pepper
¼ cup chopped parsley
3 tbsp. chopped pimiento
½ cup dry white wine
2 tbsp. lemon juice
1 tsp. salt ● (optional)
¼ tsp. dillweed
⅛ tsp. pepper
    Lemon wedges (optional)

● *HIGH SODIUM ALERT—Use fresh fish. Omit added salt.*

Cut steaks into serving-size pieces. Spray baking dish with cooking spray. Arrange onion over bottom of dish. Place fish in a single layer over onion. Combine mushrooms, tomato, green pepper, parsley and pimiento and spread over top of fish. Combine wine, lemon juice, and seasonings; pour over vegetables. Bake in a preheated 350° oven for 25 to 30 minutes or until fish flakes easily with a fork. Serve with lemon wedges, if desired.

Total		Per Serving
1121.4	Calories	140.2
28.6	Carbohydrate (g)	3.6
196.0	Protein (g)	24.5
11.9	Total Fat (g)	1.5
3.6	Saturated Fat (g)	0.5
454.0	Cholesterol (mg)	56.8
542.6	Sodium (mg)	67.8

Low-Cal Stuffing

Makes about 3 cups

1 tbsp. safflower or corn oil
¾ cup chopped onion
2¼ cups pared, chopped apple
⅓ cup chopped celery ●
⅓ cup chopped parsley
2 tbsp. lemon juice
¼ tsp. salt ● (optional)
⅛ tsp. dried thyme

● *HIGH SODIUM ALERT—Omit celery and added salt.*

Heat oil in nonstick skillet sprayed with cooking spray. Add onions to skillet; sauté until tender. Combine onions with remaining ingredients; mix thoroughly.

Total		Per ½ Cup
349.6	Calories	58.3
56.5	Carbohydrate (g)	9.4
3.8	Protein (g)	0.6
15.1	Total Fat (g)	2.5
1.0	Saturated Fat (g)	0.2
0.0	Cholesterol (mg)	0.0
74.4	Sodium (mg)	12.4

Oven-Fried Fish Fillets

Makes 4 servings

1 lb. flounder fillets or other fish fillets, fresh or frozen, defrosted ●
2 tbsp. low-fat mayonnaise ●
5 tbsp. fine dry bread crumbs ●
1 tsp. parsley flakes
½ tsp. paprika

● *HIGH SODIUM ALERT—Use fresh fish, unsalted mayonnaise and low-sodium bread crumbs.*

Cut fillets into serving-size pieces. Coat with mayonnaise on both sides. Combine bread crumbs, parsley flakes and paprika in a shallow dish. Press fish fillets into crumb mixture to coat both sides. Place on nonstick baking sheet. Bake in a preheated 450° oven 12 minutes, or until fish flakes easily with a fork.

Total		Per Serving
520.6	Calories	130.2
24.9	Carbohydrate (g)	6.2
79.9	Protein (g)	20.0
9.2	Total Fat (g)	2.3
1.5	Saturated Fat (g)	0.4
244.6	Cholesterol (mg)	61.2
622.7	Sodium (mg)	155.7

1 tsp.=5 mL   1 tbsp.=15 mL   1 cup=250 mL   1 oz.=30 g

Fish Kebabs

Makes 8 servings

- 2 lb. fresh or frozen, defrosted, cod steaks ●
- 1 cup dry white wine
- 3 tbsp. Worcestershire sauce ●
- 2 tsp. garlic salt ●
- 1/2 tsp. pepper
- 2 tsp. dried oregano
- 1 tbsp. safflower or corn oil

● *HIGH SODIUM ALERT—Substitute 1/4 tsp. garlic powder for garlic salt. Omit Worcestershire. Use fresh fish.*

Cut cod into 2-inch cubes; arrange cubes in shallow dish. Combine remaining ingredients except oil; pour mixture over fish. Cover and refrigerate 2 to 4 hours. Drain fish and reserve marinade. Thread cubes on skewers. Brush with oil. Grill over hot coals or in oven broiler, turning frequently, for 12 to 15 minutes, or until fish becomes opaque and flakes when tested with a fork. While grilling, baste occasionally with reserved marinade.

Total		Per Serving
1048.6	Calories	131.7
19.8	Carbohydrate (g)	2.5
160.3	Protein (g)	20.1
17.0	Total Fat (g)	2.1
2.0	Saturated Fat (g)	0.3
454.0	Cholesterol (mg)	56.8
5201.6	Sodium (mg)	650.2

Salmon Paysanne

Makes 8 servings

- 2 lb. salmon steaks or other fish steaks, fresh or frozen, defrosted ●
- Salt ● and white pepper to taste (optional)
- 4-oz. can sliced mushrooms, drained ●
- 1/2 cup sliced green onions
- 1/4 cup catsup ● ▲
- 1/2 tsp. liquid smoke seasoning

● *HIGH SODIUM ALERT—Use fresh fish. Omit added salt. Use unsalted mushrooms and catsup.*

▲ *HIGH SUGAR ALERT—Use sugarless catsup.*

Cut steaks into serving-size portions. Place in a single layer in a nonstick baking dish sprayed with cooking spray. Sprinkle with salt and pepper. Combine remaining ingredients and spread over top of fish. Bake in a

preheated 350° oven for 25 to 30 minutes or until fish flakes easily with a fork.

Total		Per Serving
1831.6	Calories	229.0
24.3	Carbohydrate (g)	3.1
183.0	Protein (g)	22.9
107.1	Total Fat (g)	13.4
35.3	Saturated Fat (g)	4.4
282.0	Cholesterol (mg)	35.3
1506.0	Sodium (mg)	188.3

Chilled Shrimp and Mushroom Kebabs ●●

Makes 6 servings

- 1/2 lb. fresh whole mushrooms, stems removed
- 1 cucumber, pared, quartered, cut into chunks
- 1 lb. cooked cleaned shrimp
- 3 tbsp. safflower or corn oil
- 2 tbsp. white or cider vinegar
- 1 small onion, finely chopped
- 2 tbsp. lemon juice
- 2 tbsp. water
- 1 tbsp. prepared horseradish
- Salt and pepper to taste (optional)
- 1/2 tsp. garlic powder
- 1/4 tsp. dried tarragon
- 24 cherry tomatoes

● *HIGH SODIUM ALERT—Not recommended for low-sodium diets.*

■ *HIGH CHOLESTEROL ALERT—Not recommended for low-cholesterol diets.*

Place mushroom caps in bowl with cucumber chunks and shrimp. In a small bowl beat oil with vinegar, onion, lemon juice, water, horseradish, salt, pepper, garlic powder and tarragon. Pour over mushrooms, shrimp and cucumber; stir to mix well. Refrigerate covered several hours or overnight. Drain shrimp, mushrooms and cucumber. To make kebabs, thread a tomato, mushroom, shrimp, mushroom, cucumber, mushroom, shrimp, mushroom and tomato onto each of 12 skewers.

Total		Per Serving
1204.0	Calories	200.7
60.2	Carbohydrate (g)	10.0
138.8	Protein (g)	23.1
54.9	Total Fat (g)	9.2
7.0	Saturated Fat (g)	1.2
1020.0	Cholesterol (mg)	170.0
721.1	Sodium (mg)	120.2

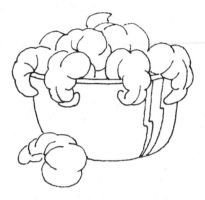

Cantonese Shrimp and Beans

Makes 6 servings

- 1 tbsp. safflower or corn oil
- 1/4 cup thinly sliced green onions
- 1 clove garlic, crushed
- 1 1/2 lb. raw, peeled, deveined shrimp, fresh or frozen, defrosted ● ■
- 1 cup chicken broth, canned or homemade ●
- 10-oz. package frozen cut green beans
- Salt ● and pepper to taste (optional)
- 1/2 tsp. ginger
- 1 tbsp. cornstarch
- 1 tbsp. cold water

● *HIGH SODIUM ALERT—Substitute unsalted water-packed tuna for shrimp. Use unsalted broth. Omit added salt.*

■ *HIGH CHOLESTEROL ALERT—Substitute water-packed tuna for shrimp.*

Spray large nonstick skillet with cooking spray. Heat oil in skillet over moderate heat; add onions, garlic and shrimp. Cook for 3 minutes, stirring frequently; if food sticks to skillet, add a little of the broth. Stir in green beans, chicken broth, salt, pepper and ginger. Simmer covered 5 to 7 minutes, or until beans are crisp-tender. Combine cornstarch and water; stir into shrimp mixture. Cook, stirring constantly, until liquid becomes thick and clear.

Total		Per Serving
875.9	Calories	146.0
38.4	Carbohydrate (g)	6.4
128.4	Protein (g)	21.4
19.7	Total Fat (g)	3.3
2.0	Saturated Fat (g)	0.3
1038.0	Cholesterol (mg)	173.0
1679.2	Sodium (mg)	279.9

Alert Symbols: ● Sodium   ■ Cholesterol   ▲ Sugar

Oven "French Fried" Scallops

Makes 4 servings

- 1 lb. scallops, fresh or frozen, defrosted ●
- 1/2 cup low-calorie French salad dressing ●
- 1/2 cup bread crumbs ●
  Paprika
  Lemon wedges or dill pickle relish ● (optional)

● *HIGH SODIUM ALERT—Substitute 1 lb. fresh fish fillets, cut into bite-size chunks, for scallops. Use unsalted salad dressing and low-sodium bread crumbs. Omit pickle relish.*

Drain scallops and pat dry with a paper towel. Dip in dressing, then roll in bread crumbs. Sprinkle with paprika. For best results, refrigerate and allow to dry before baking. Spread scallops in single layer in nonstick baking pan or cookie sheet. Bake in a very hot preheated oven (500° or more) for 8 to 10 minutes, or until golden brown. Garnish with lemon wedges or well-drained dill pickle relish, if desired.

Total		Per Serving
687.0	Calories	171.8
71.8	Carbohydrate (g)	18.0
76.4	Protein (g)	19.1
9.0	Total Fat (g)	2.3
1.5	Saturated Fat (g)	0.4
161.5	Cholesterol (mg)	40.4
2591.0	Sodium (mg)	647.8

Key Lime Mullet

Makes 8 servings

- 2 lb. mullet fillets or other fish fillets, fresh or frozen, defrosted ●
- Salt ● and pepper to taste (optional)
- 1/4 cup lime juice
- 3 tbsp. diet margarine, melted ● ■
  Paprika
  Lime wedges (optional)

● *HIGH SODIUM ALERT—Use fresh fish. Omit added salt. Use unsalted margarine.*

■ *HIGH CHOLESTEROL ALERT—Use polyunsaturated margarine.*

Cut fillets into serving-size pieces. Place in a single layer in a shallow baking dish. Sprinkle with salt and pepper. Pour lime juice over fish and refrigerate, covered, for 30 minutes, turning once. Remove fish, reserving juice. Place fish on broiler pan sprayed with cooking spray. Combine reserved juice with margarine. Brush fish with juice mixture and sprinkle with paprika. Broil about 4 inches from heat source for 8 to 10 minutes or until fish flakes easily with a fork. Serve with lime wedges, if desired.

Total		Per Serving
1490.2	Calories	186.3
5.5	Carbohydrate (g)	0.7
178.0	Protein (g)	22.3
80.6	Total Fat (g)	10.1
23.6	Saturated Fat (g)	3.0
540.0	Cholesterol (mg)	67.5
1064.5	Sodium (mg)	133.1

Barbecued Sea Steaks

Makes 4 servings

- 1 lb. fresh or frozen, defrosted, cod or halibut steaks ●
- 6-oz. can tomato juice ●
- 2 tbsp. lemon juice
- 1 tsp. Worcestershire sauce ●
- 1 tsp. instant minced onion
  Salt ● and pepper to taste (optional)
- 1/4 tsp. sugar ▲ (optional)
- 1/4 tsp. grated lemon rind
- 1/8 tsp. dried oregano
  Few drops liquid smoke seasoning (optional)
  Few drops red pepper sauce (optional)

● *HIGH SODIUM ALERT—Use fresh fish. Use unsalted tomato juice. Omit added salt and Worcestershire.*

▲ *HIGH SUGAR ALERT—Omit added sugar.*

Cut cod into 4 serving pieces. Combine remaining ingredients in small saucepan; heat to boiling. Reduce heat; simmer, uncovered, for 5 minutes. Place fish 4 inches above medium coals; grill about 7 minutes. Turn; brush with sauce. Grill 7 minutes longer, or until fish flakes easily with fork, brushing occasionally with more sauce.

Total		Per Serving
400.8	Calories	100.2
12.0	Carbohydrate (g)	3.0
81.6	Protein (g)	20.4
1.4	Total Fat (g)	0.4
0.5	Saturated Fat (g)	0.1
227.0	Cholesterol (mg)	56.8
740.0	Sodium (mg)	185.0

Skillet Fillet of Sole à la Bonne Femme

Makes 4 servings

- 1/2 cup dry sherry
- 1 tbsp. diet margarine ● ■
- 1/4 lb. sliced fresh mushrooms
- 1 bay leaf
- 2 tbsp. minced onion
- 1 lb. sole fillets, fresh or frozen, defrosted ●
  Salt ● and pepper to taste (optional)

1 tsp. = 5 mL   1 tbsp. = 15 mL   1 cup = 250 mL   1 oz. = 30 g

½ cup skim milk
1 tbsp. instant-blend flour
Paprika
2 tbsp. chopped parsley

● *HIGH SODIUM ALERT—Use fresh fish and unsalted margarine. Omit added salt.*

■ *HIGH CHOLESTEROL ALERT—Use polyunsaturated margarine.*

Spray a large nonstick skillet with cooking spray. Add 2 tablespoons sherry, the margarine and mushrooms. Cook and stir until liquid evaporates and mushrooms are lightly browned. Remove from skillet and set aside. Pour remaining sherry into the skillet. Add bay leaf and minced onion. Cut fillets into serving-size pieces. Add fillets in a single layer to skillet. Sprinkle with salt and pepper. Cover and simmer over very low heat about 8 to 10 minutes or just until fish is opaque and flakes easily with fork. Carefully remove fish to a warm platter.

Stir milk and flour together; stir into simmering poaching liquid in skillet. Cook and stir over moderate heat until the sauce is thick and bubbling. Spoon over the fish fillets; top with browned mushrooms and sprinkle with paprika and parsley.

Total		Per Serving
690.1	Calories	172.5
28.7	Carbohydrate (g)	7.2
84.7	Protein (g)	21.2
10.0	Total Fat (g)	2.5
2.2	Saturated Fat (g)	0.6
229.5	Cholesterol (mg)	57.4
554.7	Sodium (mg)	138.7

Tunaburgers

Makes 4 servings
2 cans (7 oz. each) water-packed tuna, drained, flaked ●
2 eggs, beaten ■
2 tbsp. grated extra-sharp Romano or Cheddar cheese ● ■
1 tbsp. chopped parsley
1 clove garlic, minced
Salt ● and pepper to taste (optional)
1 tbsp. safflower or corn oil
¼ cup fine dry bread crumbs ●
Lemon wedges (optional)

● *HIGH SODIUM ALERT—Use unsalted tuna, low-sodium cheese and low-sodium bread crumbs. Omit added salt.*

■ *HIGH CHOLESTEROL ALERT—Substitute 4 egg whites or ½ cup liquid egg substitute for eggs. Use low-fat cheese or omit.*

Combine tuna, eggs, cheese, parsley, garlic, salt and pepper; mix well. Shape mixture into 4 patties. Brush lightly with oil and roll in bread crumbs. Broil about 4 minutes on each side, until well-browned. Serve with lemon wedges, if desired.

Total		Per Serving
943.8	Calories	236.0
19.8	Carbohydrate (g)	5.0
131.5	Protein (g)	32.9
34.5	Total Fat (g)	8.6
7.8	Saturated Fat (g)	2.0
769.9	Cholesterol (mg)	192.5
3922.3	Sodium (mg)	980.6

Quick and Easy Yellow Perch

Makes 8 servings
2 lb. yellow perch fillets or other fish fillets, fresh or frozen, defrosted ●
2 tbsp. safflower or corn oil
2 tbsp. lemon juice
2 tbsp. chopped parsley
Salt ● and pepper to taste (optional)
Paprika
Lemon wedges (optional)

● *HIGH SODIUM ALERT—Use fresh fish. Omit added salt.*

Cut fillets into serving-size pieces. Place fish in single layer on a broil-and-serve platter sprayed with cooking spray. Combine oil, lemon juice, parsley, salt and pepper; pour over fillets and refrigerate covered for 30 minutes. Broil about 4 inches from heat for 8 to 10 minutes or until fish flakes easily with a fork.

Sprinkle with paprika. Serve with lemon wedges, if desired.

Total		Per Serving
1087.5	Calories	135.9
3.1	Carbohydrate (g)	0.4
177.3	Protein (g)	22.2
36.2	Total Fat (g)	4.5
4.7	Saturated Fat (g)	0.6
544.0	Cholesterol (mg)	68.0
620.2	Sodium (mg)	77.5

Succulent Sea Bass

Makes 8 servings
2 lb. sea bass fillets or other fish fillets, fresh or frozen, defrosted ●
½ cup unsweetened pineapple juice
¼ cup steak sauce ●
Salt ● and pepper to taste (optional)

● *HIGH SODIUM ALERT—Use fresh fish. Omit steak sauce and added salt.*

Cut fillets into serving-size pieces. Place fish in single layer in shallow baking dish. Combine remaining ingredients and pour over fish. Refrigerate covered for 30 minutes, turning once. Remove fish, reserving marinade for basting. Place fish on a broiler pan sprayed with cooking spray. Broil about 4 inches from heat source for 4 to 6 minutes. Turn carefully and brush with reserved marinade. Broil 4 to 6 minutes longer or until fish flakes easily with a fork.

Total		Per Serving
959.5	Calories	119.9
27.8	Carbohydrate (g)	3.5
174.7	Protein (g)	21.8
10.8	Total Fat (g)	1.4
3.7	Saturated Fat (g)	0.5
498.0	Cholesterol (mg)	62.3
1716.0	Sodium (mg)	214.5

Alert Symbols: ● Sodium   ■ Cholesterol   ▲ Sugar

The Secrets Of Sauces

Apple Basting Sauce

Makes 1 cup

¹/₂ cup unsweetened applesauce
¹/₂ cup dry white wine.

Combine thoroughly. (Use as a baste for meat during roasting.)

Total		Per Tablespoon
150.0	Calories	9.4
18.0	Carbohydrate (g)	1.1
0.3	Protein (g)	0.1
0.3	Total Fat (g)	0.1
0.0	Saturated Fat (g)	0.0
0.0	Cholesterol (mg)	0.0
6.5	Sodium (mg)	0.4

Oriental Marinade •

Makes about 1 ¹/₃ cups

¹/₂ cup sake wine or dry sherry
¹/₂ cup water
¹/₃ cup soy sauce
1 tsp. ground ginger
1 tsp. garlic powder

● *HIGH SODIUM ALERT—Not recommended for low-sodium diets.*

Combine all ingredients thoroughly. (Use as a marinade or basting sauce for meat, poultry or fish.)

Total		Per Tablespoon
217.3	Calories	10.3
14.5	Carbohydrate (g)	0.7
5.3	Protein (g)	0.3
0.0	Total Fat (g)	0.0
0.0	Saturated Fat (g)	0.0
0.0	Cholesterol (mg)	0.0
5865.3	Sodium (mg)	279.3

Orange Marinade

Makes about 1 cup

¹/₂ cup dry white wine
¹/₂ cup unsweetened orange juice
2 tbsp. soy sauce ●

● *HIGH SODIUM ALERT—Omit soy sauce.*

Combine all ingredients thoroughly. (Use as a marinade or barbecue baste for poultry or seafood.)

Total		Per Tablespoon
180.0	Calories	11.3
19.8	Carbohydrate (g)	1.2
3.0	Protein (g)	0.2
0.2	Total Fat (g)	0.0
0.0	Saturated Fat (g)	0.0
0.0	Cholesterol (g)	0.0
2203.0	Sodium (mg)	137.7

1 tsp. = 5 mL   1 tbsp. = 15 mL   1 cup = 250 mL   1 oz. = 30 g

Dieter's Duck Sauce for Broiled Chicken

Makes 1 cup

1½ cups canned apricot or peach nectar ▲
2 tsp. cider vinegar
2 tsp. catsup ● ▲
2 tsp. soy sauce ●

●*HIGH SODIUM ALERT—Use unsalted catsup. Omit soy sauce.*

▲*HIGH SUGAR ALERT—Use sugar-free nectar. Substitute tomato paste for catsup or use sugarless catsup.*

Combine all ingredients thoroughly in saucepan. Simmer uncovered until thick. (Use as a baste or as a sauce when serving.)

Total		Per Tablespoon
231.9	Calories	14.5
59.0	Carbohydrate (g)	3.7
1.9	Protein (g)	0.1
0.4	Total Fat (g)	0.1
0.0	Saturated Fat (g)	0.0
0.0	Cholesterol (mg)	0.0
836.7	Sodium (mg)	52.3

Mock Sour Cream Dressing

Makes 1½ cups

1 cup uncreamed small-curd cottage cheese ●
½ cup plain low-fat yogurt
2 tbsp. lemon juice
Salt ● and pepper to taste (optional)

●*HIGH SODIUM ALERT—Use unsalted cottage cheese. Omit added salt.*

Combine all ingredients in blender; cover; blend until smooth. (Serve with baked potato or as a base for dips.)

Total		Per Tablespoon
193.0	Calories	8.0
11.7	Carbohydrate (g)	0.5
29.1	Protein (g)	1.2
2.6	Total Fat (g)	0.1
1.4	Saturated Fat (g)	0.1
20.0	Cholesterol (mg)	0.8
483.7	Sodium (mg)	20.2

Low-Calorie Cream Sauce

Makes 1⅓ cups

13-oz. can evaporated skim milk
¼ cup instant-blend flour
1 tsp. chopped parsley
Pinch nutmeg
Pinch white pepper
Butter-flavored salt to taste ● (optional)

●*HIGH SODIUM ALERT—Substitute liquid butter flavoring to taste or omit.*

Combine milk and flour in nonstick saucepan. Cook and stir over very low heat until sauce begins to bubble; simmer 2 minutes. Stir in remaining ingredients. (Increase or decrease amount of flour for thicker or thinner sauce.)

Total		Per ⅓ Cup
450.5	Calories	112.6
71.6	Carbohydrate (g)	17.9
32.9	Protein (g)	8.2
0.4	Total Fat (g)	0.1
0.0	Saturated Fat (g)	0.0
0.0	Cholesterol (mg)	0.0
281.5	Sodium (mg)	70.4

Creole Sauce I

Makes 2 cups

1½ cups canned tomatoes, undrained, well broken up ●
8-oz. can sliced mushrooms, undrained ●
1 green pepper, thinly sliced
1 onion, thinly sliced
1 tbsp. flour
1 cup fat-skimmed beef or chicken broth, canned or homemade ●
Dash red pepper sauce (optional)

●*HIGH SODIUM ALERT—Use unsalted tomatoes, mushrooms and broth.*

Combine tomatoes, mushrooms, green pepper and onion in saucepan. Simmer 10 minutes. Mix flour with beef broth; stir into saucepan. Cook and stir until thick. Season with red pepper sauce.

Total		Per ¼ Cup
231.0	Calories	28.9
44.0	Carbohydrate (g)	5.5
17.3	Protein (g)	2.2
0.9	Total Fat (g)	0.1
0.0	Saturated Fat (g)	0.0
24.0	Cholesterol (mg)	3.0
2248.7	Sodium (mg)	281.1

Creole Sauce II

Makes 1½ cups

⅓ cup chopped green pepper
¼ cup chopped onion
1 small clove garlic, minced
⅛ tsp. thyme leaves, crumbled
¼ cup water
10¾-oz. can condensed tomato soup ●

●*HIGH SODIUM ALERT—Use unsalted soup.*

Cook green pepper, onion, garlic and thyme in water in saucepan until tender. Stir in soup. Cook and stir until heated through. (Serve over omelets, cooked shrimp, baked or broiled fish.)

Total		Per ¼ Cup
251.2	Calories	42.0
45.7	Carbohydrate (g)	7.6
6.3	Protein (g)	1.1
6.5	Total Fat (g)	1.1
0.0	Saturated Fat (g)	0.0
0.0	Cholesterol (mg)	0.0
2427.9	Sodium (mg)	404.7

Savory Barbecue Sauce

Makes 3 cups

1 medium onion, minced
1 small green pepper, minced
8-oz. can plain tomato sauce (check label for no added oil) ●
1 cup water
¾ cup unsweetened pineapple juice
½ cup chili sauce ● ▲
2 tbsp. prepared mustard ●
1 tsp. Worcestershire sauce ●
1 tsp. salt ●
Dash red pepper sauce

●*HIGH SODIUM ALERT—Substitute dry mustard to taste for prepared mustard. Use unsalted tomato sauce; also, substitute unsalted tomato sauce and chili powder to taste for chili sauce. Omit Worcestershire and added salt.*

▲*HIGH SUGAR ALERT—Use sugarless chili sauce.*

Combine all ingredients in saucepan. Simmer 20 minutes. (Use as sauce or baste for meat or poultry.)

Total		Per ¼ Cup
395.4	Calories	33.0
92.5	Carbohydrate (g)	7.7
12.5	Protein (g)	1.1
2.9	Total Fat (g)	0.3
0.0	Saturated Fat (g)	0.0
0.0	Cholesterol (mg)	0.0
5954.4	Sodium (mg)	496.2

Alert Symbols: ● Sodium ■ Cholesterol ▲ Sugar

Seasoned Lemon Butter for Seafood

Makes 4 servings
- 1 tbsp. butter or margarine ● ■
- Juice and grated rind of 2 fresh lemons
- 1/2 cup canned clam broth or seafood poaching liquid, strained ●
- 1 tbsp. finely chopped green onion
- 1/2 tsp. butter-flavored salt ●
- 1/8 tsp. pepper

● *HIGH SODIUM ALERT—Use unsalted butter or margarine and unsalted clam broth or poaching liquid. Omit butter-flavored salt.*

■ *HIGH CHOLESTEROL ALERT—Use polyunsaturated margarine.*

Melt butter in small saucepan. Add remaining ingredients; heat uncovered. (Use as a dipping sauce for lobster, serve over broiled or poached fish, or use as a basting sauce for broiled or grilled fish.)

Total		Per Serving
159.2	Calories	39.8
12.5	Carbohydrate (g)	3.1
3.3	Protein (g)	0.8
11.5	Total Fat (g)	2.9
6.4	Saturated Fat (g)	1.6
45.7	Cholesterol (mg)	11.4
1557.7	Sodium (mg)	389.4

Seafood Sauces

Cucumber Sauce

Makes 1 cup
- 1 cup finely diced cucumber
- 1 onion, chopped
- 1/4 cup low-calorie low-fat mayonnaise ●
- 1/4 cup plain low-fat yogurt
- 1/2 tsp. celery seeds

● *HIGH SODIUM ALERT—Use unsalted mayonnaise.*

Combine all ingredients thoroughly.

Total		Per Tablespoon
171.2	Calories	10.7
21.8	Carbohydrate (g)	1.4
4.9	Protein (g)	0.3
9.1	Total Fat (g)	0.6
0.5	Saturated Fat (g)	0.1
37.0	Cholesterol (mg)	2.3
127.2	Sodium (mg)	8.0

Slim Seafood Sauce

Makes 1 1/4 cups
- 1 cup canned condensed tomato soup ●
- 2 tbsp. lemon juice
- 2 tbsp. minced onion (or 2 tsp. dried)
- 2 tsp. prepared horseradish

● *HIGH SODIUM ALERT—Use unsalted soup.*

Combine all ingredients thoroughly and chill. (Use for dipping chilled seafood.)

Total		Per Tablespoon
199.5	Calories	10.0
36.8	Carbohydrate (g)	1.8
4.5	Protein (g)	0.2
5.3	Total Fat (g)	0.3
0.0	Saturated Fat (g)	0.0
0.0	Cholesterol (mg)	0.0
1991.5	Sodium (mg)	99.6

Dill Sauce

Makes 3/4 cup
- 1/4 cup plain low-fat yogurt
- 2 tbsp. fresh dillweed, minced
- 1/2 cup low-calorie low-fat mayonnaise ●

● *HIGH SODIUM ALERT—Use unsalted mayonnaise.*

Combine all ingredients thoroughly.

Total		Per Tablespoon
191.2	Calories	15.9
11.2	Carbohydrate (g)	0.9
2.0	Protein (g)	0.2
17.0	Total Fat (g)	1.4
0.5	Saturated Fat (g)	0.1
69.0	Cholesterol (mg)	5.8
183.2	Sodium (mg)	15.3

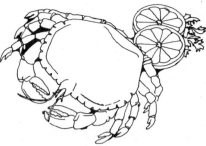

Chili Cocktail Sauce

Makes 3/4 cup
- 1/2 cup chili sauce ● ▲
- 1 tbsp. prepared horseradish
- 1 tbsp. lemon juice
- 1 tbsp. Worcestershire sauce ●
- 1 tsp. minced onion
- 1/4 tsp. salt ● (optional)

● *HIGH SODIUM ALERT—Substitute unsalted tomato sauce and chili powder to taste for chili sauce. Omit Worcestershire and added salt.*

▲ *HIGH SUGAR ALERT—Use sugarless chili sauce.*

Mix all ingredients well, and chill thoroughly. (This is a highly flavored sauce for shellfish or vegetables served as appetizers or hors d'oeuvres.)

Total		Per Tablespoon
158.3	Calories	13.2
39.8	Carbohydrate (g)	3.3
3.8	Protein (g)	0.3
0.5	Total Fat (g)	0.1
0.0	Saturated Fat (g)	0.0
0.0	Cholesterol (mg)	0.0
2010.1	Sodium (mg)	167.5

Lemon Cocktail Sauce

Makes 3/4 cup
- 2/3 cup low-calorie low-fat mayonnaise ●
- 1 tbsp. minced chives
- 1 tbsp. prepared horseradish
- 1 tbsp. prepared mustard ●
- 2 tbsp. lemon juice

● *HIGH SODIUM ALERT—Use unsalted mayonnaise. Substitute dry mustard to taste for prepared mustard.*

Combine all ingredients thoroughly.

Total		Per Tablespoon
238.8	Calories	19.9
15.4	Carbohydrate (g)	1.3
1.2	Protein (g)	0.1
22.3	Total Fat (g)	1.9
0.0	Saturated Fat (g)	0.0
85.3	Cholesterol (mg)	7.1
404.9	Sodium (mg)	33.7

1 tsp. = 5 mL   1 tbsp. = 15 mL   1 cup = 250 mL   1 oz. = 30 g

Vegetables For All Seasons

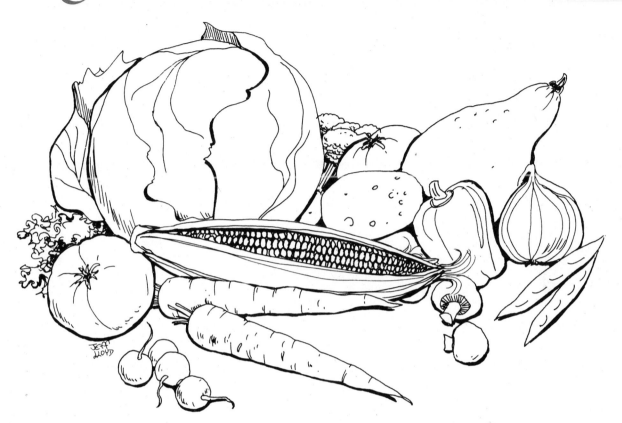

Italian Green Beans

Makes 3 servings

10-oz. package frozen Italian or whole green beans, defrosted
6-oz. can (3/4 cup) tomato juice ●
2 tbsp. chopped onion or 2 tsp. instant minced onion
1 tsp. dried oregano
Salt ● and pepper to taste (optional)
1 tbsp. grated extra-sharp Romano cheese ● ■

● *HIGH SODIUM ALERT—Use unsalted tomato. Use low-sodium cheese. Omit added salt.*

■ *HIGH CHOLESTEROL ALERT—Use low-fat cheese, or omit.*

Combine all ingredients except cheese in small nonstick skillet or saucepan. Simmer covered 3 minutes. Uncover and continue to simmer until most of the liquid has evaporated. Sprinkle with cheese.

Hint: For Greek Green Beans, substitute dried mint for the oregano and crumbled feta cheese for the Romano in the ingredients listed above.

Total		Per Serving
140.6	Calories	46.9
26.8	Carbohydrate (g)	8.9
8.8	Protein (g)	2.9
2.1	Total Fat (g)	0.7
1.3	Saturated Fat (g)	0.4
6.4	Cholesterol (mg)	2.1
442.6	Sodium (mg)	147.5

Green Beans and Bacon Canadian-Style ●

Makes 6 servings

2-oz. Canadian bacon, diced
1 lb. fresh green beans, diagonally sliced
1 small onion, thinly sliced
1/4 cup water
Salt and pepper to taste (optional)

● *HIGH SODIUM ALERT—Not recommended for low-sodium diets.*

Spray nonstick saucepan with cooking spray. Fry bacon in saucepan over moderate heat, stirring constantly, until lightly browned. Remove from saucepan; blot; reserve. Combine green beans, onion, and water in the saucepan. Cook covered 12 minutes, or until beans are crisp-tender. Drain liquid from saucepan; sprinkle beans with salt and pepper. Add reserved bacon; cook and stir over moderate heat until heated through.

Total		Per Serving
331.6	Calories	55.3
39.9	Carbohydrate (g)	6.7
25.5	Protein (g)	4.3
10.9	Total Fat (g)	1.8
3.0	Saturated Fat (g)	0.5
47.2	Cholesterol (mg)	7.9
1488.2	Sodium (mg)	248.0

Alert Symbols: ● Sodium   ■ Cholesterol   ▲ Sugar

Skillet Green Beans Amandine

Makes 3 servings

- 1 tbsp. slivered blanched almonds
- 1 lb. fresh green beans or 10-oz. package frozen whole green beans, defrosted
- 1/4 cup fat-skimmed chicken broth, canned or homemade ●
- Salt ● and pepper to taste (optional)

● *HIGH SODIUM ALERT—Use unsalted broth. Omit added salt.*

Spread almonds in nonstick skillet. Shake skillet gently over moderate heat until almonds are toasted. Remove almonds; reserve. Combine green beans and chicken broth in the skillet. Simmer uncovered until most of the liquid has evaporated and beans are crisp-tender. Sprinkle with reserved almonds, the salt and pepper.

Total		Per Serving
223.5	Calories	74.5
34.1	Carbohydrate (g)	11.4
10.7	Protein (g)	3.6
4.8	Total Fat (g)	1.6
0.4	Saturated Fat (g)	0.1
3.5	Cholesterol (mg)	1.2
212.8	Sodium (mg)	70.9

German Sweet-and-Sour Green Beans●

Makes 4 servings

- 1 oz. Canadian bacon, diced
- 1/3 cup chopped onion
- 2 tbsp. vinegar
- 1 tbsp. flour
- 2 tsp. sugar ▲
- 16-oz. can French-style green beans, drained, 1/3 cup liquid reserved

● *HIGH SODIUM ALERT—Not recommended for low-sodium diets.*

▲ *HIGH SUGAR ALERT—Use sugar substitute.*

Spray nonstick saucepan with cooking spray. Fry bacon in saucepan until crisp. Add onion; cook 2 minutes. Combine vinegar, flour, sugar and reserved bean liquid; stir into saucepan. Cook and stir until thickened. Stir in beans and heat through.

Total		Per Serving
231.4	Calories	57.9
36.4	Carbohydrate (g)	9.1
13.4	Protein (g)	3.4
5.7	Total Fat (g)	1.4
1.5	Saturated Fat (g)	0.4
23.6	Cholesterol (mg)	5.9
1526.5	Sodium (mg)	381.6

Quickie Green Beans with Mushrooms

Makes 4 servings

- 1 tbsp. diet margarine ● ■
- 2-oz. can sliced mushrooms, drained ●
- 16-oz. can green beans, undrained ●

● *HIGH SODIUM ALERT—Use unsalted margarine and vegetables.*

■ *HIGH CHOLESTEROL ALERT—Use polyunsaturated margarine.*

Melt margarine in nonstick saucepan or small skillet. Add mushrooms; brown lightly, stirring occasionally with wooden spoon. Add the green beans (including liquid). Heat to boiling; cook uncovered until most of the liquid has evaporated.

Total		Per Serving
142.0	Calories	35.5
20.6	Carbohydrate (g)	5.1
5.7	Protein (g)	1.4
6.5	Total Fat (g)	1.6
1.0	Saturated Fat (g)	0.2
0.0	Cholesterol (mg)	0.0
1424.0	Sodium (mg)	356.0

Saucy Green Beans●

Makes 3 servings

- 10-oz. package frozen French-cut green beans
- 1/3 cup water
- 1 tbsp. instant cream of mushroom soup powder from single-serving packet

● *HIGH SODIUM ALERT—Not recommended for low-sodium diets.*

Combine green beans and water in saucepan; cook covered until tender. Stir soup powder into saucepan. Cook and stir until sauce thickens.

Total		Per Serving
154.0	Calories	51.3
26.0	Carbohydrate (g)	8.7
5.8	Protein (g)	1.9
4.3	Total Fat (g)	1.4
2.6	Saturated Fat (g)	0.9
5.0	Cholesterol (mg)	1.7
1021.0	Sodium (mg)	340.0

1 tsp. = 5 mL   1 tbsp. = 15 mL   1 cup = 250 mL   1 oz. = 30 g

Cider-Pickled Green Beans

Makes 6 servings

1 lb. sliced fresh green beans
1 small onion, sliced, separated into rings
½ cup defrosted undiluted frozen unsweetened apple juice or cider concentrate
½ cup cider vinegar
½ cup boiling water
1½ tsp. salt ● (optional)
1 tsp. celery seed
¼ tsp. dill seed
Pinch ground turmeric

● *HIGH SODIUM ALERT—Omit added salt.*

Combine all ingredients in non-aluminum saucepan; simmer until beans are just tender. Cool. Refrigerate covered at least 12 hours before serving.

Total		Per Serving
407.0	Calories	67.8
104.2	Carbohydrate (g)	17.4
9.7	Protein (g)	1.6
0.0	Total Fat (g)	0.0
0.0	Saturated Fat (g)	0.0
0.0	Cholesterol (mg)	0.0
39.0	Sodium (mg)	6.5

Pickled Beets●

Makes 4 servings

16-oz. can sliced beets, undrained
1 cup apple cider
½ cup cider vinegar
½ cup sliced onion
1 tbsp. mixed pickling spice
Salt and freshly ground pepper to taste (optional)

●*HIGH SODIUM ALERT—Not recommended for low-sodium diets.*

Combine all ingredients in saucepan and heat to boiling. Cool to room temperature. Chill covered several hours before serving.

Total		Per Serving
300.0	Calories	75.0
74.8	Carbohydrate (g)	18.7
4.9	Protein (g)	1.2
0.5	Total Fat (g)	0.1
0.0	Saturated Fat (g)	0.0
0.0	Cholesterol (mg)	0.0
1078.0	Sodium (mg)	269.5

Honeyed Beets●

Makes 4 servings

¼ cup unsweetened apple juice
2 tbsp. cider vinegar
1 tbsp. honey ▲
2 tsp. cornstarch or arrowroot
2 cans (8 oz. each) sliced beets, drained
Salt and pepper to taste (optional)

● *HIGH SODIUM ALERT—Not recommended for low-sodium diets.*

▲ *HIGH SUGAR ALERT—Substitute sugar substitute for honey.*

Combine apple juice, vinegar, honey and cornstarch in nonstick saucepan. Cook, stirring occasionally, over moderate heat until simmering. Stir in beets, salt and pepper. Simmer 3 minutes.

Total		Per Serving
225.3	Calories	56.3
57.1	Carbohydrate (g)	14.3
2.9	Protein (g)	0.7
0.3	Total Fat (g)	0.1
0.0	Saturated Fat (g)	0.0
0.0	Cholesterol (mg)	0.0
695.5	Sodium (mg)	173.9

Broccoli in Mock Butter Sauce

Makes 6 servings

10-oz. package frozen broccoli spears
½ cup boiling water
1 tsp. cornstarch or arrowroot
1 tsp. butter-flavored salt ●
2 tbsp. cold water

● *HIGH SODIUM ALERT—Substitute ¼ tsp. liquid butter flavoring for salt.*

Cook broccoli in the boiling water in saucepan 5 minutes, or until just tender. Drain broccoli, reserving cooking liquid. Combine cornstarch, salt and the cold water. Stir cornstarch mixture into cooking liquid; simmer until sauce thickens and bubbles. Pour over broccoli.

Total		Per Serving
93.7	Calories	31.2
17.1	Carbohydrate (g)	5.7
9.1	Protein (g)	3.?
0.9	Total Fat (g)	0.3
0.0	Saturated Fat (g)	0.0
0.0	Cholesterol (mg)	0.0
1955.0	Sodium (mg)	651.7

Alert Symbols: ● Sodium   ■ Cholesterol   ▲ Sugar

Broccoli or Spinach Supreme

Makes 3 servings

10-oz. package frozen chopped broccoli or spinach ●
1/2 cup fat-skimmed chicken broth, canned or homemade ●
3 tbsp. low-calorie low-fat mayonnaise ●
2 tsp. instant minced onion (optional)

● *HIGH SODIUM ALERT—Use broccoli, not spinach. Use unsalted broth and mayonnaise.*

Place vegetables in saucepan. Stir remaining ingredients together; add to vegetables. Simmer covered, stirring occasionally, until vegetables are defrosted. Uncover and continue to simmer, stirring occasionally, until most of the liquid has evaporated.

Total		Per Serving
153.0	Calories	51.0
18.8	Carbohydrate (g)	6.3
10.6	Protein (g)	3.5
6.9	Total Fat (g)	2.3
0.0	Saturated Fat (g)	0.0
31.0	Cholesterol (mg)	10.3
466.0	Sodium (mg)	155.3

Brussels Sprouts in Orange Sauce

Makes 6 servings

4 cups fresh Brussels sprouts
6-oz. can unsweetened orange juice
1/2 cup water
1/2 tsp. cornstarch or arrowroot
1/4 tsp. cinnamon
Salt ● and pepper to taste (optional)

● *HIGH SODIUM ALERT—Omit added salt.*

Combine all ingredients in saucepan. Simmer covered 6 to 7 minutes until sprouts are nearly tender. Uncover and continue to simmer, stirring occasionally, until most of the liquid has evaporated.

Total		Per Serving
405.7	Calories	67.6
79.7	Carbohydrate (g)	13.3
34.8	Protein (g)	5.8
2.7	Total Fat (g)	0.5
0.0	Saturated Fat (g)	0.0
0.0	Cholesterol (mg)	0.0
97.5	Sodium (mg)	16.3

Dilled Brussels Sprouts

Makes 3 servings

10-oz. package frozen or 1 pint fresh Brussels sprouts
1/2 cup fat-skimmed beef broth, canned or homemade ●
1 tsp. dill seed
1 tsp. instant minced onion (optional)
Salt ● and pepper to taste (optional)

● *HIGH SODIUM ALERT—Use unsalted broth. Omit added salt.*

Combine all ingredients in saucepan; simmer covered 8 to 10 minutes, or until sprouts are nearly tender. Uncover and continue to simmer until most of the liquid has evaporated.

Total		Per Serving
117.0	Calories	39.0
22.2	Carbohydrate (g)	7.4
11.9	Protein (g)	4.0
0.6	Total Fat (g)	0.2
0.0	Saturated Fat (g)	0.0
12.0	Cholesterol (mg)	4.0
436.0	Sodium (mg)	145.3

Red Cabbage with Apples

Makes 8 servings

1 small head red cabbage (about 1 lb.), shredded
2 large apples, pared, thinly sliced
1/2 cup unsweetened apple juice
1/4 cup lemon juice
1 onion, sliced
2 tbsp. raisins
2 tbsp. brown sugar ▲
Salt ● and pepper to taste (optional)

● *HIGH SODIUM ALERT—Omit added salt.*

▲ *HIGH SUGAR ALERT—Omit sugar, or stir in liquid sugar substitute just before serving.*

Toss all ingredients together in nonstick saucepan. Simmer covered 30 minutes.

Total		Per Serving
624.5	Calories	78.0
157.6	Carbohydrate (g)	19.7
12.5	Protein (g)	1.6
2.1	Total Fat (g)	0.3
0.0	Saturated Fat (g)	0.0
0.0	Cholesterol (mg)	0.0
146.7	Sodium (mg)	18.3

Oriental Stir-Fried Bok Choy

Makes 6 servings

1 tbsp. safflower or corn oil
1 clove garlic, minced
1 large head bok choy (celery cabbage), cut into large chunks
1 tbsp. soy sauce ●
1 tbsp. dry white wine

● *HIGH SODIUM ALERT—Omit soy sauce.*

Heat oil in wok or large nonstick skillet. Sauté garlic until brown. Add the bok choy; sprinkle with soy sauce and wine. Cook and stir over high heat 1 minute. Serve immediately.

Total		Per Serving
261.0	Calories	43.5
22.9	Carbohydrate (g)	3.8
12.2	Protein (g)	2.0
15.4	Total Fat (g)	2.6
1.0	Saturated Fat (g)	0.2
0.0	Cholesterol (mg)	0.0
1277.5	Sodium (mg)	212.9

1 tsp. = 5 mL   1 tbsp. = 15 mL   1 cup = 250 mL   1 oz. = 30 g

Cabbage in Tomato-Pineapple Sauce

Makes 6 servings

2 cups plain tomato sauce (check label for no added oil) ●
1/2 cup juice-packed crushed pineapple
1/4 cup fat-skimmed beef broth, canned or homemade, ● or water
1 medium head cabbage (about 1 1/2 lb.)

● *HIGH SODIUM ALERT—Use unsalted tomato sauce. Use unsalted broth or the water.*

Combine tomato sauce, pineapple and beef broth in skillet. Cut cabbage into 8 wedges, attached to the core. Place wedges in skillet. Simmer covered 8 to 10 minutes, or until cabbage is crisp-tender. Don't overcook. Serve cabbage with the sauce.

Total		Per Serving
389.0	Calories	64.8
92.8	Carbohydrate (g)	15.5
17.3	Protein (g)	2.9
2.1	Total Fat (g)	0.3
0.0	Saturated Fat (g)	0.0
6.0	Cholesterol (mg)	1.0
3683.5	Sodium (mg)	613.9

Confetti Cabbage

Makes 4 servings

1 onion, chopped
1 tbsp. diet margarine ● ■
3 cups shredded cabbage

1 cup shredded carrots ●
1/2 cup water
1/2 tsp. dried oregano
1/8 tsp. garlic powder
Salt ● and pepper to taste (optional)

● *HIGH SODIUM ALERT—Use unsalted margarine. Substitute additional cabbage for carrots. Omit added salt.*

■ *HIGH CHOLESTEROL ALERT—Use polyunsaturated margarine.*

Sauté onion in margarine in large skillet until just transparent. Stir in remaining ingredients. Cook covered over moderate heat 5 minutes. Uncover and simmer until most of the liquid has evaporated.

Total		Per Serving
187.0	Calories	46.7
32.1	Carbohydrate (g)	8.0
5.9	Protein (g)	1.5
6.5	Total Fat (g)	1.6
1.0	Saturated Fat (g)	0.2
0.0	Cholesterol (mg)	0.0
215.0	Sodium (mg)	53.7

Hawaiian Carrots●

Makes 6 servings

2 cups fresh or frozen sliced carrots
1 cup fat-skimmed chicken broth, canned or homemade ●
1/4 cup minced onion
1/4 cup chopped green pepper
8-oz. can juice-packed pineapple chunks, drained, juice reserved
2 tsp. cornstarch or arrowroot
Salt and pepper to taste (optional)

● *HIGH SODIUM ALERT—Not recommended for low-sodium diets.*

Place carrots and chicken broth in saucepan; simmer covered 10 minutes, or until carrots are nearly tender. Add onion and green pepper. Cook uncovered 2 minutes.

Drain liquid from saucepan. Add pineapple. Cook 1 minute. Mix cornstarch with reserved pineapple juice until well blended; stir into simmering vegetables. Cook and stir until mixture simmers and thickens. Sprinkle with salt and pepper.

Total		Per Serving
307.7	Calories	51.3
70.6	Carbohydrate (g)	11.8
8.1	Protein (g)	1.3
1.7	Total Fat (g)	0.3
0.0	Saturated Fat (g)	0.0
14.0	Cholesterol (mg)	2.3
838.0	Sodium (mg)	139.7

Quick Maple "Candied" Carrots●

Makes 6 servings

16-oz. can sliced carrots, undrained
1 tbsp. maple syrup ▲
2 tsp. diet margarine ■
Dash lemon juice (optional)
Salt and pepper to taste (optional)

● *HIGH SODIUM ALERT—Not recommended for low-sodium diets.*

■ *HIGH CHOLESTEROL ALERT—Use polyunsaturated margarine.*

▲ *HIGH SUGAR ALERT—Use sugarless syrup substitute.*

Heat carrots in small saucepan; drain well. Stir in remaining ingredients; heat through.

Total		Per Serving
210.3	Calories	52.6
42.3	Carbohydrate (g)	10.6
2.7	Protein (g)	0.7
4.9	Total Fat (g)	1.2
0.7	Saturated Fat (g)	0.2
0.0	Cholesterol (mg)	0.0
1145.3	Sodium (mg)	286.4

Alert Symbols: ● Sodium ■ Cholesterol ▲ Sugar

Baked Corn on the Cob

Makes 4 servings

4 ears fresh or frozen corn
4 tsp. diet margarine ● ■
  Salt ● and coarsely ground pepper
    to taste (optional)

● *HIGH SODIUM ALERT—Use unsalted margarine. Omit added salt.*

■ *HIGH CHOLESTEROL ALERT—Use polyunsaturated margarine.*

Husk corn and rinse well (or defrost at room temperature, if using frozen corn). Place each ear on a sheet of heavy-duty foil, or use a double thickness of regular foil. Spread each ear with 1 tsp. margarine. Sprinkle with salt and pepper. Wrap each ear in foil and secure ends. Bake in a preheated 300° oven 15 to 20 minutes, or place on a rack in a covered grill and turn frequently. Unwrap after 15 minutes to check for doneness.

Total		Per Serving
346.5	Calories	86.6
64.0	Carbohydrate (g)	16.0
12.0	Protein (g) ^	3.0
12.0	Total Fat (g)	3.0
1.2	Saturated Fat (g)	0.3
0.0	Cholesterol (mg)	0.0
146.3	Sodium (mg)	36.6

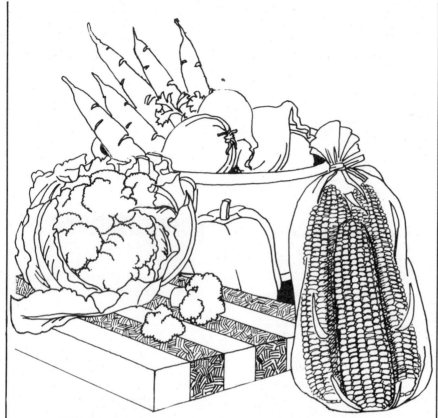

Sherried Carrots•

Makes 6 servings

1-lb. package frozen small whole
  carrots, defrosted
½ cup dry sherry
½ cup water
2 tbsp. diet margarine ■
  Salt and pepper to taste (optional)
1 tbsp. minced fresh parsley or 1
  tsp. parsley flakes

● *HIGH SODIUM ALERT—Not recommended for low-sodium diets.*

■ *HIGH CHOLESTEROL ALERT—Use polyunsaturated margarine.*

Combine all ingredients except parsley in shallow nonstick skillet. Simmer covered about 10 minutes, or until carrots are crisp-tender. Uncover and continue to simmer until liquid has evaporated into a glaze. Sprinkle with parsley and serve.

Total		Per Serving
457.0	Calories	76.2
53.5	Carbohydrate (g)	8.9
5.1	Protein (g)	0.8
12.9	Total Fat (g)	2.1
2.0	Saturated Fat (g)	0.3
0.0	Cholesterol (mg)	0.0
439.0	Sodium (mg)	73.2

Quick Creamed Cauliflower

Makes 3 servings

10-oz. package frozen cauliflower
½ cup fat-skimmed chicken broth,
  canned or homemade ●
½ cup evaporated skim milk
2 tbsp. instant-blend flour
  Salt ● and pepper to taste
    (optional)
  Paprika (optional)

● *HIGH SODIUM ALERT—Use unsalted broth. Omit added salt.*

Combine cauliflower and chicken broth in saucepan. Simmer covered 10 to 12 minutes, or until cauliflower is tender. Combine milk and flour; mix well. Stir into saucepan; cook and stir until sauce simmers and bubbles. Sprinkle with salt, pepper and paprika before serving.

Total		Per Serving
231.7	Calories	77.2
39.5	Carbohydrate (g)	13.2
18.1	Protein (g)	6.0
0.8	Total Fat (g)	0.3
0.0	Saturated Fat (g)	0.0
12.0	Cholesterol (mg)	4.0
532.4	Sodium (mg)	177.5

Creole Corn

Makes 8 servings

16-oz. can stewed tomatoes,
  undrained, broken up ●
1 small green pepper, chopped
1 onion, chopped
1 stalk celery, chopped ●
2 cups fresh or defrosted frozen
  kernel corn
  Salt ● and pepper to taste
    (optional)

● *HIGH SODIUM ALERT—Use unsalted tomatoes. Omit celery and added salt.*

Simmer tomatoes, green pepper, onion and celery in nonstick saucepan 20 minutes. Stir in corn, salt and pepper. Cook 5 minutes.

Total		Per Serving
473.2	Calories	59.1
108.4	Carbohydrate (g)	13.5
17.5	Protein (g)	2.2
4.4	Total Fat (g)	0.5
0.0	Saturated Fat (g)	0.0
0.0	Cholesterol (mg)	0.0
1596.4	Sodium (mg)	199.5

1 tsp. = 5 mL   1 tbsp. = 15 mL   1 cup = 250 mL   1 oz. = 30 g

Corn Pudding

Makes 8 servings

- 3 eggs ■
- 1½ cups skim milk
- 1 tbsp. cornstarch
- 1½ cups drained canned or defrosted frozen corn ●
- 1 tsp. salt ●
  Pinch black pepper
  Dash red pepper sauce or cayenne pepper
- 3 tbsp. bacon bits ● ■

● *HIGH SODIUM ALERT—Use frozen, not canned, corn. Omit added salt and bacon bits.*

■ *HIGH CHOLESTEROL ALERT—Substitute ¾ cup liquid egg substitute for eggs. Use imitation bacon bits.*

Beat eggs, milk and cornstarch together. Stir in corn, salt, black pepper and red pepper sauce. Pour into ovenproof baking dish. Sprinkle with bacon bits. Bake in a preheated 300° oven 50 to 60 minutes, or until set.

Total		Per Serving
702.5	Calories	87.8
75.1	Carbohydrate (g)	9.4
43.2	Protein (g)	5.4
28.0	Total Fat (g)	3.5
9.0	Saturated Fat (g)	1.1
776.5	Cholesterol (mg)	97.1
3242.0	Sodium (mg)	405.3

Oven-Fried Eggplant I

Makes 6 servings

- 1 medium eggplant (about 1 lb.), pared
  Cold water
- 3 tbsp. low-calorie low-fat mayonnaise ●
- 3 tbsp. water
- 6 tbsp. grated Parmesan cheese ● ■
- ¼ cup Italian-seasoned bread crumbs ●

● *HIGH SODIUM ALERT—Use unsalted mayonnaise, low-sodium cheese and low-sodium bread crumbs.*

■ *HIGH CHOLESTEROL ALERT—Use low-fat cheese.*

Cut eggplant into ½-inch thick slices. Soak slices in cold water to cover 15 to 20 minutes. Drain and blot dry. Fork-blend mayonnaise and 3 tablespoons water until smooth. Dip eggplant slices on both sides into mayonnaise mixture; press

lightly into cheese, then into bread crumbs, lightly coating both sides. Spray shallow nonstick baking pan with cooking spray. Arrange eggplant in single layer in pan. Bake in a preheated 475° oven 5 minutes. Turn slices over and bake 3 to 4 minutes, or until eggplant is golden and crisp on the outside, tender inside.

Total		Per Serving
391.7	Calories	65.3
42.2	Carbohydrate (g)	7.0
22.8	Protein (g)	3.8
16.4	Total Fat (g)	2.7
5.5	Saturated Fat (g)	0.9
51.5	Cholesterol (mg)	8.6
1278.2	Sodium (mg)	213.0

Oven-Fried Eggplant II

Makes 8 servings

- 1 large eggplant (about 1½ lb.), pared
  Cold water
- 2 tbsp. safflower or corn oil
- 2 tbsp. lemon juice
- ½ tsp. salt ●
- ½ cup Italian-seasoned bread crumbs ●

● *HIGH SODIUM ALERT—Omit added salt. Use low-sodium bread crumbs.*

Cut eggplant into ½-inch thick slices. Soak slices in cold water to cover 15 to 20 minutes. Drain and blot dry. Combine oil, lemon juice and salt in shallow dish. Dip eggplant slices on both sides into oil mixture, then into bread crumbs. Arrange eggplant in single layer on nonstick baking sheet sprayed with cooking spray. Bake in a preheated 400° oven 10 to 15 minutes, turning once.

Total		Per Serving
592.0	Calories	74.0
70.4	Carbohydrate (g)	8.8
14.8	Protein (g)	1.8
30.8	Total Fat (g)	3.8
2.0	Saturated Fat (g)	0.2
0.0	Cholesterol (mg)	0.0
2972.2	Sodium (mg)	371.5

Marinated Mushrooms

Makes 6 servings

- 1 lb. fresh mushrooms, sliced
- ¼ cup water
- ¼ cup fresh lemon juice
- 1 tbsp. safflower or corn oil
- 2 tsp. dried oregano
- 1 tsp. grated lemon rind
- 1 clove garlic, minced
  Salt ● and pepper to taste (optional)

● *HIGH SODIUM ALERT—Omit added salt.*

Combine all ingredients in glass bowl or plastic bag. Refrigerate covered, stirring occasionally, 8 hours or overnight. Drain mushrooms before serving.

Total		Per Serving
272.1	Calories	45.3
26.2	Carbohydrate (g)	4.4
12.6	Protein (g)	2.1
15.4	Total Fat (g)	2.6
1.0	Saturated Fat (g)	0.2
0.0	Cholesterol (mg)	0.0
69.6	Sodium (mg)	11.6

"Buttery" Spinach ●

Makes 2 servings

- 10-oz. package frozen leaf spinach, defrosted
- ¼ cup water
- ½ tsp. butter-flavored salt
  Pinch ground nutmeg or mace

● *HIGH SODIUM ALERT—Not recommended for low-sodium diets.*

Combine all ingredients in saucepan. Cook covered 3 minutes.

Total		Per Serving
69.0	Calories	34.5
11.9	Carbohydrate (g)	6.0
8.8	Protein (g)	4.4
0.9	Total Fat (g)	0.4
0.0	Saturated Fat (g)	0.0
0.0	Cholesterol (mg)	0.0
1110.0	Sodium (mg)	555.0

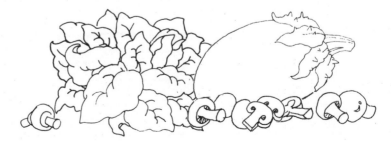

Alert Symbols: ● Sodium ■ Cholesterol ▲ Sugar

Mashed Squash

Makes 4 servings

- 1 medium acorn squash, halved, seeded
- 1 tbsp. maple syrup ▲
- ½ tsp. pumpkin pie spice
  Butter-flavored salt to taste ● (optional)
  Pepper to taste (optional)

● *HIGH SODIUM ALERT—Omit added salt.*

▲ *HIGH SUGAR ALERT—Use sugarless syrup substitute.*

Place squash halves cut sides down on baking sheet. Bake in a preheated 400° oven 30 minutes, or until tender. Scoop out squash into mixing bowl; beat with electric mixer. Stir in syrup, pumpkin pie spice, salt and pepper.

Total		Per Serving
244.0	Calories	61.0
62.0	Carbohydrate (g)	15.5
6.6	Protein (g)	1.6
0.4	Total Fat (g)	0.1
0.0	Saturated Fat (g)	0.0
0.0	Cholesterol (mg)	0.0
6.0	Sodium (mg)	1.6

Baked Tomatoes

Makes 6 servings

- 3 large tomatoes, cut crosswise into halves
- 3 tbsp. Italian-seasoned bread crumbs ●
- 2 tsp. olive oil ■
- 1 tsp. onion powder

● *HIGH SODIUM ALERT—Use low-sodium bread crumbs.*

■ *HIGH CHOLESTEROL ALERT—Substitute safflower or corn oil for olive oil.*

Place tomatoes cut-sides up on baking sheet. Combine remaining ingredients; sprinkle over tomato halves. Bake in a preheated 375° oven about 12 minutes, or until crumbs are golden.

Total		Per Serving
306.4	Calories	51.1
48.7	Carbohydrate (g)	8.1
10.5	Protein (g)	1.8
10.2	Total Fat (g)	1.7
1.3	Saturated Fat (g)	0.2
0.9	Cholesterol (mg)	0.1
596.4	Sodium (mg)	99.4

Sautéed Zucchini

Makes 3 servings

- 1 medium zucchini, sliced, or 10-oz. package frozen sliced zucchini, defrosted
- 1 tbsp. diet margarine ● ■
  Butter-flavored salt to taste ● (optional)
  Freshly ground pepper to taste (optional)
- 2 tsp. minced fresh parsley

● *HIGH SODIUM ALERT—Use unsalted margarine. Omit added salt.*

■ *HIGH CHOLESTEROL ALERT—Use polyunsaturated margarine.*

Arrange zucchini slices in single layer in small nonstick skillet or saucepan. Add margarine, salt and pepper. Simmer covered about 4 minutes, or until just tender. Uncover and continue to cook, stirring occasionally, until the liquid has evaporated and zucchini slices are evenly coated. Sprinkle with parsley before serving.

Total		Per Serving
99.4	Calories	33.1
10.3	Carbohydrate (g)	3.4
3.5	Protein (g)	1.2
6.3	Total Fat (g)	2.1
1.0	Saturated Fat (g)	0.3
0.0	Cholesterol (mg)	0.0
114.4	Sodium (mg)	38.1

Slow-Baked Italian Zucchini

Makes 12 servings

- 3 cups sliced zucchini
- 1 cup fat-skimmed chicken broth, canned or homemade ●
- 6-oz. can tomato paste
- 1 onion, chopped
- 1 tsp. dried oregano or mixed Italian seasoning
- 1 clove garlic, minced
- 2 tsp. Italian-seasoned bread crumbs ●
- 2 tbsp. grated extra-sharp Romano cheese ● ■ (optional)

● *HIGH SODIUM ALERT—Use unsalted broth and plain bread crumbs. Use low-sodium cheese, or omit.*

■ *HIGH CHOLESTEROL ALERT—Use low-fat cheese, or omit.*

Combine zucchini, broth, tomato paste, onion, oregano and garlic in casserole. Sprinkle with bread crumbs and cheese. Bake uncovered in a preheated 350° oven 2 hours.

Total		Per Serving
283.3	Calories	23.6
61.4	Carbohydrate (g)	5.1
15.4	Protein (g)	1.3
0.5	Total Fat (g)	0.0
0.0	Saturated Fat (g)	0.0
26.0	Cholesterol (mg)	2.2
830.7	Sodium (mg)	69.2

1 tsp. = 5 mL   1 tbsp. = 15 mL   1 cup = 250 mL   1 oz. = 30 g

Zucchini Piquant

Makes 4 servings

2 medium zucchini or yellow summer squash, sliced
1/2 cup low-calorie low-fat Russian or Thousand Island salad dressing ●
1/4 cup water
2 tsp. instant minced onion

● *HIGH SODIUM ALERT—Use unsalted dressing.*

Combine all ingredients in nonstick saucepan. Simmer uncovered, stirring occasionally, until most of the liquid has evaporated and zucchini slices are evenly coated. Serve hot.

Total		Per Serving
317.0	Calories	79.3
48.3	Carbohydrate (g)	12.1
5.4	Protein (g)	1.4
8.5	Total Fat (g)	2.1
0.0	Saturated Fat (g)	0.0
0.0	Cholesterol (mg)	0.0
1565.0	Sodium (mg)	391.3

Orange-Spiked Zucchini and Carrots•

Makes 7 servings

1 lb. zucchini, cut into 1/4-inch slices
10-oz. package frozen sliced carrots, defrosted
1 cup unsweetened orange juice
1 stalk celery, finely chopped
2 tbsp. chopped onion
Salt and pepper to taste (optional)

● *HIGH SODIUM ALERT—Not recommended for low-sodium diets.*

Combine all ingredients in nonstick saucepan. Simmer covered 10 to 12 minutes, or until zucchini is tender. Uncover and simmer until most of the liquid has evaporated.

Total		Per Serving
334.8	Calories	47.8
76.4	Carbohydrate (g)	10.9
11.4	Protein (g)	1.6
2.2	Total Fat (g)	0.3
0.0	Saturated Fat (g)	0.0
0.0	Cholesterol (mg)	0.0
195.5	Sodium (mg)	27.9

Oriental Stir-Fried Vegetables

Makes 4 servings

1 lb. fresh broccoli, asparagus spears, green beans or sliced zucchini
1/2 onion, thinly sliced
2-oz. can sliced mushrooms, undrained ●
2 tbsp. soy sauce, ● white wine or water (optional)
2 tsp. safflower oil

● *HIGH SODIUM ALERT—Use unsalted mushrooms. Substitute wine or water for soy sauce.*

Slice broccoli or asparagus spears into 1 1/2-inch lengths. Combine all ingredients in nonstick skillet. Cook and stir uncovered until liquid has evaporated and vegetables are crisp-tender.

Total		Per Serving
258.3	Calories	64.6
33.3	Carbohydrate (g)	8.3
18.5	Protein (g)	4.6
10.2	Total Fat (g)	2.5
0.7	Saturated Fat (g)	0.2
0.0	Cholesterol (mg)	0.0
317.5	Sodium (mg)	79.4

Stir-Fried Peppers and Onions

Makes 4 servings

2 red or green bell peppers (or 1 of each), cut into narrow strips
1 large Spanish onion, sliced
2 tbsp. soy sauce ● (optional)
2 tbsp. white wine
2 tsp. safflower or corn oil

● *HIGH SODIUM ALERT—Omit soy sauce.*

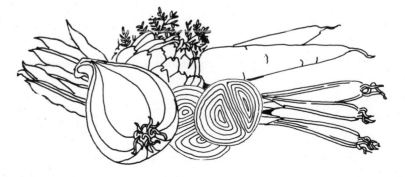

Combine all ingredients in nonstick skillet. Simmer covered over moderate heat 2 minutes. Uncover and continue to cook, stirring frequently, until most of the liquid has evaporated and vegetables just begin to brown slightly.

Total		Per Serving
204.3	Calories	51.1
24.1	Carbohydrate (g)	6.0
4.5	Protein (g)	·1.1
9.7	Total Fat (g)	2.4
0.7	Saturated Fat (g)	0.2
0.0	Cholesterol (mg)	0.0
14.7	Sodium (mg)	3.7

French Carrot Medley•

Makes 6 servings

2 cups fresh or frozen sliced carrots
6-oz. can (3/4 cup) unsweetened orange juice
4-oz. can sliced mushrooms, undrained
4 stalks celery, sliced
2 tbsp. chopped onion
1/2 tsp. dillweed
Salt and pepper to taste (optional)
2 tsp. cornstarch or arrowroot
1/4 cup cold water

● *HIGH SODIUM ALERT—Not recommended for low-sodium diets.*

Combine all ingredients except cornstarch and water in saucepan. Simmer covered 12 to 15 minutes, or until carrots are tender. Combine cornstarch with water. Stir into simmering vegetables; cook and stir until sauce thickens and bubbles.

Total		Per Serving
260.3	Calories	43.4
58.7	Carbohydrate (g)	9.9
8.8	Protein (g)	1.5
1.0	Total Fat (g)	0.2
0.0	Saturated Fat (g)	0.0
0.0	Cholesterol (mg)	0.0
796.0	Sodium (mg)	132.7

Alert Symbols: ● Sodium ■ Cholesterol ▲ Sugar

Pasta, Rice And Potatoes

Despite the fattening reputation of potatoes, rice, spaghetti, macaroni, noodles and other pasta products, these foods are virtually fat-free. They only become fattening when topped with rich sauces or combined with fatty ingredients. If you combine them with low-fat, low-calorie ingredients or with homemade, fat-skimmed sauces, there is no reason not to enjoy potato, pasta or rice dishes.

All spaghetti-type products, despite differences in shape—shells, strips, tubes, wheels or whatever—"weigh in" at 105 calories per ounce of dry pasta. If you cook spaghetti products longer than the recommended time—14 to 20 minutes to the tender stage, rather than 8 to 10 minutes to the firm stage or *al dente*—they will absorb more water and swell to a larger size. For that reason, one cupful of tender-cooked spaghetti is lower in calories than a cupful cooked *al dente*—155 calories instead of 215 calories.

Protein-enriched pasta products made with high-protein soy flour are a valuable aid to *Lean Cuisine*. They are no lower in calories, but their added protein content enables you to make a meal using less meat, while providing sufficient protein.

Remember, if you are on a low-sodium diet, to use *no* salt in the water when cooking pasta, potatoes or rice. Also, since regular egg noodles do contain cholesterol, be sure to use cholesterol-free noodles (made without egg yolks) if you are on a cholesterol-restricted diet.

LEAN CUISINE GUIDE TO PASTA, RICE AND POTATOES*

	Calories	Carbohydrate (g)	Protein (g)	Fat (g)
Egg Noodles, cooked	100	18.7	3.3	1.2
Macaroni, cooked al dente	96	19.6	3.3	0.4
Macaroni, tender-cooked	78	16.1	2.4	0.3
Spaghetti, cooked al dente	96	19.6	3.3	0.4
Spaghetti, tender-cooked	78	16.1	2.4	0.3
Rice, brown, cooked	116	24.9	2.5	0.6
Rice, white, cooked	93	20.4	2.9	0.1
Rice, instant, cooked	90	20.0	2.8	Trace
Potato, baked (skin not eaten)	108	24.6	2.9	0.2
Potato, unpared, boiled	104	23.3	2.9	0.1
Potato, pared, boiled	88	19.6	2.6	0.1

Source: U.S. Department of Agriculture, Agricultural Research Service, *Nutritive Values of American Foods* (Agriculture Handbook No. 456), 1975. *Figures reflect content of 1/2 cup serving pasta and rice and of 1 medium potato (approximately 3 potatoes per pound).

Baked Macaroni and Cheese with Mushrooms

Makes 10 servings

3 1/2 cups tender-cooked protein-enriched elbow macaroni ●
8-oz. can mushroom stems and pieces, drained ●
4-oz. can pimientos ●, drained, minced
1 cup skim milk
1 tsp. cornstarch or arrowroot
1 cup shredded low-fat diet sharp cheese (about 4 oz.) ●
1 onion, chopped
2 tsp. prepared mustard ●
1 tsp. Worcestershire sauce ●
Salt ● and pepper to taste (optional)
1 tbsp. seasoned bread crumbs ●

● *HIGH SODIUM ALERT—Cook macaroni without salt. Use unsalted mushrooms and low-sodium cheese and bread crumbs. Substitute dry mustard to taste for prepared mustard. Omit Worcestershire and added salt.*

Combine macaroni, mushrooms and pimientos in 1 1/2-quart baking dish. Mix milk with cornstarch in nonstick saucepan. Cook and stir over low heat until simmering. Stir in cheese, onion, mustard, Worcestershire, salt and pepper; cook and stir until cheese is completely melted. Stir sauce into macaroni mixture. Top with bread crumbs. Bake in a preheated 350° oven 25 minutes, or until hot and bubbly.

Total		Per Serving
986.7	Calories	98.7
159.8	Carbohydrate (g)	16.0
64.4	Protein (g)	6.4
13.5	Total Fat (g)	1.4
5.2	Saturated Fat (g)	0.5
45.0	Cholesterol (mg)	4.5
4862.8	Sodium (mg)	486.3

Noodle Lasagna

Makes 8 servings

4 oz. uncooked wide egg noodles ● ■
1 cup low-fat cottage cheese ●
1 lb. lean beef round, trimmed of fat, ground
28-oz. can tomatoes, undrained, well broken up ●
6-oz. can tomato paste
1 onion, chopped
1 clove garlic, minced, or 1/8 tsp. garlic powder
2 tsp. dried oregano
Salt ● and pepper to taste (optional)
1 cup shredded part-skim pizza cheese (about 4 oz.) ●
1/4 cup grated Parmesan cheese ● ■

● *HIGH SODIUM ALERT—Cook noodles without salt. Use unsalted tomatoes and low-sodium cheeses. Omit added salt.*

■ *HIGH CHOLESTEROL ALERT—Use cholesterol-free noodles. Omit Parmesan.*

Cook noodles according to package directions. Rinse under cold water; drain. Combine with cottage cheese. Spray nonstick skillet with cooking spray. Brown meat in skillet. Pour off fat. Stir in tomatoes, tomato paste, onion, garlic, oregano, salt and pepper. Simmer covered about 1 1/2 hours, stirring occasionally. Pour 1/3 of the sauce into casserole; top with half the noodle mixture, then half the pizza cheese. Repeat layers; top with remaining sauce. Sprinkle with Parmesan. Bake in a preheated 325° oven 1 hour.

Total		Per Serving
2164.6	Calories	270.6
168.8	Carbohydrate (g)	21.1
191.4	Protein (g)	23.9
80.4	Total Fat (g)	10.1
40.4	Saturated Fat (g)	5.1
506.6	Cholesterol (mg)	63.3
4328.0	Sodium (mg)	541.0

One-Step Skillet Spaghetti and Meat Sauce

Makes 4 servings

8 oz. lean beef round, trimmed of fat, ground
2 cups water
16-oz. can plain tomato sauce (check label for no added oil) ●
1 onion, chopped
1 tsp. dried oregano
Garlic salt ● and pepper to taste (optional)
4 oz. uncooked thin spaghetti, broken up

● *HIGH SODIUM ALERT—Use unsalted tomato sauce. Substitute garlic powder to taste for garlic salt.*

Spray large nonstick skillet with cooking spray. Spread the meat in a thin layer in skillet. Cook over moderate heat until underside is browned. Break up into large chunks and turn over. When meat is brown, add 1 cup of the water, then pour off the liquid into a cup. Set liquid aside and allow the fat to rise to the surface. Meanwhile, stir remaining ingredients except spaghetti into skillet. Heat to boiling. Add the broken spaghetti a little at a time, stirring after each addition. Skim fat from the reserved drained liquid. Stir the fat-skimmed liquid into skillet. Simmer uncovered, stirring frequently, until most of the liquid is absorbed and spaghetti is tender and coated with a thick sauce. Serve straight from the skillet.

Total		Per Serving
1012.1	Calories	253.0
128.6	Carbohydrate (g)	32.2
70.7	Protein (g)	17.7
24.6	Total Fat (g)	6.2
10.9	Saturated Fat (g)	2.7
147.5	Cholesterol (mg)	36.9
3239.7	Sodium (mg)	809.9

Alert Symbols:　● Sodium　■ Cholesterol　▲ Sugar

Alfie's Fettucine

Makes 8 servings

8 oz. uncooked wide egg noodles ● ■
1 cup low-fat cottage cheese, at room temperature ●
½ cup grated Parmesan cheese ● ■
¼ cup minced fresh parsley
Salt ● and coarsely ground pepper to taste (optional)

● *HIGH SODIUM ALERT—Cook noodles without salt. Use low-sodium cheese. Omit added salt.*

■ *HIGH CHOLESTEROL ALERT—Use cholesterol-free noodles. Substitute a low-fat cheese.*

Boil noodles according to package directions. Drain and return to the same pot. Quickly toss together with remaining ingredients. Serve immediately.

Total		Per Serving
1255.5	Calories	156.9
174.4	Carbohydrate (g)	21.8
78.5	Protein (g)	9.8
24.1	Total Fat (g)	3.0
12.9	Saturated Fat (g)	1.6
275.8	Cholesterol (mg)	34.5
3900.3	Sodium (mg)	487.5

Chinese Fried Rice

Makes 8 servings

2 eggs, beaten ■
2 large onions, chopped
2 tsp. safflower or corn oil
¼ cup soy sauce ● (optional)
3 stalks celery, chopped ●
1 red or green bell pepper, chopped
1 clove garlic, minced
3 green onions, chopped
1 cup instant rice
1 cup boiling water

● *HIGH SODIUM ALERT—Substitute ¼ cup water for the soy sauce. Substitute additional bell pepper for the celery or omit.*

■ *HIGH CHOLESTEROL ALERT—Use ½ cup liquid egg substitute.*

Spray large nonstick skillet with cooking spray. Add the eggs and cook without stirring over low heat until set. Break up with a fork. Remove from skillet; reserve. Combine the 2 onions, oil and 2 tbsp. of the soy sauce in the skillet. Cook and stir until onion is brown.

Add remaining ingredients and heat to boiling. Reduce heat; simmer 1 minute. Stir in reserved egg. Remove from heat; cover tightly, let stand 5 minutes. Stir before serving.

Total		Per Serving
753.6	Calories	94.2
116.8	Carbohydrate (g)	14.6
27.0	Protein (g)	3.4
21.7	Total Fat (g)	2.7
4.0	Saturated Fat (g)	0.5
504.0	Cholesterol (mg)	63.0
303.0	Sodium (mg)	37.9

Quick Spanish Rice

Makes 8 servings

1 large onion, finely chopped
1 stalk celery, finely chopped ●
1 red or green bell pepper, diced
8-oz. can plain tomato sauce (check label for no added oil) ●
8-oz. can tomatoes, well broken up ●
1¼ cups fat-skimmed chicken, turkey or beef broth ●, canned or homemade
1 tsp. prepared mustard ●
1 bay leaf
½ tsp. dried oregano
2 cups instant rice

● *HIGH SODIUM ALERT—Omit celery. Use unsalted tomato sauce, tomatoes and broth. Substitute dry mustard to taste for prepared mustard.*

Combine all ingredients except rice in nonstick saucepan. Simmer covered 10 minutes. Stir in rice. Simmer covered over very low heat, stirring occasionally, about 5 minutes.

Total		Per Serving
934.4	Calories	116.8
203.5	Carbohydrate (g)	25.4
27.6	Protein (g)	3.5
2.1	Total Fat (g)	0.3
0.0	Saturated Fat (g)	0.0
17.5	Cholesterol (mg)	2.2
2875.9	Sodium (mg)	359.5

Rice with Currants

Makes 6 servings

1 cup instant rice
1 cup water
5 tbsp. dried currants
Pinch cinnamon
Salt ● and pepper to taste (optional)

● *HIGH SODIUM ALERT—Omit added salt.*

Combine rice, water, currants and cinnamon in saucepan. Heat to boiling. Remove from heat; let stand 5 minutes. Season with salt and pepper to taste.

Total		Per Serving
382.8	Calories	63.8
85.3	Carbohydrate (g)	14.2
8.0	Protein (g)	1.3
0.2	Total Fat (g)	0.0
0.0	Saturated Fat (g)	0.0
0.0	Cholesterol (mg)	0.0
2.6	Sodium (mg)	0.4

Apple-Curry Rice

Makes 6 servings

½ cup tomato juice ●
½ cup unsweetened apple juice
1 cup instant rice
1 tsp. curry powder
1 red apple, unpared, diced

● *HIGH SODIUM ALERT—Use unsalted tomato juice.*

Combine all ingredients except apple in saucepan. Heat to boiling. Remove from heat; stir in apple. Cover tightly; let stand 5 minutes.

Total		Per Serving
516.5	Calories	86.1
118.2	Carbohydrate (g)	19.7
8.1	Protein (g)	1.3
1.0	Total Fat (g)	0.2
0.0	Saturated Fat (g)	0.0
0.0	Cholesterol (mg)	0.0
248.0	Sodium (mg)	41.3

1 tsp. = 5 mL   1 tbsp. = 15 mL   1 cup = 250 mL   1 oz. = 30 g

Pineapple Rice

Makes 6 servings

1 cup unsweetened pineapple juice
1 cup instant rice
2 tbsp. soy sauce ● (optional)

● *HIGH SODIUM ALERT—Omit soy sauce.*

Combine all ingredients in saucepan, and heat to boiling. Remove from heat; cover tightly. Let stand 5 minutes.

Total		Per Serving
	Calories	
490.0	Calories	81.7
112.4	Carbohydrate (g)	18.7
8.1	Protein (g)	1.3
0.5	Total Fat (g)	0.1
0.0	Saturated Fat (g)	0.0
0.0	Cholesterol (mg)	0.0
3.0	Sodium (mg)	0.5

Orange-Raisin Rice

Makes 6 servings

1 cup unsweetened orange juice
1 cup instant rice
3 tbsp. golden raisins
Pinch pumpkin pie spice
1 tsp. Chopped parsley
Salt ● and pepper to taste
(optional)

● *HIGH SODIUM ALERT—Omit added salt.*

Combine orange juice, rice and raisins in saucepan. Heat to boiling. Remove from heat; cover tightly. Let stand 5 minutes. Stir in remaining ingredients.

Total		Per Serving
555.0	Calories	92.5
128.3	Carbohydrate (g)	21.4
9.4	Protein (g)	1.6
0.4	Total Fat (g)	0.1
0.0	Saturated Fat (g)	0.0
0.0	Cholestrol (mg)	0.0
9.0	Sodium (mg)	1.5

Easy Onion Rice

Makes 6 servings

1 cup canned condensed onion
soup ●
1 cup instant rice

● *HIGH SODIUM ALERT—Use unsalted soup.*

Pour soup into nonstick saucepan. Skim fat from soup. Heat to boiling. Stir in rice. Remove from heat; cover tightly. Let stand 5 minutes.

Total		Per Serving
487.0	Calories	81.2
88.9	Carbohydrate (g)	14.8
17.9	Protein (g)	3.0
5.3	Total Fat (g)	0.9
0.0	Saturated Fat (g)	0.0
48.0	Cholesterol (mg)	8.0
2145.0	Sodium (mg)	357.5

Raisin-Curry Rice

Makes 6 servings

½ cup tomato juice ●
½ cup unsweetened pineapple juice
1 cup instant rice
3 tbsp. golden raisins
1 tsp. curry powder

● *HIGH SODIUM ALERT—Use unsalted tomato juice.*

Combine all ingredients in saucepan, and heat to boiling. Remove from heat; cover tightly. Let stand 5 minutes.

Total		Per Serving
523.5	Calories	87.2
121.4	Carbohydrate (g)	20.2
9.2	Protein (g)	1.5
0.4	Total Fat (g)	0.1
0.0	Saturated Fat (g)	0.0
0.0	Cholesterol (mg)	0.0
251.0	Sodium (mg)	41.8

Tuna and Macaroni Salad

Makes 8 luncheon-size servings

8 oz. protein-enriched elbow
macaroni, tender-cooked ●
7-oz. can water-packed tuna,
drained, flaked ●
½ cup diced celery ●
¼ cup diagonally-sliced green onion

½ cup low-calorie low-fat
mayonnaise ●
½ cup plain low-fat yogurt
⅛ tsp. dillweed
Salt ● and pepper to taste
(optional)
Paprika

● *HIGH SODIUM ALERT—Cook macaroni without salt. Use unsalted tuna and mayonnaise. Substitute cucumber or green pepper for celery. Omit added salt.*

Rinse macaroni in cold water; drain. Combine all ingredients except paprika. Cover and chill thoroughly. Sprinkle with paprika just before serving.

Total		Per Serving
1333.5	Calories	166.7
189.7	Carbohydrate (g)	23.7
89.4	Protein (g)	11.2
22.7	Total Fat (g)	2.8
1.0	Saturated Fat (g)	0.1
200.0	Cholesterol (mg)	25.0
4614.3	Sodium (mg)	576.8

Macaroni Salad

Makes 12 servings

8 oz. protein-enriched elbow
macaroni, tender-cooked ●
1 onion, chopped
2 stalks celery, diced ●
2 carrots, shredded ●
1 small red or green bell pepper,
finely chopped
⅓ cup plain low-fat yogurt
⅓ cup low-calorie low-fat
mayonnaise ●
1 tbsp. lemon juice
1 tsp. prepared mustard ●
12 medium stuffed green (Spanish)
olives, sliced ●
Salt ● and freshly ground pepper
to taste (optional)
Paprika

● *HIGH SODIUM ALERT—Cook macaroni without salt. Substitute additional bell pepper for celery and carrots. Use unsalted mayonnaise. Substitute dry mustard to taste for prepared mustard. Omit olives and added salt.*

Rinse macaroni with cold water; drain. Combine all ingredients except paprika; cover and chill thoroughly.

Total		Per Serving
1151.9	Calories	96.0
211.0	Carbohydrate (g)	17.6
36.5	Protein (g)	3.0
21.0	Total Fat (g)	1.8
0.7	Saturated Fat (g)	0.1
49.3	Cholesterol (mg)	4.1
4106.6	Sodium (mg)	342.2

Alert Symbols: ● Sodium   ■ Cholesterol   ▲ Sugar

Macaroni-Apple Salad

Makes 4 servings

2 cups tender-cooked protein-enriched elbow macaroni, rinsed, drained, chilled ●
2 red apples, diced
1 cup diced celery ●
¼ cup low-calorie low-fat mayonnaise ●
¼ cup plain low-fat yogurt
¼ cup chopped walnuts
4 large lettuce leaves

● *HIGH SODIUM ALERT—Cook macaroni without salt. Substitute cucumber for celery. Use unsalted mayonnaise.*

Combine macaroni, apples, celery, mayonnaise and yogurt; cover and chill. Serve on lettuce leaves; garnish with nuts.

Total		Per Serving
778.8	Calories	194.7
116.8	Carbohydrate (g)	29.2
19.6	Protein (g)	4.9
29.8	Total Fat (g)	7.5
1.5	Saturated Fat (g)	0.4
37.0	Cholesterol (mg)	9.3
1243.3	Sodium (mg)	310.8

Macaroni-Salmon Salad

Makes 8 servings

15-oz. can salmon ●
2 cups tender-cooked protein-enriched elbow macaroni ●
1 cup seeded and diced cucumber
1 cup chopped celery ●
½ cup chopped green pepper
½ cup chopped onion
1 cup low-calorie low-fat mayonnaise ●
1½ tsp. dillweed
Salt ● and coarsely ground pepper to taste (optional)
Chilled lettuce leaves
4 tomatoes, quartered

● *HIGH SODIUM ALERT—Cook macaroni without salt. Use unsalted salmon and mayonnaise. Substitute additional diced cucumber and green pepper for celery. Omit added salt.*

Rinse macaroni in cold water; drain. Drain salmon; remove skin and center bone; flake slightly. Combine salmon with macaroni, cucumber, celery, green pepper, onion, mayonnaise, dillweed, salt and pepper; cover and chill thoroughly. Spoon salad into lettuce-lined bowl. Garnish with tomatoes.

Total		Per Serving
1479.0	Calories	184.9
136.3	Carbohydrate (g)	17.0
107.2	Protein (g)	13.4
59.1	Total Fat (g)	7.4
5.0	Saturated Fat (g)	0.6
278.0	Cholesterol (mg)	34.8
3131.5	Sodium (mg)	391.4

Hot German Potato Salad

Makes 6 servings

2 tbsp. safflower or corn oil
⅓ cup finely chopped onion
1 tbsp. flour
1½ tsp. salt ●
¼ tsp. dry mustard
¼ cup water
3 tbsp. cider vinegar
½ cup diced celery ●
3 tbsp. pickle relish ●
3 tbsp. chopped green pepper
2½ cups diced cooked pared potatoes ●

● *HIGH SODIUM ALERT—Omit added salt and celery. Cook potatoes without salt. Use unsalted relish.*

Heat oil in nonstick skillet. Add onion; brown lightly. Combine flour, salt, mustard, water and vinegar; stir mixture into onion. Cook over low heat until sauce thickens. Combine celery, pickle relish and green pepper with potatoes. Add the hot dressing; mix lightly but thoroughly. Turn into baking dish; bake covered in a preheated 350° oven about 20 minutes.

Total		Per Serving
659.4	Calories	109.9
93.9	Carbohydrate (g)	15.7
9.7	Protein (g)	1.6
28.7	Total Fat (g)	4.8
2.0	Saturated Fat (g)	0.3
0.0	Cholesterol (mg)	0.0
4531.8	Sodium (mg)	755.3

Caesar Potato Salad

Makes 8 servings

4 potatoes, pared, cooked, cubed ●
¼ cup low-calorie low-fat Italian salad dressing ●
1 egg, beaten ■
4 pitted black olives, sliced ●
8 tsp. grated Parmesan cheese ● ■ (optional)
1 tbsp. Worcestershire sauce ●
2 tsp. prepared mustard ●
Garlic salt to taste ● (optional)

● *HIGH SODIUM ALERT—Cook potatoes without salt. Use unsalted salad dressing and low-sodium cheese. Omit olives and Worcestershire. Substitute dry mustard to taste for prepared mustard and garlic powder to taste for garlic salt.*

■ *HIGH CHOLESTEROL ALERT—Use ¼ cup liquid egg substitute and low-fat cheese.*

Combine all ingredients in large bowl. Cover and chill thoroughly.

Total		Per Serving
496.5	Calories	62.1
82.5	Carbohydrate (g)	10.3
17.3	Protein (g)	2.2
13.9	Total Fat (g)	1.7
2.6	Saturated Fat (g)	0.3
252.0	Cholesterol (mg)	31.5
2817.7	Sodium (mg)	352.2

Patio Potato Salad

Makes 12 servings

6 medium potatoes, pared, cooked, cubed ●
3 tbsp. lemon juice
2 onions, chopped
6 hard-cooked eggs, quartered ■
1 green pepper, chopped
Pepper to taste (optional)
5 tbsp. low-calorie low-fat mayonnaise ●

● *HIGH SODIUM ALERT—Cook potatoes without salt. Use unsalted mayonnaise.*

■ *HIGH CHOLESTEROL ALERT—Omit eggs.*

Combine all ingredients in large bowl. Cover and chill thoroughly.

Total		Per Serving
1236.0	Calories	103.0
154.1	Carbohydrate (g)	12.8
57.9	Protein (g)	4.8
46.6	Total Fat (g)	3.9
12.0	Saturated Fat (g)	1.0
1552.0	Cholesterol (mg)	129.3
2392.0	Sodium (mg)	199.3

1 tsp. = 5 mL   1 tbsp. = 15 mL   1 cup = 250 mL   1 oz. = 30 g

Hot German Apple and Potato Salad

Makes 8 servings

3 medium potatoes, pared, cooked, cubed ●
3 unpared apples, diced
2 stalks celery, finely chopped ●
2 tbsp. chopped fresh parsley
3 tbsp. cider vinegar
1 tsp. grated lemon rind
1 tsp. caraway seeds (optional)
1 tsp. sugar ▲ (optional)
Salt ● and pepper to taste (optional)

● *HIGH SODIUM ALERT—Cook potatoes without salt. Omit celery and added salt.*

▲ *HIGH SUGAR ALERT—Use sugar substitute.*

Toss all ingredients together in large nonstick skillet. Cook and stir over low heat 2 or 3 minutes, or until heated through. Serve immediately.

Total		Per Serving
492.0	Calories	61.5
119.5	Carbohydrate (g)	14.9
7.8	Protein (g)	1.0
0.3	Total Fat (g)	0.0
0.0	Saturated Fat (g)	0.0
0.0	Cholesterol (mg)	0.0
1063.0	Sodium (mg)	132.9

Flavored Potatoes

Makes 4 servings

1 cup fat-skimmed beef or chicken broth, canned or homemade ●
1/2 cup skim milk
1 cup instant potato flakes
Salt ● and pepper to taste (optional)

● *HIGH SODIUM ALERT—Use unsalted broth. Omit added salt.*

Combine broth and milk in saucepan. Cook and stir over low heat until hot. Stir in potato flakes, salt and pepper. Remove from heat. Beat with fork or wire whisk until fluffy.

Total		Per Serving
239.0	Calories	59.8
46.8	Carbohydrate (g)	11.7
12.7	Protein (g)	3.2
0.3	Total Fat (g)	0.1
0.0	Saturated Fat (g)	0.0
26.5	Cholesterol (mg)	6.6
885.5	Sodium (mg)	221.4

Creamy Stuffed Baked Potatoes

Makes 6 servings

3 large baking potatoes
3/4 cup plain low-fat yogurt
1/4 cup low-calorie low-fat blue cheese salad dressing ●
1 tbsp. grated onion

● *HIGH SODIUM ALERT—Use unsalted dressing.*

Bake potatoes 1 hour in a preheated 400° oven. After removing potatoes, increase oven temperature setting to 450°. Slice potatoes lengthwise in half. Scoop out potato; reserve shells.

Combine potato, yogurt, salad dressing and onion; beat until fluffy. Divide among reserved shells. Place filled potato shells on baking sheet and return to oven. Bake at 450° 12 to 15 minutes.

Total		Per Serving
574.7	Calories	95.8
109.7	Carbohydrate (g)	18.3
19.9	Protein (g)	3.3
7.2	Total Fat (g)	1.2
3.5	Saturated Fat (g)	0.6
27.0	Cholesterol (mg)	4.5
807.2	Sodium (mg)	134.5

Parslied Potatoes

Makes 4 servings

4 medium potatoes, pared
Salt to taste ● (optional)
2 tbsp. diet margarine ● ■
2 tbsp. minced fresh parsley or 2 tsp. parsley flakes

● *HIGH SODIUM ALERT—Omit added salt. Use unsalted margarine.*

■ *HIGH CHOLESTEROL ALERT—Use polyunsaturated margarine.*

Place potatoes in saucepan with water to cover. Add salt to taste; heat to boiling. Simmer 12 to 15 minutes, or until tender. Drain. Toss with margarine to coat. Sprinkle with parsley.

Hint: For Dilled Potatoes, substitute chopped fresh dill (or 2 teaspoons dillweed) for parsley. To make Lemon-Minted Potatoes, add 2 teaspoons lemon juice to the margarine, and substitute chopped fresh mint (or 2 tsp. dried mint) for parsley.

Total		Per Serving
516.0	Calories	129.0
93.0	Carbohydrate (g)	23.3
11.4	Protein (g)	2.9
12.4	Total Fat (g)	3.1
2.0	Saturated Fat (g)	0.5
0.0	Cholesterol (mg)	0.0
240.0	Sodium (mg)	60.0

Alert Symbols: ● Sodium   ■ Cholesterol   ▲ Sugar

Slimmer Sweets
And Treats

Choosing Ice Cream Alternatives

There's a confusing array of frozen desserts available to dieters. What to choose depends on what you want to avoid: calories, cholesterol, fat, sugar? Don't be misled—read the nutrition labels carefully. A dessert that's almost fat-free may be high in sugar and nearly as fattening as your favorite ice cream. A "dietetic" or low-sugar sweet may be rich with butterfat.

If You Want to Avoid Cholesterol, choose ice, ice milk, low-fat frozen yogurt or sherbet. Avoid ice cream and especially avoid frozen custard, which contains egg yolks.

If You Want to Avoid Fat, choose ice, low-fat frozen yogurt, low-fat ice milk or sherbet. Avoid ice cream, especially expensive brands.

If You Want to Avoid Sugar, choose sugar-free dietetic ice milk or ice cream. Avoid ices, sherbets, frozen yogurt and regular ice cream or ice milk.

If You Want to Avoid Calories, choose low-fat ice milk—the lower the fat content, the better.

LEAN CUISINE GUIDE TO FROZEN DESSERTS *

	Calories	Fat (g)	Cholesterol (mg)
Ice, lemon or lime	177	0.0	0.0
Ice Cream			
Regular, hardened, vanilla	269	14.3	59.0
Extra-rich, hardened, vanilla	349	23.7	88.0
Soft-serve, French vanilla (frozen custard)	377	22.5	153.0
Sugarless, strawberry	261	12.0	42.0
Ice Milk			
Hardened, vanilla	184	5.6	18.0
Soft-serve, vanilla	223	4.6	13.0
99% fat-free, vanilla	163	1.6	NA
Sugarless, strawberry	186	5.3	17.0
Sherbet, orange	270	3.8	14.0
Yogurt			
Low-fat frozen vanilla	180	2.0	11.0
Low-fat frozen strawberry	210	2.0	11.0

Source: U.S. Department of Agriculture, Agricultural Research Service, *Composition of Foods: Dairy and Egg Products,* 1976; and individual manufacturers.
* *Figures reflect nutrition content of 1 cup (8 fluid ounces) of particular commercial product. Brands may vary.*
NA: Data not available.

1 tsp. = 5 mL   1 tbsp. = 15 mL   1 cup = 250 mL   1 oz. = 30 g

Nectar Whip

Makes 8 servings

2 envelopes unflavored gelatin
1/2 cup cold water
1/4 cup honey ▲
12-oz. can unsweetened peach or
    apricot nectar ▲
2 tsp. lemon juice
3 egg whites

▲ *HIGH SUGAR ALERT—Replace honey with sugar substitute to taste. Check nectar label for added sugar.*

Combine gelatin and water in a saucepan. Wait 1 minute, then cook over low heat, stirring constantly, until gelatin dissolves. Remove from heat. Stir in honey, peach nectar and lemon juice. Chill, stirring occasionally until mixture is syrupy-thick. Add egg whites to gelatin. Beat at high speed with electric mixer until light and fluffy. Chill until firm.

Total		Per Serving
536.7	Calories	67.1
115.1	Carbohydrate (g)	14.4
24.8	Protein (g)	3.1
0.0	Total Fat (g)	0.0
0.0	Saturated Fat (g)	0.0
0.0	Cholesterol (mg)	0.0
164.0	Sodium (mg)	20.5

Strawberry Apple Fizz

Makes 4 servings

3 oz. unsweetened frozen apple
    juice concentrate, defrosted,
    undiluted
1 envelope unflavored gelatin
1 cup boiling water
1 1/2 cups frozen whole unsweetened
    strawberries, not defrosted

Put apple juice in blender container and sprinkle on gelatin. Wait 1 minute, than add boiling water. Cover and blend until gelatin granules are dissolved. Add frozen berries. Cover and blend until liquified. Pour into 4 glass dessert cups and chill until set. (Dessert separates into layers.) For variety use other fruits and juices, except pineapple.

Total		Per Serving
280.0	Calories	70.0
64.7	Carbohydrate (g)	16.2
7.5	Protein (g)	1.9
0.3	Total Fat (g)	0.1
0.0	Saturated Fat (g)	0.0
0.0	Cholesterol (mg)	0.0
12.5	Sodium (mg)	3.1

Banana Orange Gelatin

Makes 4 servings

1 large ripe banana
1/4 cup cold water
1 envelope unflavored gelatin
1 cup boiling water
6-oz. can unsweetened frozen
    orange juice concentrate, partly
    defrosted, undiluted

Slice banana into a glass bowl. Put cold water in mixing bowl or blender container. Sprinkle on gelatin. Wait 1 minute until gelatin softens, then add boiling water. Stir or blend until gelatin granules are thoroughly dissolved. Add orange juice concentrate and mix or blend well. Pour over banana slices. Chill until set.

Total		Per Serving
510.0	Calories	127.5
112.5	Carbohydrate (g)	28.1
15.2	Protein (g)	3.8
0.0	Total Fat (g)	0.0
0.0	Saturated Fat (g)	0.0
0.0	Cholesterol (mg)	0.0
14.5	Sodium (mg)	3.6

Peach Soufflé ▲

Makes 6 servings

4 egg whites
1/8 tsp. cream of tartar
1/4 tsp. salt ● (optional)
4 tbsp. sugar
2 jars (4 3/4 oz. each) strained baby
    food peaches with tapioca ●
1/2 tsp. vanilla
    Whipped Milk Topping (recipe in
    this chapter) (optional)

● *HIGH SODIUM ALERT—Omit added salt. Use unsalted peaches.*

▲ *HIGH SUGAR ALERT—Not recommended for low-sugar diets.*

Beat egg whites until foamy. Add cream of tartar and salt; continue beating until soft peaks form.

Gradually add sugar, beating until stiff peaks form. Gently fold in peaches and vanilla. Spray a 1 1/2-quart soufflé dish or casserole with cooking spray. Spoon peach mixture into soufflé dish. Set in a pan of warm water and bake in a preheated 325° oven for 40 to 50 minutes, or until firm. Serve immediately, garnished with Whipped Milk Topping, if desired.

Total		Per Serving
470.1	Calories	78.4
107.4	Carbohydrate (g)	17.9
18.7	Protein (g)	3.1
0.0	Total Fat (g)	0.0
0.0	Saturated Fat (g)	0.0
0.0	Cholesterol (mg)	0.0
228.4	Sodium (mg)	38.1

Fresh Fruit Whip

Makes 8 servings

4-serving envelope regular or low-
    calorie gelatin dessert mix (any
    flavor) ● ▲
1 cup boiling water
4 to 6 ice cubes
    Pinch salt ●
1 egg white
1 cup fresh fruit (except pineapple,
    papaya or mango), cut into bite-
    size pieces or slices

● *HIGH SODIUM ALERT—Use low-sodium gelatin dessert mix. Substitute cream of tartar for added salt.*

▲ *HIGH SUGAR ALERT—Use sugar-free gelatin dessert mix.*

Dissolve gelatin in boiling water. Stir in ice cubes until melted. Chill until partially set. Add salt to egg white; beat until stiff. In another bowl, beat gelatin at high speed until doubled. Gently but thoroughly fold in beaten egg white, a little at a time. Fold in fruit. Chill until set.

Total		Per Serving
395.0	Calories	49.4
91.3	Carbohydrate (g)	11.4
13.0	Protein (g)	1.6
0.2	Total Fat (g)	0.0
0.0	Saturated Fat (g)	0.0
0.0	Cholesterol (mg)	0.0
586.5	Sodium (mg)	73.3

Alert Symbols: ● Sodium   ■ Cholesterol   ▲ Sugar

Chilled Orange Soufflé ▲

Makes 8 servings

1 envelope unflavored gelatin
½ cup sugar
1 cup water
6-oz. can frozen unsweetened orange juice concentrate, undiluted, defrosted
½ cup ice water
½ cup instant nonfat dry milk crystals
2 tbsp. lemon juice
Whipped Milk Topping (recipe in this chapter) (optional)
Cantaloupe, green grapes, blueberries or other fresh fruit (optional)

▲ *HIGH SUGAR ALERT—Not recommended for low-sugar diets.*

Mix together unflavored gelatin and ¼ cup of the sugar in saucepan; stir in 1 cup water. Place over low heat, stirring constantly, until gelatin is dissolved. Remove from heat; stir in orange juice concentrate. Chill, stirring occasionally, until mixture is the consistency of unbeaten egg white. While mixture is chilling, pour ½ cup ice water into a mixing bowl; add nonfat dry milk crystals. Beat until soft peaks form, about 3 to 4 minutes. Add lemon juice. Continue beating until firm peaks form, about 3 to 4 minutes longer. Gradually add remaining ¼ cup sugar. Fold in gelatin mixture. Turn into serving bowl; chill until firm. Garnish with Whipped Milk Topping and fresh fruit, if desired.

Total		Per Serving
900.5	Calories	112.6
206.4	Carbohydrate (g)	25.8
23.2	Protein (g)	2.9
0.4	Total Fat (g)	0.1
0.0	Saturated Fat (g)	0.0
7.5	Cholesterol (mg)	0.9
190.0	Sodium (mg)	23.7

Baked Custard

Makes 8 servings

4 eggs, slightly beaten ■
3½ cups skim milk
7 tbsp. sugar ▲
2 tsp. vanilla
Salt or butter-flavored salt ● (optional)
Pinch ground cinnamon (optional)

● *HIGH SODIUM ALERT—Omit added salt.*

■ *HIGH CHOLESTEROL ALERT—Use 1 cup liquid egg substitute.*

▲ *HIGH SUGAR ALERT—Use equivalent sugar substitute.*

Combine ingredients and mix well. Pour into 8 oven proof custard cups. Set cups in a shallow baking pan. Add 1 inch hot water to pan. Bake in a preheated 350° oven 40 to 45 minutes until a knife inserted near the edge comes out clean. Chill.

Total		Per Serving
981.0	Calories	122.6
131.3	Carbohydrate (g)	16.4
55.5	Protein (g)	6.9
24.0	Total Fat (g)	3.0
8.0	Saturated Fat (g)	1.0
1025.5	Cholesterol (mg)	128.2
688.5	Sodium (mg)	86.1

Chocolate Tapioca ■

Makes 6 servings

2 eggs, separated
2 cups water
3 single-serving envelopes low-calorie hot cocoa mix
2 tbsp. quick-cooking tapioca
1 tbsp. sugar ▲ (optional)
Pinch salt ● or cream of tartar
2 tsp. vanilla

● *HIGH SODIUM ALERT— Use cream of tartar instead of salt.*

■ *HIGH CHOLESTEROL ALERT—Not recommended for low-cholesterol diets.*

▲ *HIGH SUGAR ALERT—Omit added sugar.*

Blend egg yolks with ½ cup of the water in a nonstick saucepan. Stir in cocoa mix, tapioca, sugar and remaining 1½ cups water. Cook and stir over moderate heat until mixture simmers. Remove from heat and cool. Beat egg whites with salt or cream of tartar until soft peaks form. Stir vanilla into tapioca mixture. Gently but thoroughly fold in egg whites. Spoon into 6 dessert cups and chill thoroughly.

Total		Per Serving
430.9	Calories	71.8
52.4	Carbohydrate (g)	8.7
30.1	Protein (g)	5.0
13.2	Total Fat (g)	2.2
4.6	Saturated Fat (g)	0.8
519.0	Cholesterol (mg)	86.5
479.1	Sodium (mg)	79.9

Stove-Top Blueberry Rice Pudding

Makes 10 servings

1 cup uncooked rice
2 cups water
2 eggs, beaten ■
3 tbsp. sugar ▲ (optional)
⅛ tsp. salt or butter-flavored salt ● (optional)
13-oz. can evaporated skim milk
2 tsp. vanilla
1 cup fresh blueberries

● *HIGH SODIUM ALERT—Omit added salt or butter-flavored salt.*

■ *HIGH CHOLESTEROL ALERT—Use ½ cup liquid egg substitute.*

▲ *HIGH SUGAR ALERT—Use equivalent sugar substitute, or omit.*

Place rice and water in 3-qt. saucepan. Heat to boiling. Cover; lower heat. Simmer over low heat 20 minutes or until rice is cooked. Meanwhile, combine eggs, sugar, salt and evaporated milk. Stir into cooked rice. Cook and stir over medium heat until mixture thickens. Remove from heat. Stir in vanilla and blueberries. Serve hot or cold.

Total		Per Serving
1302.0	Calories	130.2
229.3	Carbohydrate (g)	22.9
56.0	Protein (g)	5.6
13.8	Total Fat (g)	1.4
4.0	Saturated Fat (g)	0.4
520.9	Cholesterol (mg)	52.1
588.0	Sodium (mg)	58.8

1 tsp. = 5 mL   1 tbsp. = 15 mL   1 cup = 250 mL   1 oz. = 30 g

Chocolate Pudding

Makes 4 servings

2 cups skim milk
2 tbsp. unsweetened cocoa
3 tbsp. sugar ▲
2½ tbsp. cornstarch
¼ tsp. salt ● (optional)
2 tsp. vanilla

● *HIGH SODIUM ALERT—Omit added salt.*

▲ *HIGH SUGAR ALERT—Use equivalent sugar substitute; add after cooking, along with the vanilla.*

Scald 1½ cups of the milk. Combine the cocoa, sugar, cornstarch and salt. Blend in the remaining ½ cup cold milk into cocoa mixture. Mix well. Stir into the scalded milk. Cook over very low heat, stirring constantly, until the mixture is thick. Remove from the heat. Stir in the vanilla. Cool. Spoon into 4 individual dessert dishes and chill.

Total		Per Serving
433.3	Calories	108.3
89.7	Carbohydrate (g)	22.4
20.9	Protein (g)	5.2
1.1	Total Fat (g)	0.3
0.6	Saturated Fat (g)	0.1
10.0	Cholesterol (mg)	2.5
254.9	Sodium (mg)	63.7

Homemade Fat-Free Strawberry Ice Milk

Makes 8 servings

2 tsp. unflavored gelatin
1 cup cold water
¾ cup instant dry nonfat milk crystals
1½ cups skim milk
⅔ cup sugar ▲
2 tsp. vanilla
1 tbsp. lemon juice
1 cup fresh or frozen unsweetened strawberries, mashed or pureed

▲ *HIGH SUGAR ALERT—Use equivalent sugar substitute.*

Soften the gelatin in ½ cup of the cold water. Combine ¼ cup of the milk crystals with the skim milk and heat gently in a saucepan. Add the gelatin mixture and heat until dissolved. Stir in ½ cup of the sugar until dissolved. Stir in the vanilla. Chill until slightly thickened. Beat the remaining ½ cup milk crystals with the remaining ½ cup of cold water until it begins to thicken slightly. Add the lemon juice and remaining sugar and beat 5 minutes or until the consistency of whipped cream. Fold in the chilled gelatin mixture. Spoon into refrigerator trays. Freeze until the edges are set. Remove to mixer bowl and beat on high speed until fluffy. Cover and freeze until firm. Allow to soften slightly before serving.

Hints: For Vanilla Ice Milk, omit strawberries.

For Banana Ice Milk, substitute 2 very ripe bananas, mashed, for strawberries.

For Chocolate Ice Milk, omit strawberries. Add 3 tablespoons unsweetened cocoa and 3 additional tablespoons sugar (or equivalent sugar substitute) when adding the ½ cup sugar to the warm milk mixture.

Total		Per Serving
931.7	Calories	116.5
196.6	Carbohydrate (g)	24.6
35.6	Protein (g)	4.4
0.0	Total Fat (g)	0.0
0.0	Saturated Fat (g)	0.0
18.7	Cholesterol (mg)	2.3
464.3	Sodium (mg)	58.0

Rum-Peach Sherbet

Makes 8 servings

2 cups canned juice-packed sliced peaches, drained, juice reserved
Water
1 tsp. lemon juice
1 envelope unflavored gelatin
2 tbsp. honey ▲
2 tsp. rum flavoring
Pinch salt ● (optional)

● *HIGH SODIUM ALERT—Omit added salt.*

▲ *HIGH SUGAR ALERT—Use equivalent sugar substitute, or omit.*

Measure reserved juice; add water to make 1½ cups liquid. Combine peach juice, lemon juice and gelatin in saucepan. Wait 1 minute. Heat gently until gelatin is dissolved. Combine all ingredients in blender. Cover and blend on high speed. Pour in a shallow bowl and freeze 1 hour. Remove to mixer bowl and beat on high speed until fluffy. Cover and freeze until firm. Allow to soften slightly before serving.

Total		Per Serving
436.3	Calories	54.5
90.4	Carbohydrate (g)	11.3
10.0	Protein (g)	1.3
0.4	Total Fat (g)	0.1
0.0	Saturated Fat (g)	0.0
0.0	Cholesterol (mg)	0.0
48.0	Sodium (mg)	6.0

Alert Symbols: ● Sodium   ■ Cholesterol   ▲ Sugar

Easy Fruit Juice Tapioca

Makes 6 servings

2½ cups unsweetened pineapple juice (or other unsweetened fruit juice)
4 tbsp. quick-cooking tapioca
Dash salt ● (optional)
Pinch ground cinnamon or apple pie spice (optional)

● *HIGH SODIUM ALERT—Omit added salt.*

Combine all ingredients in saucepan. Wait 5 minutes, then cook and stir over low heat until mixture simmers and boils. Remove from heat and cover. Wait 30 minutes, then stir well. Spoon into 6 dessert cups and chill several hours.

Total		Per Serving
471.2	Calories	78.5
117.7	Carbohydrate (g)	19.6
2.7	Protein (g)	0.4
0.0	Total Fat (g)	0.0
0.0	Saturated Fat (g)	0.0
0.0	Cholesterol (mg)	0.0
6.2	Sodium (mg)	1.0

Pronto Orange Ice

Makes 4 servings

4-serving envelope regular or low-calorie orange flavored gelatin dessert mix ● ▲
½ cup hot water
1 cup orange juice

● *HIGH SODIUM ALERT—Use low-sodium gelatin dessert mix.*

▲ *HIGH SUGAR ALERT—Use sugar-free gelatin dessert mix.*

Dissolve gelatin mix in hot water. Stir in orange juice. Pour into shallow container; freeze until slushy. Remove to mixer bowl; beat on high speed until fluffy. Cover and freeze firm. Soften slightly before serving.

Total		Per Serving
437.0	Calories	109.3
103.7	Carbohydrate (g)	25.9
9.7	Protein (g)	2.4
0.2	Total Fat (g)	0.1
0.0	Saturated Fat (g)	0.0
0.0	Cholesterol (mg)	0.0
272.0	Sodium (mg)	68.0

Peach Cottage Cake

Makes 8 servings

8 or 9 vanilla wafers ● ▲
2 cups juice-packed peach slices
½ cup low-fat cottage cheese ●
2 eggs ■
7 tbsp. free-pouring brown sugar ▲
2 tsp. vanilla
Cinnamon or apple pie spice

● *HIGH SODIUM ALERT—Use unsalted wafers and cottage cheese.*

■ *HIGH CHOLESTEROL ALERT—Use 4 egg whites or ½ cup liquid egg substitute.*

▲ *HIGH SUGAR ALERT—Use dietetic cookies and brown sugar substitute.*

Arrange the wafers in the bottom of an 8-inch nonstick cake pan. Drain the peaches and reserve ½ cup of the juice. Layer peaches on top of the wafers. Put cottage cheese, eggs, reserved peach juice, sugar and vanilla in blender; cover and blend until smooth. Pour mixture over the peaches. Sprinkle with cinnamon or spice. Bake in a preheated 325° oven for 1 hour or until set. Serve warm or chilled.

Total		Per Serving
898.7	Calories	112.3
149.9	Carbohydrate (g)	18.7
52.8	Protein (g)	4.1
18.5	Total Fat (g)	2.3
5.9	Saturated Fat (g)	0.7
526.5	Cholesterol (mg)	65.8
647.0	Sodium (mg)	80.9

Lime or Lemon Sherbet ▲

Makes 16 servings

1 envelope unflavored gelatin
1 cup sugar
1½ cups water
6 egg whites
1 tbsp. grated lemon or lime rind
¾ cup lemon or lime juice

▲ *HIGH SUGAR ALERT—Not recommended for low-sugar diets.*

Combine gelatin and ½ cup of the sugar in small saucepan. Stir in water. Heat to boiling, stirring until gelatin is completely dissolved; set aside. Beat egg whites at high speed until soft peaks form. Gradually add remaining sugar; beat until stiff. Continue to beat while adding the warm gelatin mixture in a thin steady stream. Beat in rind and juice. Pour into shallow metal trays. Freeze until slushy, stirring occasionally. Transfer to large chilled mixer bowl. With chilled beaters, quickly beat at high speed until smooth and fluffy. Return to trays; cover and freeze until firm. Allow to soften slightly before serving.

Total		Per Serving
942.4	Calories	58.9
215.6	Carbohydrate (g)	13.5
28.4	Protein (g)	1.8
0.1	Total Fat (g)	0.0
0.0	Saturated Fat (g)	0.0
0.0	Cholesterol (mg)	0.0
297.8	Sodium (mg)	18.6

1 tsp. = 5 mL   1 tbsp. = 15 mL   1 cup = 250 mL   1 oz. = 30 g

Lean Pie Crust

Makes 8 servings

1/2 cup sifted all-purpose flour
1/4 tsp. salt ●
1/4 tsp. baking powder ●
1/4 cup diet margarine at room
temperature ● ■

●*HIGH SODIUM ALERT—Omit added salt and baking powder. Use unsalted margarine.*

■*HIGH CHOLESTEROL ALERT—Use polyunsaturated margarine.*

Stir flour, salt and baking powder together. Add margarine. Cut in with fork or pastry blender and continue mixing until no pastry sticks to the sides of the bowl. Shape into a ball. Wrap and refrigerate to chill for an hour or more. Roll the dough out on a floured board. If prebaking, heat oven to 425° and bake about 12 minutes, until golden. This recipe makes single crust to line an 8- or 9-inch pie plate. For a 2-crust pie, double the recipe.

Total		Per Serving
410.0	Calories	51.3
43.9	Carbohydrate (g)	5.5
6.1	Protein (g)	0.8
24.5	Total Fat (g)	3.1
4.0	Saturated Fat (g)	0.5
0.0	Cholesterol (mg)	0.0
1056.3	Sodium (mg)	132.0

Graham Cracker Crust

Makes 8 servings

3/4 cup plain graham cracker
crumbs ● ▲
3 tbsp. diet margarine, softened ● ■

●*HIGH SODIUM ALERT—Use low-sodium graham crackers or low-sodium cookies to make crumbs. Use unsalted margarine.*

■*HIGH CHOLESTEROL ALERT—Use polyunsaturated margarine.*

▲*HIGH SUGAR ALERT—Use sugar-free cookies to make crumbs.*

Fork-blend crumbs and margarine thoroughly. Press mixture firmly and evenly onto the bottom and sides of nonstick 8- or 9-inch pie plate for pie crust or 8-inch springform pan for cheesecake crust.

For pie crust, bake in a preheated 400° oven 5 minutes. Cool before filling. For cheesecake, chill unbaked crust about 45 minutes before filling.

Total		Per Serving
395.0	Calories	49.4
46.7	Carbohydrate (g)	5.8
5.1	Protein (g)	0.6
24.0	Total Fat (g)	3.0
4.4	Saturated Fat (g)	0.6
4.4	Cholesterol (mg)	0.6
757.5	Sodium (mg)	94.7

Angel Pie Shell ▲

Makes 8 servings

2 egg whites
Pinch salt ● or cream of tartar
1/2 tsp. vanilla
7 tbsp. sugar

●*HIGH SODIUM ALERT—Use cream of tartar.*

▲*HIGH SUGAR ALERT—Not recommended for low-sugar diets.*

With an electric mixer, beat egg whites in non-plastic bowl until frothy. Add salt or cream of tartar. Beat until soft peaks form. Add vanilla. Beat in sugar, 1 tbsp. at a time. Continue beating until stiff peaks form. Spread meringue on bottom and sides of a 9-inch nonstick pie pan which has been sprayed with cooking spray. Bake in preheated 275° oven 1 hour, or until crisp. Turn off oven. Leave shell in the oven 30 minutes; remove and cool. (Pile shell with fresh fruit, frozen yogurt or low-fat ice milk, or use as a base for refrigerator pie filling.)

Total		Per Serving
373.0	Calories	46.6
89.2	Carbohydrate (g)	11.2
8.0	Protein (g)	1.0
0.0	Total Fat (g)	0.0
0.0	Saturated Fat (g)	0.0
0.0	Cholesterol (mg)	0.0
362.5	Sodium (mg)	45.3

Banana-Raspberry Layer Cake ▲

Makes 16 servings

1/2 cup evaporated skim milk, chilled
10-oz. package fresh or defrosted
frozen raspberries, drained,
juice reserved
Water
1 envelope unflavored gelatin
1/4 cup cold water
Red food coloring (optional)
1 large packaged angel cake
2 ripe bananas, thinly sliced
Fresh raspberries (optional)

▲*HIGH SUGAR ALERT—Not recommended for low-sugar diets.*

Pour milk into ice cube tray and freeze until ice crystals begin to form around edges. Measure reserved raspberry juice; add enough water to juice to make 1 cup. In a saucepan, combine gelatin with 1/4 cup cold water to soften. Wait 1 minute; then heat gently until gelatin dissolves. Stir in reserved juice and refrigerate until cool. In mixing bowl, combine chilled gelatin mixture with milk, and beat until peaks form. If desired, add a few drops of food coloring. Fold in berries. Slice angel cake horizontally into 3 layers. Frost first layer with raspberry mixture; top with half of the banana slices. Add second layer; frost and top with remaining banana slices. Add third layer. Spread top of cake with remaining raspberry mixture. Garnish with a few fresh raspberries, if desired. Chill thoroughly.

Total		Per Serving
2131.4	Calories	133.2
481.8	Carbohydrate (g)	30.1
56.8	Protein (g)	3.6
2.7	Total Fat (g)	0.2
0.0	Saturated Fat (g)	0.0
5.0	Cholesterol (mg)	0.3
1080.0	Sodium (mg)	67.5

Alert Symbols: ● Sodium ■ Cholesterol ▲ Sugar

Refrigerator Cheesecake

Makes 12 servings

Graham Cracker Crust (recipe in this chapter)
- 2 envelopes unflavored gelatin
- 1/2 cup cold water
- 2 eggs, separated ■
- 3/4 cup skim milk
- 4 tbsp. sugar ▲
- 1/4 tsp. salt ●
- 1 cup low-fat cottage cheese ●
- 2 tsp. lemon juice
- 1 tsp. grated lemon rind
- 2 tsp. vanilla
- 4 tbsp. honey ▲
- 1/2 cup nonfat instant dry milk crystals
- 1/2 cup ice-cold water

●*HIGH SODIUM ALERT—Omit added salt. Use unsalted cottage cheese.*

■*HIGH CHOLESTEROL ALERT—Use 1/3 cup liquid egg substitute for egg yolks, plus the 2 egg whites as specified in recipe.*

▲*HIGH SUGAR ALERT—Replace sugar and honey with equivalent sugar substitute.*

Prepare unbaked Graham Cracker Crust in 8-inch springform pan. Place in refrigerator to chill. Sprinkle gelatin over 1/2 cup of cold water in a large bowl to soften. Beat egg yolks in the top of a double boiler until fluffy; add skim milk, sugar and salt. Place over hot water. Cook, stirring constantly, until thick. Add gelatin mixture; stir until dissolved. Remove from heat and pour into blender. Add cheese, lemon juice, rind, vanilla and honey. Cover and blend until smooth. Chill until slightly thickened. In a small bowl, beat egg whites until stiff but not dry. In another bowl, beat nonfat dry milk with 1/2 cup ice-cold water until creamy. Gently but thoroughly, fold beaten egg whites into cheese mixture. Gently fold in the whipped milk mixture. Spoon cheesecake mixture into prepared crust. Chill several hours until set.

Total		Per Serving
1455.3	Calories	121.3
201.9	Carbohydrate (g)	16.8
77.9	Protein (g)	6.5
38.0	Total Fat (g)	3.2
9.6	Saturated Fat (g)	0.8
534.6	Cholesterol (mg)	44.5
2632.8	Sodium (mg)	219.4

Brandied Pineapple Pie ■

Makes 8 servings

Graham Cracker Crust, baked (recipe in this chapter)
- 8-oz. can cold juice-packed pineapple tidbits, (*not* fresh or frozen), drained, juice reserved
- 1 envelope unflavored gelatin
- 1 1/2 cups skim milk
- 5 tsp. sugar ▲
- Pinch salt ●
- 3 eggs, separated
- 2 tsp. brandy flavoring

●*HIGH SODIUM ALERT—Omit added salt.*

■*HIGH CHOLESTEROL ALERT—Not recommended for low-cholesterol diets.*

▲*HIGH SUGAR ALERT—Replace sugar with equivalent sugar substitute.*

Prepare Graham Cracker Crust in 8- or 9-inch pie plate. Set aside to cool. Measure 1/4 cup of the reserved pineapple juice; sprinkle gelatin on juice to soften. Combine milk, sugar, salt and beaten egg yolks in the top of a double boiler. Cook and stir over boiling water until mixture thickens slightly. Stir in gelatin mixture and brandy flavoring. Chill until mixture begins to set. Beat egg whites until stiff. Gently, but thoroughly, fold whites into milk mixture. Spread pineapple in prepared pie shell; cover with chiffon mixture. Chill until set.

Hint: For Brandied Pineapple Parfaits, omit pie shell; layer pineapple and chiffon mixture in 6 parfait glasses. Chill until set.

Total		Per Serving
1066.2	Calories	133.3
123.7	Carbohydrate (g)	15.5
43.6	Protein (g)	5.5
43.0	Total Fat (g)	5.4
10.4	Saturated Fat (g)	1.3
763.5	Cholesterol (mg)	95.4
1406.5	Sodium (mg)	175.8

Yogurt Peach Quiche

Makes 8 servings

Lean Pie Crust (recipe in this chapter)
- 2 1/2 cups thinly sliced pared fresh or juice-packed peaches canned, drained
- 2 eggs ■
- 1 cup low-fat vanilla yogurt ▲
- 1/4 cup sugar ▲
- 1/8 tsp. salt ● (optional)
- Cinnamon

●*HIGH SODIUM ALERT—Omit added salt.*

■*HIGH CHOLESTEROL ALERT—Use 4 egg whites or 1/2 cup liquid egg substitute.*

▲*HIGH SUGAR ALERT—Substitute plain low-fat yogurt and vanilla flavoring for vanilla yogurt. Use sugar substitute in place of sugar.*

Line an 8-inch nonstick pie pan with pastry. Add peaches in a single layer. Beat eggs slightly; add yogurt, sugar and salt to eggs. Mix well; pour over peaches. Sprinkle with cinnamon. Bake in a preheated 450° oven for 15 minutes. Reduce heat to 325° and bake 30 minutes longer, or until custard is set.

Hint: For Yogurt Peach Custard, omit pie shell; layer fruit and filling in 6 ovenproof custard cups. Bake in preheated 350° oven until set, about 30 to 40 minutes.

Total		Per Serving
1125.0	Calories	140.6
166.8	Carbohydrate (g)	20.9
32.5	Protein (g)	4.1
40.0	Total Fat (g)	5.0
9.8	Saturated Fat (g)	1.2
515.0	Cholesterol (mg)	64.4
1338.3	Sodium (mg)	167.3

1 tsp. = 5 mL   1 tbsp. = 15 mL   1 cup = 250 mL   1 oz. = 30 g

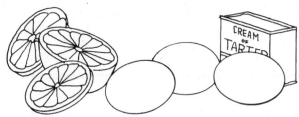

Frozen Yogurt Baked Alaska Pie ▲

Makes 8 servings

1 pint vanilla or strawberry low-fat frozen yogurt
Lean Pie Crust, prebaked (recipe in this chapter)
3 egg whites
Pinch salt ● or cream of tartar
6 tbsp. confectioners sugar
2 cups sliced fresh strawberries, or other fresh fruit

● *HIGH SODIUM ALERT—Use cream of tartar.*

▲ *HIGH SUGAR ALERT—Not recommended for low-sugar diets.*

Soften yogurt; spread in the bottom of 8-inch baked pastry shell. Freeze solid. Beat egg whites with salt or cream of tartar until soft peaks form. Gradually add sugar, beating until stiff and glossy. Remove pie from freezer. Arrange berries over yogurt. Pile meringue over berries and spread to edges of crust. Place pie on cookie sheet. Bake in preheated 500° oven about 3 minutes. Serve immediately.

Total		Per Serving
1102.5	Calories	137.8
180.3	Carbohydrate (g)	22.5
34.8	Protein (g)	4.6
35.0	Total Fat (g)	4.4
7.6	Saturated Fat (g)	1.0
22.0	Cholesterol (mg)	2.8
1709.3	Sodium (mg)	213.7

Fresh Fruit Bavarian Cream

Makes 8 servings

Graham Cracker Crust, baked (recipe in this chapter)
1 cup evaporated skim milk
2 four-serving packages regular or low-calorie gelatin dessert mix (any flavor) ● ▲
Pinch salt ● (optional)
1½ cups boiling water
1 cup sliced fresh strawberries or other fruit

● *HIGH SODIUM ALERT—Omit added salt. Use low-sodium gelatin dessert mix.*

▲ *HIGH SUGAR ALERT—Use sugar-free gelatin dessert mix.*

Prepare Graham Cracker Crust in an 8- or 9-inch pie pan. Set aside to cool. Pour evaporated skim milk into ice cube tray or metal mixing bowl. Put in freezer until ice crystals begin to form around edges. (Chill beater blades in freezer also.) Dissolve gelatin mix and salt in boiling water. Chill until syrupy. Beat the chilled skim milk at high speed until stiff, about 8 to 10 minutes. Gently but thoroughly, fold milk into gelatin mixture until well blended. Arrange fruit in bottom of pie shell. Cover with filling. Refrigerate several hours until set.

Hint: For Bavarian Cream Parfaits, omit pie crust; layer fruit and filling in 6 parfait glasses. Chill until set.

Total		Per Serving
1294.7	Calories	161.8
239.9	Carbohydrate (g)	30.0
40.7	Protein (g)	5.1
24.9	Total Fat (g)	3.1
4.4	Saturated Fat (g)	0.6
10.0	Cholesterol (mg)	1.3
1579.7	Sodium (mg)	197.5

Blender Chocolate "Cream Cheese" Pie ▲

Makes 8 servings

Graham Cracker Crust, baked (recipe in this chapter)
4 tbsp. cold water
1 envelope unflavored gelatin
1 cup boiling water
1 tsp. instant coffee (optional)
2 cups skim milk
1 cup low-fat cottage cheese ●
4-serving package chocolate instant pudding mix ●

● *HIGH SODIUM ALERT—Use unsalted cottage cheese and low-sodium pudding mix.*

▲ *HIGH SUGAR ALERT—Not recommended for low-sugar diets.*

Prepare baked Graham Cracker Crust in an 8- or 9-inch pie pan. Set aside to cool. Combine cold water and gelatin in blender container. Wait 1 minute, then add boiling water and instant coffee. Cover and blend on high speed until gelatin is completely dissolved, scraping sides of container occasionally. Add the milk and cheese; cover and blend on high speed until smooth and creamy. Add the pudding mix, cover and blend until smooth. Spoon into crumb crust. Chill several hours.

Total		Per Serving
1237.0	Calories	154.6
192.9	Carbohydrate (g)	24.1
63.1	Protein (g)	7.9
28.0	Total Fat (g)	3.5
5.6	Saturated Fat (g)	0.7
29.4	Cholesterol (mg)	3.7
2364.5	Sodium (mg)	295.6

Fresh Blueberry Pie

Makes 8 servings

4 cups fresh blueberries
3 tbsp. honey ▲ (optional)
1½ tbsp. cornstarch
Pinch salt ● (optional)
Lean Pie Crust, prebaked (recipe in this chapter)

● *HIGH SODIUM ALERT—Omit added salt.*

▲ *HIGH SUGAR ALERT—Use equivalent sugar substitute in place of honey, or omit.*

In a nonstick saucepan, combine 2 cups of the berries with honey, cornstarch and salt. Simmer over low heat for 10 minutes, stirring occasionally, until berries are soft and slightly thickened. Remove from heat and stir in remaining raw blueberries. Allow to cool. Spoon into crust and chill thoroughly before serving.

Total		Per Serving
806.8	Calories	100.8
141.0	Carbohydrate (g)	17.6
10.5	Protein (g)	1.3
28.5	Total Fat (g)	3.6
4.0	Saturated Fat (g)	0.5
0.0	Cholesterol (mg)	0.0
1065.7	Sodium (mg)	133.2

Alert Symbols:　● Sodium　■ Cholesterol　▲ Sugar

Pumpkin Pie

Makes 8 servings.
Lean Pie Crust (recipe in this chapter)
1 cup canned or cooked plain pumpkin (not pie filling)
2 eggs ■
1¼ cups skim milk
1 tbsp. cornstarch
⅓ cup honey ▲
¼ tsp. salt ● (optional)
1½ tsp. pumpkin pie spice, or: 1 tsp. ground cinnamon, ⅛ tsp. allspice, ⅛ tsp. ground ginger, ⅛ tsp. ground nutmeg and ⅛ tsp. ground cloves

● *HIGH SODIUM ALERT—Omit added salt.*

■ *HIGH CHOLESTEROL ALERT—Use 4 egg whites or ½ cup liquid egg substitute.*

▲ *HIGH SUGAR ALERT—Replace honey with sugar substitute to equal ½ cup sugar.*

Fit pastry into an 8-inch nonstick pie pan. Combine remaining ingredients in blender or bowl and blend or beat on high speed until smooth. Pour into prepared pie crust; bake preheated in 350° oven for 1 hour or until filling is set.

Hint: For Pumpkin Custard, omit pie crust; spoon filling into 6 ovenproof custard cups. Bake in preheated 350° oven until set, about 30 to 40 minutes.

Total		Per Serving
1136.1	Calories	142.0
175.3	Carbohydrate (g)	21.9
37.1	Protein (g)	4.6
37.2	Total Fat (g)	4.6
8.0	Saturated Fat (g)	1.0
510.2	Cholesterol (mg)	63.8
1347.3	Sodium (mg)	168.4

Yogurt Egg Nog Pie ■▲

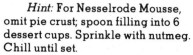

Makes 8 servings
Graham Cracker Crust, baked (recipe in this chapter)
1 envelope unflavored gelatin
½ cup sugar
¼ tsp. salt ● (optional)
3 tbsp. cornstarch
1 cup low-fat vanilla yogurt
¼ cup orange liqueur
¼ cup water
3 egg yolks, beaten
3 maraschino cherries, chopped
3 egg whites, stiffly beaten
¼ tsp. ground nutmeg or allspice

● *HIGH SODIUM ALERT—Omit added salt.*

■ *HIGH CHOLESTEROL ALERT—Not recommended for low-cholesterol diets.*

▲ *HIGH SUGAR ALERT—Not recommended for low-sugar diets.*

Prepare Graham Cracker Crust in 8- or 9-inch pie plate. Set aside to cool. Combine gelatin, sugar, salt and cornstarch in top of double boiler. Stir in yogurt, orange liqueur and water. Place over simmering water. Cook, stirring constantly, until thickened. Blend half the hot mixture into beaten egg yolks in a small bowl. Stir egg-yolk mixture into remaining yogurt mixture. Cook 2 minutes over simmering water. Remove from heat; cool. Stir in cherries. Chill until mixture is slightly thickened. Gently but thoroughly fold in stiffly beaten egg whites. Spoon mixture into pie shell. Sprinkle with nutmeg. Chill until firm.

Hint: For Nesselrode Mousse, omit pie crust; spoon filling into 6 dessert cups. Sprinkle with nutmeg. Chill until set.

Total		Per Serving
1550.9	Calories	193.9
221.2	Carbohydrate (g)	27.7
41.0	Protein (g)	5.1
45.0	Total Fat (g)	5.6
12.2	Saturated Fat (g)	1.5
767.0	Cholesterol (mg)	95.9
1097.6	Sodium (mg)	137.2

Slim and Speedy Chocolate Cream Pie

Makes 8 servings
Graham Cracker Crust, (recipes in this chapter)
2 envelopes unflavored gelatin
1½ cups skim milk
½ cup boiling water
¼ cup sugar ▲
2 tbsp. unsweetened cocoa
2 tsp. vanilla
1 pint chocolate low-fat ice milk ▲

▲ *HIGH SUGAR ALERT—Replace sugar with equivalent sugar substitute. Substitute sugar-free dietetic frozen dessert for ice milk.*

Prepare Graham Cracker Crust in an 8- or 9-inch pie plate. Set aside to cool. Combine gelatin and ⅓ cup of the skim milk in container of blender. Wait 1 minute, then add boiling water. Cover and blend until gelatin is completely dissolved. Add remaining milk, sugar, cocoa and vanilla; cover and blend. Add ice milk; cover and blend until smooth and creamy. Refrigerate a few minutes until mixture thickens. Fill pie crust with chilled filling. Chill until completely set.

Hint: For Chocolate Mini-Mousse, omit pie crust; spoon filling into 6 dessert cups or a large bowl. Chill until set.

Total		Per Serving
1223.2	Calories	152.9
184.2	Carbohydrate (g)	23.0
45.5	Protein (g)	5.7
39.1	Total Fat (g)	4.9
13.0	Saturated Fat (g)	1.6
59.5	Cholesterol (mg)	7.4
1139.4	Sodium (mg)	142.4

1 tsp. = 5 mL   1 tbsp. = 15 mL   1 cup = 250 mL   1 oz. = 30 g

One Crust Apple Pie

Makes 8 servings

Lean Pie Crust (recipe in this chapter)

5 cups thinly-sliced pared cooking apples

3/4 cup white raisins

3 tbsp. honey ▲ (optional)

1 tsp. lemon juice

1 tbsp. cornstarch

Pinch salt ● (optional)

1 tsp. apple pie spice or: 1/2 tsp. ground cinnamon, 1/4 tsp. ground nutmeg and 1/4 tsp. allspice

● *HIGH SODIUM ALERT—Omit added salt.*

▲ *HIGH SUGAR ALERT—Use equivalent sugar substitute in place of honey, or omit.*

Line an 8-inch nonstick pie pan with pastry. Combine remaining ingredients and mix well. Turn into pastry-lined pie plate. Cut a foil circle large enough to cover apples, but not pastry. Or, invert another pie pan over filling. Bake in a preheated 375° oven 1 hour, or until apples are tender.

Total		Per Serving
1046.2	Calories	130.8
212.2	Carbohydrate (g)	26.5
10.2	Protein (g)	1.3
26.2	Total Fat (g)	3.3
4.0	Saturated Fat (g)	0.5
0.0	Cholesterol (mg)	0.0
1095.9	Sodium (mg)	137.0

Banana Yogurt Pie▲

Makes 8 servings

Graham Cracker Crust, baked (recipe in this chapter)

1 envelope unflavored gelatin

2 tbsp. cold water

1/2 cup boiling water

3 tbsp. sugar

1 1/2 cups low-fat vanilla yogurt

2 small bananas, thinly sliced

Ground cinnamon

▲ *HIGH SUGAR ALERT—Not recommended for low-sugar diets.*

Prepare Graham Cracker Crust in 8- or 9-inch pie pan. Set aside to cool. Combine gelatin and cold water in blender container. Wait 1 minute, then add boiling water and sugar; cover and blend. Add yogurt; cover and blend. Refrigerate mixture 15 minutes. Spread half of the chilled filling in the pie crust; cover with a layer of banana slices; then top with remaining filling, sprinkle with cinnamon. Chill until set.

Total		Per Serving
1020.0	Calories	127.5
172.6	Carbohydrate (g)	21.6
30.5	Protein (g)	3.8
45.4	Total Fat (g)	5.7
7.1	Saturated Fat (g)	0.9
16.5	Cholesterol (mg)	2.1
991.5	Sodium (mg)	123.9

French Cream Cheese Cake

Makes 12 servings

Graham Cracker Crust (recipe in this chapter)

1 1/2 lbs. low-fat low-calorie cream cheese, or Neuchâtel cheese, softened ●

6 tbsp. sugar ▲

Pinch salt, or butter-flavored salt ● (optional)

3 eggs, or 1 egg and 4 egg whites ■

1/4 cup skim milk

1 tbsp. cornstarch

2 tsp. vanilla

3/4 tsp. grated orange or lemon rind

● *HIGH SODIUM ALERT—Use low-sodium cheese. Omit added salt.*

■ *HIGH CHOLESTEROL ALERT—Use 3/4 cup liquid egg substitute.*

▲ *HIGH SUGAR ALERT—Use equivalent sugar substitute.*

Prepare Graham Cracker Crust in an 8-inch springform pan. Place in refrigerator to chill. Combine remaining ingredients in blender. Cover and blend until smooth, 2 or 3 minutes, or until mixture is consistency of heavy cream. Spoon into crumb crust. Bake in preheated 250° oven for 1 hour. Turn oven off; open door, allow cheesecake to cool in oven 1 hour. Chill thoroughly.

Total		Per Serving
2773.5	Calories	231.1
156.1	Carbohydrate (g)	11.6
92.5	Protein (g)	7.7
200.4	Total Fat (g)	16.7
111.2	Saturated Fat (g)	9.3
1285.2	Cholesterol (mg)	107.1
3685.0	Sodium (mg)	307.1

Raisin Chip Chewies●

Makes about 50 cookies

1/2 cup diet margarine ■

1/3 cup firmly packed brown sugar ▲

1 1/2 tsp. vanilla

1 egg ■ or 2 egg whites

1 1/4 cups sifted all-purpose flour

1/2 tsp. baking soda

1/2 tsp. salt

1/2 tsp. ground cinnamon or apple pie spice

1/2 cup dark raisins

● *HIGH SODIUM ALERT—Not recommended for low-sodium diets.*

■ *HIGH CHOLESTEROL ALERT—Use polyunsaturated margarine. Use 2 egg whites.*

▲ *HIGH SUGAR ALERT—Use equivalent brown sugar substitute.*

Beat together margarine, brown sugar, vanilla and eggs with electric blender. Stir flour, baking soda, salt and cinnamon together; add to margarine mixture. Stir in raisins and mix well. Use a measuring teaspoon to drop level spoonfuls of dough on nonstick cookie sheets. Bake in a preheated 375° oven for 8 minutes, or until cookies are golden brown. Cool.

Total		Per Cookie
1507.1	Calories	30.1
237.8	Carbohydrate (g)	4.8
22.9	Protein (g)	0.5
55.3	Total Fat (g)	1.1
10.0	Saturated Fat (g)	0.2
252.0	Cholesterol (mg)	5.0
2528.2	Sodium (mg)	50.6

Alert Symbols: ● Sodium   ■ Cholesterol   ▲ Sugar

Cocoa Kisses ▲

Makes about 8 dozen

- 3 egg whites
- 1/2 tsp. cream of tartar
- 1 cup sugar
- 2 tbsp. unsweetened cocoa

▲ *HIGH SUGAR ALERT—Not recommended for low-sugar diets.*

Beat the egg whites until foamy. Add cream of tartar; beat until soft peaks form. Gradually beat in sugar, a few tablespoons at a time. Beat until stiff. Fold in cocoa. Drop batter by level teaspoonsful on nonstick cookie sheets which have been sprayed with cooking spray. Bake in a preheated 275° oven 18 to 20 minutes. Cool before removing from pans. Store in a very dry place.

Total		Per Serving
842.1	Calories	8.8
207.5	Carbohydrate (g)	2.2
14.9	Protein (g)	0.2
1.1	Total Fat (g)	0.0
0.6	Saturated Fat (g)	0.0
0.0	Cholesterol (mg)	0.0
248.9	Sodium (mg)	2.6

Baked Apples Stuffed with Raisins

Makes 6 servings

- 1/2 cup raisins
- 1/2 cup white wine or unsweetened fruit juice
- 6 baking apples, cored

Combine wine and raisins in small bowl; let soak 1 hour. Drain raisins and reserve wine. Stuff apples with raisins. Stand apples in baking pan just large enough to hold them. Pour on reserved wine. Bake in a preheated 350° oven, basting frequently with wine, about 20 to 25 minutes.

Total		Per Serving
789.5	Calories	131.6
180.9	Carbohydrate (g)	30.2
3.6	Protein (g)	0.6
4.9	Total Fat (g)	0.8
0.0	Saturated Fat (g)	0.0
0.0	Cholesterol (mg)	0.0
29.5	Sodium (mg)	4.9

Maple Baked Pears

Makes 8 servings

- 4 fresh ripe pears (D'Anjou or Bosc), cored, cut into halves
- 1 tbsp. lemon juice
- 1/2 cup water
- 8 tsp. maple syrup or honey ▲
- 1/4 tsp. ground cinnamon or apple pie spice

▲ *HIGH SUGAR ALERT—Use dietetic syrup.*

Place pears cut-side down in baking pan. Add lemon juice and water. Bake in a preheated 350° oven for 10 minutes. Turn pears cut-side up and spoon 1 tsp. maple syrup in center of each pear. Sprinkle with cinnamon and bake 8 to 10 minutes longer, basting occasionally.

Total		Per Serving
633.0	Calories	79.1
160.8	Carbohydrate (g)	20.1
5.7	Protein (g)	0.7
3.2	Total Fat (g)	0.4
0.0	Saturated Fat (g)	0.0
0.0	Cholesterol (mg)	0.0
20.0	Sodium (mg)	2.5

Honey Glazed Pears ▲

Makes 8 servings

- 4 fresh ripe pears (D'Anjou or Bosc)
- 2 tbsp. honey
- 1/2 cup water

▲ *HIGH SUGAR ALERT—Not recommended for low-sugar diets.*

Halve and core pears; don't pare them. Combine honey and water in a skillet. Place pear halves cut-side down in skillet. Cover and simmer for 6 to 8 minutes. Uncover; turn pear halves cut-side up and continue to simmer 10 to 15 minutes, basting often. Serve warm or chilled.

Total		Per Serving
618.0	Calories	77.3
156.4	Carbohydrate (g)	19.6
5.6	Protein (g)	0.7
3.2	Total Fat (g)	0.4
0.0	Saturated Fat (g)	0.0
0.0	Cholesterol (mg)	0.0
18.0	Sodium (mg)	2.2

1 tsp. = 5 mL   1 tbsp. = 15 mL   1 cup = 250 mL   1 oz. = 30 g

Cherry Yogurt Jubilee

Makes 8 servings

1 qt. low-fat vanilla frozen yogurt ▲
16-oz. can juice-packed pitted dark red cherries, undrained
2 tsp. cornstarch or arrowroot
 Few drops red food coloring (optional)
3 tbsp. brandy

▲ *HIGH SUGAR ALERT—Substitute low-fat, sugar-free vanilla ice milk for the frozen yogurt.*

Scoop yogurt into 8 sherbet glasses (place in freezer until serving time). Combine cherries, cornstarch, and food coloring in a chafing dish. Stir over moderate flame until sauce simmers and clears. Pour brandy on the sauce. Carefully ignite the vapors with a long match. Spoon flaming cherries over yogurt and serve immediately.

Total		Per Serving
990.2	Calories	123.8
172.9	Carbohydrate (g)	21.6
31.8	Protein (g)	4.0
16.9	Total Fat (g)	2.1
7.2	Saturated Fat (g)	0.9
44.0	Cholesterol (mg)	5.5
516.7	Sodium (mg)	64.6

Peaches Jubilee

Makes 4 servings

16-oz. can juice-packed peach halves, drained, juice reserved
1 tsp. cornstarch or arrowroot
1 jigger heated brandy

Combine reserved peach juice with cornstarch in small saucepan. Cook and stir over low heat until sauce simmers and thickens. Add peach halves and simmer until thoroughly heated through. Arrange peach halves in chafing dish or on platter, cut-side up. Cover with sauce; add heated brandy. Light and serve flaming.

Total		Per Serving
333.6	Calories	83.4
53.5	Carbohydrate (g)	13.4
3.7	Protein (g)	0.9
0.4	Total Fat (g)	0.1
0.0	Saturated Fat (g)	0.0
0.0	Cholesterol (mg)	0.0
37.0	Sodium (mg)	9.3

Cantaloupe Compote

Makes 6 servings

1 large ripe cantaloupe
1 cup fresh blueberries
6 tbsp. unsweetened frozen pineapple juice concentrate, defrosted, undiluted

Make melon balls with melon ball cutter. Combine with remaining ingredients in a bowl. Cover and chill.

Total		Per Serving
434.8	Calories	72.5
107.6	Carbohydrate (g)	17.9
6.5	Protein (g)	1.9
1.5	Total Fat (g)	0.3
0.0	Saturated Fat (g)	0.0
0.0	Cholesterol (mg)	0.0
68.0	Sodium (mg)	11.3

Banana Cheese Parfaits

Makes 8 servings

7½ or 8 oz. part-skim ricotta cheese ●
2 egg yolks ■
2 tbsp. sugar ▲
1 tsp. vanilla
3 tbsp. orange liqueur ▲
4 small bananas, sliced

● *HIGH SODIUM ALERT—Use low-sodium cheese.*

■ *HIGH CHOLESTEROL ALERT—Use ¹/3 cup liquid egg substitute.*

▲ *HIGH SUGAR ALERT—Substitute defrosted unsweetened orange juice concentrate with sugar substitute to taste for orange liqueur.*

Combine cheese, egg yolks, sugar, vanilla and orange liqueur in a deep bowl or blender. Beat or blend on high speed until thick and fluffy. Chill. At serving time, slice the bananas into 8 parfait glasses and spoon on the chilled cheese topping.

Total		Per Serving
982.8	Calories	122.9
132.5	Carbohydrate (g)	16.6
33.2	Protein (g)	4.2
26.2	Total Fat (g)	3.3
14.5	Saturated Fat (g)	1.8
570.6	Cholesterol (mg)	71.3
289.3	Sodium (mg)	36.2

Blushing Pears

Makes 4 servings

16-oz. can juice-packed pear halves, drained, juice reserved
½ cup red Concord wine
½ cup unsweetened orange juice
¼ tsp. apple pie spice

Arrange the pears in 4 individual stemmed glasses. Combine pear juice with remaining ingredients in a saucepan and bring to a boil. Lower heat and simmer, uncovered, until reduced by half. Remove from heat; let cool slightly. Pour liquid over the pears. Chill before serving.

Total		Per Serving
381.0	Calories	95.3
78.0	Carbohydrate (g)	19.5
2.0	Protein (g)	0.5
1.1	Total Fat (g)	0.3
0.0	Saturated Fat (g)	0.0
0.0	Cholesterol (mg)	0.0
41.7	Sodium (mg)	10.4

Alert Symbols: ● Sodium ■ Cholesterol ▲ Sugar

Strawberries a l'Orange

Makes 4 servings

1 pint ripe fresh strawberries
3 oz. frozen unsweetened orange juice concentrate, defrosted, undiluted
1 tbsp. orange liqueur ▲

▲ *HIGH SUGAR ALERT—Omit liqueur; add a little sugar substitute, if desired.*

Wash and hull the berries; leave whole. Combine with orange juice and liqueur and mix well. Chill. Spoon into 4 stemmed wine glasses.

Total		Per Serving
356.0	Calories	89.0
76.4	Carbohydrate (g)	19.1
4.8	Protein (g)	1.2
1.6	Total Fat (g)	0.4
0.0	Saturated Fat (g)	0.0
0.0	Cholestrol (mg)	0.0
5.0	Sodium (mg)	1.3

Raw Fruit Glaze for Cheesecake or Pie

Makes 8 servings

1 tbsp. cornstarch
1 cup unsweetened peach juice, or other unsweetened fruit juice
Sugar to taste ▲ (optional)
2 cups sliced fresh peaches, or other sliced fruit or whole berries

▲ *HIGH SUGAR ALERT—Use sugar substitute to taste.*

Blend cornstarch with juice in small saucepan. Cook over low heat, stiring constantly, until clear and thickened. Add sugar; stir until sugar is dissolved. Set aside to cool. Arrange peach slices on top of cheesecake or pie. Spoon sauce over fruit.

Total		Per Serving
275.9	Calories	34.5
69.3	Carbohydrate (g)	8.7
2.5	Protein (g)	0.3
1.4	Total Fat (g)	0.2
0.0	Saturated Fat (g)	0.0
0.0	Cholesterol (mg)	0.0
6.0	Sodium (mg)	0.8

Quick Strawberry Sauce

Makes about 1 cup

10-oz. package frozen unsweetened strawberries, defrosted, drained, juice reserved. ▲
1 tsp. cornstarch

▲ *HIGH SUGAR ALERT—Use unsweetened strawberries.*

Blend reserved juice and cornstarch in small saucepan. Heat to boiling, stirring constantly. Boil 1 minute. Remove from heat; stir in strawberries. Cool completely. (Spoon over low-fat frozen yogurt or ice milk.

Total		Per Tablespoon
168.6	Calories	10.5
43.1	Carbohydrate (g)	2.7
1.0	Protein (g)	0.1
1.0	Total Fat (g)	0.1
0.0	Saturated Fat (g)	0.0
0.0	Cholesterol (mg)	0.0
3.0	Sodium (mg)	0.2

Whipped Milk Topping

Makes 2 cups

2/3 cup evaporated skim milk
3 tbsp. sugar ▲
2 tsp. vanilla

▲ *HIGH SUGAR ALERT—Use equivalent sugar substitute.*

Pour milk into ice cube tray. Chill in freezer until slushy. Scrape the slushy milk into pre-chilled mixing bowl. Using pre-chilled beaters, beat at high speed until fluffy. Add sugar and vanilla and beat until stiff. (Serve as topping on plain cake, fruit gelatin or other desserts.)

Total		Per Tablespoon
301.7	Calories	9.4
62.0	Carbohydrate (g)	1.9
12.3	Protein (g)	0.4
0.0	Total Fat (g)	0.0
0.0	Saturated Fat (g)	0.0
7.0	Cholesterol (mg)	0.2
186.7	Sodium (mg)	5.8

1 tsp. = 5 mL   1 tbsp. = 15 mL   1 cup = 250 mL   1 oz. = 30 g

Whipped Cheese Dessert Topping

Makes 1 1/3 cups

1 cup low-fat large-curd cottage
   cheese ●
3 to 5 tbsp. skim milk
   Pinch salt or butter-flavored salt ●
   (optional)
2 tsp. vanilla
2 tbsp. confectioner's sugar ▲

● *HIGH SODIUM ALERT—Use unsalted cheese.
Omit added salt or butter-flavored salt.*

▲ *HIGH SUGAR ALERT—Use equivalent sugar
substitute.*

Combine all ingredients in blender.
Cover and blend until smooth.

Total		Per Tablespoon
282.9	Calories	13.5
30.2	Carbohydrates (g)	1.4
31.7	Protein (g)	1.5
2.0	Total Fat (g)	0.1
1.2	Saturated Fat (g)	0.1
20.3	Cholesterol (mg)	1.0
853.8	Sodium (mg)	40.7

Boozeless Egg Nog

Makes 6 servings

1 egg ■
1 egg white
3 cups skim milk
2 tsp. vanilla
2 tsp. rum or brandy flavoring
2 tbsp. sugar ▲
   Ground nutmeg

■ *HIGH CHOLESTEROL ALERT—Use 1/4 cup
liquid egg substitute.*

▲ *HIGH SUGAR ALERT—Use equivalent sugar
substitute.*

Combine all ingredients, except
nutmeg, in blender. Cover and
blend on high speed until frothy.
Chill thoroughly. Sprinkle with
ground nutmeg before serving.

Total		Per Serving
521.0	Calories	86.8
65.8	Carbohydrate (g)	11.0
37.0	Protein (g)	6.2
6.0	Total Fat (g)	1.0
2.0	Saturated Fat (g)	0.3
267.0	Cholesterol (mg)	44.5
490.0	Sodium (mg)	81.7

Quick Dessert Sauce

Makes 2 1/2 cups

2 1/2 cups skim milk
4-serving envelope regular or low-
   calorie pudding mix, any
   flavor ● ▲

● *HIGH SODIUM ALERT—Use low-sodium
pudding mix.*

▲ *HIGH SUGAR ALERT—Use sugar-free
pudding mix.*

Stir the milk into the pudding mix in
a nonstick saucepan. Cook and stir
over low heat until the mixture
simmers and thickens. (Use hot or
cold over fruit, ice milk or frozen
yogurt.) Store covered in
refrigerator.

Total		Per Tablespoon
633.0	Calories	15.8
133.4	Carbohydrate (g)	3.3
25.9	Protein (g)	0.6
2.4	Total Fat (g)	0.1
1.3	Saturated Fat (g)	0.1
12.5	Cholesterol (mg)	0.3
822.5	Sodium (mg)	20.6

Strawberry Topping

Makes 6 servings

2 cups fresh or frozen whole
   unsweetened strawberries
3/4 cup water

Combine ingredients in blender
and cover. Turn blender on and off
repeatedly until coarsely chopped.
(Spoon over low-fat cottage cheese,
ice milk or fruit.)

Total		Per Serving
110.0	Calories	18.3
26.0	Carbohydrate (g)	4.3
2.0	Protein (g)	0.3
2.0	Total Fat (g)	0.3
0.0	Saturated Fat (g)	0.0
0.0	Cholesterol (mg)	0.0
2.0	Sodium (mg)	0.3

Tangy Fruit Topping

Makes 1 1/4 cups

4 oz. low-fat low-calorie cream
   cheese, softened ●
3/4 cup plain low-fat yogurt
1/4 cup unsweetened frozen pineapple
   or orange juice concentrate,
   defrosted, undiluted
1 tsp. grated orange or lemon rind
   (optional)

● *HIGH SODIUM ALERT—Use low-sodium
cheese.*

Combine ingredients and beat until
fluffy. (Serve on fresh fruit.)

Total		Per Tablespoon
516.7	Calories	25.8
44.2	Carbohydrate (g)	2.2
8.2	Protein (g)	0.4
29.4	Total Fat (g)	1.5
18.3	Saturated Fat (g)	0.9
103.0	Cholesterol (mg)	5.2
547.7	Sodium (mg)	27.4

Blueberry Topping

Makes about 1 1/2 cups

1 pint fresh or frozen unsweetened
   blueberries
2 tbsp. sugar ▲
1 tsp. cornstarch
1/4 tsp. ground cinnamon

▲ *HIGH SUGAR ALERT—Omit sugar; after
cooking, stir in equivalent sugar substitute.*

Combine all ingredients in small
saucepan. Cook and stir 2 minutes
over low heat. Cool completely.

Total		Per Tablespoon
354.6	Calories	14.8
88.6	Carbohydrate (g)	3.7
2.9	Protein (g)	0.1
2.1	Total Fat (g)	0.1
0.0	Saturated Fat (g)	0.0
0.0	Cholesterol (mg)	0.0
4.0	Sodium (mg)	0.2

Alert Symbols: ● Sodium   ■ Cholesterol   ▲ Sugar

Grape Jelly ▲

Makes 1 1/2 cups
1 envelope unflavored gelatin
3/4 cup cold water
6-oz. can frozen grape juice
   concentrate, defrosted,
   undiluted

▲ *HIGH SUGAR ALERT — Not recommended for low-sugar diets.*

Sprinkle gelatin on cold water in a saucepan; wait until softened, about 1 minute. Add grape juice concentrate. Cook and stir until mixture boils. Store in a covered jar in refrigerator.

Total		Per Tablespoon
420.0	Calories	17.5
100.0	Carbohydrate (g)	4.2
7.3	Protein (g)	0.3
0.0	Total Fat (g)	0.0
0.0	Saturated Fat (g)	0.0
0.0	Cholesterol (mg)	0.0
12.0	Sodium (mg)	0.5

Pureed Pineapple Preserves

Makes about 2 cups
16-oz. can juice-packed crushed
   pineapple, drained, juice
   reserved
1 envelope unflavored gelatin

Pour reserved juice into a small saucepan. Sprinkle gelatin on juice. Heat gelatin-juice mixture over low heat, only until gelatin melts. Pour into blender; add crushed pineapple. Cover and blend until

smooth. Spoon into jars. Cover and store in refrigerator or freezer.

Total		Per Tablespoon
305.0	Calories	9.5
70.0	Carbohydrate (g)	2.2
8.0	Protein (g)	0.3
2.0	Total Fat (g)	0.1
0.0	Saturated Fat (g)	0.0
0.0	Cholesterol (mg)	0.0
12.0	Sodium (mg)	0.4

Fresh Raspberry Jam

Makes about 2 cups
1 tbsp. unflavored gelatin
2 tbsp. cold water
3 pints fresh raspberries, or other
   fresh berries, crushed
1 cup sugar (or less, to taste) ▲
1 1/2 tbsp. lemon juice
1/2 cup liquid pectin

▲ *HIGH SUGAR ALERT—Omit sugar; after heating, stir in equivalent sugar substitute.*

Soften the gelatin in the cold water. Combine berries with sugar and lemon juice in a saucepan. Heat to boiling. Cook and stir for 1 minute. Stir in pectin and gelatin. Boil for 3 minutes, stirring constantly. Pour into jelly jars. Cover and store in refrigerator.

Total		Per Tablespoon
1372.0	Calories	42.9
341.4	Carbohydrate (g)	10.7
17.8	Protein (g)	0.6
4.8	Total Fat (g)	0.2
0.0	Saturated Fat (g)	0.0
0.0	Cholesterol (mg)	0.0
17.0	Sodium (mg)	0.5

Easy Strawberry Preserves

Makes about 2 cups
1 pint strawberries, hulled
1 cup cold water
4-serving envelope regular or low-
   calorie strawberry gelatin
   dessert mix ● ▲

● *HIGH SODIUM ALERT—Use low-sodium gelatin dessert mix.*

▲ *HIGH SUGAR ALERT—Use sugar-free gelatin dessert mix.*

Crush the strawberries in a saucepan. Add the water and gelatin dessert mix. Cook and stir until gelatin is completely dissolved. Simmer gently uncovered for 2 minutes. Pour into 3 jelly jars. Cover and store in refrigerator.

Total		Per Tablespoon
436.0	Calories	13.6
102.2	Carbohydrate (g)	3.2
10.3	Protein (g)	0.3
1.6	Total Fat (g)	0.5
0.0	Saturated Fat (g)	0.0
0.0	Cholesterol (mg)	0.0
273.0	Sodium (mg)	8.5

Peach Jam

Makes about 4 cups
3 cans (16 oz. each) juice-packed
   sliced peaches, drained, juice
   reserved
1 envelope unflavored gelatin
1/2 cup sugar ▲

▲ *HIGH SUGAR ALERT — Omit sugar; add equivalent sugar substitute to gelatin mixture after cooking.*

Puree drained peaches in blender. Measure puree; add enough reserved juice to make 3 cups. Set aside. Measure another 1/4 cup reserved juice into a saucepan. Sprinkle gelatin on juice. When gelatin is softened, add sugar and heat to boiling, stirring until gelatin is completely dissolved. Combine with peach puree. Store in covered jars in refrigerator or freezer.

Total		Per Tablespoon
1070.0	Calories	16.7
253.5	Carbohydrate (g)	4.0
17.0	Protein (g)	0.3
1.2	Total Fat (g)	0.0
0.0	Saturated Fat (g)	0.0
0.0	Cholesterol (mg)	0.0
117.0	Sodium (mg)	1.8

1 tsp. = 5 mL   1 tbsp. = 15 mL   1 cup = 250 mL   1 oz. = 30 g

Metric Equivalents

METRIC EQUIVALENTS FOR OVEN TEMPERATURES

Fahrenheit	Celsius	Fahrenheit	Celsius
250 F	120 C	400 F	200 C
275 F	140 C	425 F	220 C
300 F	150 C	450 F	230 C
325 F	160 C	475 F	250 C
350 F	180 C	500 F	260 C
375 F	190 C	550 F	290 C

METRIC EQUIVALENTS FOR VOLUME AND WEIGHT MEASURES

Volume Measure	Metric Equivalent
1/4 teaspoon	1 mL
1/2 teaspoon	2 mL
1 teaspoon	5 mL
1 tablespoon (3 teaspoons)	15 mL
2 tablespoons (1 fluid ounce)	30 mL
1/4 cup (4 tablespoons) (2 fluid ounces)	60 mL
1/3 cup	80 mL
1/2 cup (8 tablespoons) (4 fluid ounces)	125 mL
2/3 cup	160 mL
3/4 cup (6 fluid ounces)	180 mL
1 cup (8 fluid ounces)	250 mL
1 pint (2 cups)	500 mL
1 quart (4 cups)	1 L

Weight Measure	Metric Equivalent
1 ounce	30 g
2 ounces	60 g
3 ounces	85 g
1/4 pound (4 ounces)	115 g
1/2 pound (8 ounces)	225 g
3/4 pound (12 ounces)	340 g
1 pound (16 ounces)	450 g

METRIC EQUIVALENTS FOR DIMENSIONS

1/2 inch	1.5 cm	4 inches	10 cm
1 inch	2.5 cm	5 inches	13 cm
1 1/2 inches	4 cm	9 inches	23 cm
2 inches	5 cm	11 inches	28 cm
3 inches	8 cm	13 inches	33 cm

METRIC ABBREVIATIONS

mL = milliliter
L = liter (1000 milliliters)
g = gram
kg = kilogram
cm = centimeter

Index